The Essential Elements of Sex

9 Secrets to a Lifetime of Intimacy

Eryn-Faye Frans, LL.B.

iUniverse, Inc.
Bloomington

The Essential Elements of Sex:
9 Secrets to a Lifetime of Intimacy

iUniverse books may be ordered through booksellers or by contacting:

iUniverse
1663 Liberty Drive
Bloomington, IN 47403
www.iuniverse.com
1-800-Authors (1-800-288-4677)

Logo design by Scott Mallone of Haydon Innovation. (www.haydoninnovation.com)

ISBN: 978-1-4759-5529-3 (sc)
ISBN: 978-1-4759-5530-9 (e)

Library of Congress Control Number: 2012919099

Printed in the United States of America

iUniverse rev. date: 12/6/2012

Contents

For Eric – my lover, best friend, partner and husband of my youth.
I love you.

Acknowledgments

———◆●◆———

I lost my mother to ovarian cancer when I was eighteen and my father to brain cancer when I was twenty-one. I didn't have them for long enough, but they made a tremendous impact on my life for the short number of years they were here. The two of them modeled courage, boldness, compassion and empathy – all qualities essential in my profession. But more importantly, they demystified the subject of sex. Nothing was taboo in our household, and conversations about sexual intimacy were handled in a factual and candid manner. The act of sex was to be saved for marriage, but conversations about the topic were meant for all ages and stages in life. I have no doubt I would not be who I am today had it not been for their influences. Thank you, George and Bonnie Mallone.

Thank you, Eric Frans, my husband of fourteen years. The first interaction we had was a debate that extended to a two-hour intellectual brawl. He won the argument and my heart. For years, Eric has seen qualities deep within me long before I recognized them myself. He has managed to love me *as I am*, while never allowing me to settle with *where I am*. Always reminding me of my greater self and calling this forth from within me, he is my closest friend and biggest fan. Thanks, Babe.

Riley, you have been amazing during the writing of this book. Your dad and I often say to each other, "If we were only able to have one child, Riley was the one to have!" You have shown enormous patience when I asked you to bring your homework into my office so I could get in an extra few hours of work. Exhibiting compassion and understanding far beyond your years, you have stopped to ask how the book is coming. I love the person you are today, and I am so excited to see the woman you will become.

My advisory team has provided countless hours of support, encouragement and advice. They never hesitate to speak into my life, and yet never cease cheering me on. I greatly value their insight and wisdom in both my personal and professional lives. Thank you, Dr. Paddy Ducklow, Laura North and Celeste Wade.

Thank you to the team at The Meeting House. Matt Vincent, Tim Day and Bruxy Cavey, you have all made our church a place to call home even in the midst of busy seasons of teaching at other churches. You have cultivated a soft place to land, and we relish our times with you.

As I have run the course and developed it into a book, there have been numerous people who have helped me by opening doors, and providing a huge source of encouragement. Thank you, Bruce and Barbara Applequist, Pat and Rex Bolin, Scott and Hoda Mallone, Meredyth Mallone, Jonathan and Courtney Applequist, Christopher Applequist, Jethro and Roberta Taylor, Brian and Colleen McKenzie, Ben and Jennifer Nyland, Corwin Hiebert and Eileen Rothe, Tim and Carol Dorn, Brian and Ellie Bonsma, Susan Knight, Sherman and Sarah Hu, Dr. Dave Currie, Christie Rayburn, Laura Hudson, Jackie Graham, Tammy Nash, Darlene Dueck, Heather Harbaugh, Louise Taylor, Ruth Lamb, Jessica Samuels, Alison Caldwell-Johnson, Phil and Amber Smith, Tim Tang and Joanne Wong, Lucas and Judy Chang, Regina Li, Sonja Bristow, Rob and Janet Thiessen, Jamie and Katrina Holtom, Wayne and Patricia Russell and Randy Neilson.

There are two other women I want to thank specially – Eleanor Mumford and Darlene Howath. Eleanor inspired me with the concept of the Three Cs when I was only eighteen. Darlene, a retired ER nurse, answered countless phone calls when I had questions about the nitty-gritties of sex early in my career. Both of you were instrumental in shaping my profession by educating me about the necessity of balancing both the art and science of sexual intimacy.

Last, but certainly not least, thank you to all the men and women who have written, called and emailed to ask when this book was coming out. Your faith in me challenged me to continue in those moments when I was ready to throw in the towel. You kept me focused on the big picture, and this document would not have made it off my computer without you. Thank you.

ERYN-FAYE FRANS
TORONTO, ONTARIO
SEPTEMBER 2012

Introduction

———•◆•———

"Without dreams, there can be no courage.
And without courage, there can be no action."
Wim Wenders – Director and Photographer

The woman in front of me was in tears, completely undone by my presentation. We had retreated into the ordering room so that she could make a private purchase, but it was obvious that she needed far more than product. She, like so many women and men that I would meet over the years, felt isolated and alone in her struggle to connect with her spouse. "I thought I was the only one who felt this way. I thought something was wrong with me. What can I do to change my marriage? How can I make our sex life better?" But she's not alone – and neither are you.

We sit at a precipice in history. Never before has there been such a cynical attitude toward marriage. He doesn't meet your needs? Then dump him and move on. She doesn't put out in the bedroom? The lady from accounting certainly will. Heaven knows your family and friends will support any decision that you make – as long as you are happy.

And while this cavalier attitude towards relationships is what culture presents on the surface, it belies the real pain and isolation that lie below the surface. No woman goes into marriage wanting the pain of emotional disconnection. No man sets out to cheat on his wife. No woman looks forward to crying herself to sleep at night. No man chooses the heartache his kids feel as their mother walks out the door.

Men and women truly want to connect with their spouses, but they have lost their way. In our disposable marriage society, it becomes easy to neglect the building blocks that make a relationship work. It is easy to overlook the small choices, made consistently, that weave strength into the fabric of a successful relationship. And yet, if we do not make changes in our patterns of behavior, we will lose one of the most precious gifts we can give each other – intimacy that grows and deepens over a lifetime.

Since you are reading this book, I believe you are searching for something more. Well done – that is the first step. And while sexual intimacy is topic of this book, the changes that you make in this area of your relationship will reverberate throughout the entirety of your marriage. Over the course of this book, I will outline the information crucial to the foundation of your sexual relationship, and then describe the nine essential elements necessary to build a strong, sustainable partnership onto it: communication, ritual, mystery, respect, pleasure, trust, creativity, passion and attraction. Finally, I will give you the tools to keep the changes going so that your relationship can continue to thrive over the years together.

My Journey

I didn't grow up dreaming of being a Passion Coach®. When my teachers asked me what I wanted to be when I grew up, I didn't write about speaking to couples who were feeling alone and isolated in the most intimate area of their relationship. In fact, I didn't identify with any profession in the helping field. Teacher and counselor never even made my list.

Law, as far as I could see as a young woman, was my path to doing justice for the downtrodden in this world. As I completed my law degree at the University of Glasgow, I had dreams of working at the European Court of Justice.

Unbeknownst to me, God had a different plan. The calling to defend the downtrodden, to act justly, and to love mercy was certainly at the core of who I was created to be. It is just that law wasn't the path He had for me. My path was something that took years, many tears and hardships, and ultimately courage to discover.

Riley's Birth

When Eric and I first got married, we had what I like to describe as an average or normal sex life. My husband, of course, takes great offense to these adjectives, and teases me regularly to upgrade my description to great or even awesome. We laugh together and then I return to calling it average because it really, truly was. We had our good moments and our bad moments, times when everything just clicked in the bedroom and times when it was disastrous, bursts of creativity, and periods of boredom. Our sex life had an ebb and flow to it we accepted as normal.

It was all of these things, that is, until I gave birth to our daughter Riley. It took fifty-three hours to deliver her, which culminated with an episiotomy and forceps extraction. To top it off, I can only guess the doctor who stitched me up was late for his tee time, because the repair job he did was atrocious. My pelvic floor was a mess.

Of course, in the midst of giving birth, the only focus is the health and well being of the child, and so it was many weeks before Eric and I realized my body was not bouncing back the way they describe in books. In response to the pain and discomfort of intercourse (not to mention the myriad of other challenges that accompany a newborn), we quietly slipped into a sexless marriage.

Having no experience with the impact a sexless marriage can have on your relationship, my husband and I danced around the question "How do we resolve this?" We weren't sure who we could talk to, and we certainly had never heard of other couples facing what we were. Our communication skills, which had always been excellent, became strained.

Fortunately, we had an incredible family doctor. Once I worked up the courage to tell her what was happening to me, she immediately went to work on correcting the damage that had been done. Never once did she belittle what I had to say, despite the fact I had never given birth before and so didn't know what normal looked like. Her empathetic and proactive approach to my issues reassured me, and together we found solutions that resulted in my body being able to heal, slowly but surely, over time.

A year later, Riley was diagnosed with severe chronic neutropenia, a rare blood disorder where the doctors were very concerned she would not be able to ward off bacterial infections. They told us we needed to keep her away from groups of children. Daycare was obviously not an option and I couldn't bring myself to seriously consider a nanny. But Riley's restrictions meant we could not engage in Mom's Day Out, the local recreation center or our church nursery. Even local parks were avoided because I could never tell when a swarm of kids would descend on the place. I was incredibly isolated and bored to tears.

Determined not to dissolve into a puddle of depression over my daughter's condition, I launched an intellectual stimulation program for myself. Every day, I would turn on the TV or go online to various news sources, and read up on what was happening in the rest of the world so when Eric returned home, we could discuss something besides my diaper duties. Dinner each night would go something like this: "So, Darling, have you heard what is happening in Russia? Oh, and please pass the mashed potatoes."

The Party Industry

It was around this time I watched a segment on *The Today Show* about in-home parties that address sexual intimacy. Sex toy parties, if you will. I have to admit, I was horrified and intrigued all at once. Horrified because this was not an area of our relationship Eric and I had explored, but intrigued because I instantly realized the lady onscreen had invitations to speak to women in their homes about the most taboo of topics. And it dawned on me – had I known this woman when Eric and I were struggling after Riley's birth, things might have been easier. She could not have healed my pelvic floor more quickly, but she could have helped me find some workarounds. More importantly, she would have *talked* to me. She would have been a *safe* person to open up to.

In hindsight, I find this revelation deeply disturbing. I was a pastor's kid married to a church elder. I ran in Christian circles, had Christian friends, my husband worked for a Christian organization. To put it mildly, we were smack-dab in the middle of the proverbial Christian ghetto. And yet there was no one we felt safe enough to approach when we were struggling. I had remained quiet and alone with my turmoil until this lady appeared on my TV screen. Somehow, she broke through my shame.

In that moment, I felt a nudge. A nudge to share my story with other ladies. I had a picture in my mind of standing in someone's living room, sharing about the importance of the Three Cs – commitment, communication and consummation. I could see myself talking to these women about the value of healthy connection in marriage. Bedroom toys would be my invitation into the inner lives of women – if I could only figure out how they worked!

After much prayer and research, I presented the idea to Eric. He was quite shocked. In fact, he was speechless for a bit, which is highly unusual for him. But then he surprised me. Instead of saying, "You're crazy!" he offered me a challenge. "Go do your market research. If there is truly a need out there, I will support you. Oh, and start by talking to my mother. If you can talk to her about sex, you can talk to anyone."

So, I created a list of women in my life and systematically took them to coffee. I talked to women in their twenties to sixties, newlyweds, mothers, grandmothers, pastors' wives, marriage counselors and sex therapists. And yes, I even broached the topic with my conservative, evangelical Texan mother-in-law.

With all these women, I would share my story and the reason why this business idea intrigued me. I would then ask them, "Do you think there is any need for something like this?" Every time, without fail, women opened up their hearts to me and told me their own stories. It was as if they had been waiting to be asked, and the dam had been released. They all had different stories because they were from different walks of life, but they all said the same thing: "We need to talk about this more." I realized there needed to be a forum where we could discuss these things, realize we are not alone, and also get the resources we need to address these issues.

I did indeed join an organization and began to sell bedroom accoutrements. I was extremely good at it – one of the best in the country. When other women in the organization would ask how I was so successful in my sales numbers, I would scratch my head because I truly didn't care what I sold. When I went to annual conferences and they would encourage us to reduce our presentation time to thirty minutes, I would scratch my head because my *introduction* alone was thirty minutes. I had my audience captive, and that was the time in which I did the teaching on what it took to have a healthy relationship. Far from being a deterrent, I was doing parties as often as five nights a week.

Those days in the trenches were extremely educational for me. Of course, I learned an incredible amount about how the body works. Whenever I got a question to which I did not have an answer, I would ask my mentor, who was a former emergency room nurse, or look it up in a book. I was in a natural environment to dip into vast knowledge about sexuality. The resources I was able to access, along with the myriad of books I read on the subject during this season, were invaluable.

But I learned far more than just the nitty-gritties of sex. In the privacy of the ordering room, woman after woman – usually in tears – would open up about her life and her secret struggle for genuine intimacy. They weren't there just for the toys – they were there because they deeply longed to connect with their spouses and needed to find out how to do so. While they might be able to have casual conversations with their friends about sex, no one in their world was creating space for real, honest, candid and solutions-oriented conversations about intimacy. And the question they all asked was, "Am I alone in my struggle?"

Coaching

It was this constant question that prompted me to begin a coaching business. I obviously could not give the amount of time these women wanted in a party ordering room. So, I began to meet with them at Starbucks. While we sipped our lattés, I would listen to their stories, answer their questions, and give them tips that had worked for other women. And yet, even though Starbucks serves superb coffee, I quickly realized it was not the best venue for women to open up about their sex lives. We began to meet privately in my home.

It was at this time I was invited to join the team at the TV show *Marriage Uncensored with Dave and Christie*. It was an amazing time professionally because I was constantly surrounded by experts in the field of marriage and family from all over Canada and the U.S. I had the privilege and honor to ask them questions, read their books, spend time with them, and learn. Furthermore, my job at the organization was to answer questions from the viewership that pertained to issues of sexuality. Questions regarding pornography, infidelity, body issues, correctness in the bedroom, talking to kids about sex, forgiveness, trust and so forth flooded in from around the world. And yet, this experience was very similar to my time in the party industry. At their essence, the questions were the same. "Am I alone? Who can walk beside me as I battle for intimacy?"

I realized at this time that there was a dearth of quality information on the subject for the average person to access. Most people do not walk into their local bookstore and say, "Can you please point me to your section on sex?" It's uncomfortable. I know this from frequent personal experience.

I once walked into a Christian bookstore, emptied out their section, and plunked the books down next to the register. "I think you are going to have to restock all of your sex books," I told the girl behind the counter. She was so embarrassed, she didn't know how to respond. All of a sudden, she was incredibly efficient in processing my purchase and ushering me out the door.

When we are seeking information on this sensitive subject, it is very difficult to access. Even if you can find your way to the sex section, it is mostly full of unhelpful books, accompanied by racy photos. If you venture into the relationship section, the books deal with interpersonal dynamics, but at the expense of the details necessary when having candid conversations about sexual intimacy. That, in my experience, is not what people are looking for. People want solid information, which gets into the nitty-gritties, but not by neglecting the art of genuine connection. Often, books sacrifice one on the altar of the other.

I therefore launched a website to tackle both aspects. You could go to my website to learn more about the G-spot or how to communicate with your spouse. You could get tips on his love language or the basics of oral sex. To forge genuine intimacy, we must understand both. There is a rawness to sexuality – it entails body parts and fluids and technique. There is also a softness – conversations and whispers and secrets between a husband and wife. One without the other creates imbalance. And yet, when the two come together – the joining of the science and art of sexual intimacy – it is the most powerful combination known to humankind.

After the website launched, this combination drew the attention of a wide range of people. I began to get clients from beyond the borders of my own world. They came to me from all over Canada, the U.S. and even Europe. People from all different nationalities and backgrounds were seeking answers.

Even so, I began to notice a disturbing trend amongst my Christian clients. The rudder of their sex life was fear. Everything they did or did not do was directed by fear. As I began to unpack this pattern with client after client, I realized that the core was fear they would sin. That they would be ungodly. And so they responded to that fear by doing nothing and staying silent until they ended up in a coaching session with me.

The Essential Elements of Sex™

In response to this trend, I wrote and piloted a course I entitled *The Essential Elements of Sex,* designed specifically for Christians. The course is biblically and research based because I found Christians were sorely lacking information from both sources. Not only were they unaware of the passages in Scripture there to guide our relationships with our spouses, they were also oblivious to the advances the scientific community has made in the field of sexuality. I also tried to hold the science and spirituality of sexuality in tandem.

As I taught the course, it changed marriages. The men were hopeful – sometimes for the first time in years – and the women were excited. They couldn't wait to get home and do the Bedwork I had assigned. I also had participants assess their personal satisfaction week after week. At the end of the course, the average participant moved up four points. This may not seem like a lot when written on paper, but when couples came into the course ranking their sex life at a four out of ten and leaving with an eight, this was very exciting to them.

As I began to teach at venues across Canada and the U.S., requests came in to produce more materials. Not every church was at the place on their journey to invite the Passion Coach to teach their congregation, but they wanted the material for their congregants. As such, this book was born. In essence, it is a version of the course I teach. Just like the course, it is designed as a workbook for people to do, either individually or as a couple.

It is broken into three sections: Laying the Foundation, The Essential Elements and Making It Last. The first section gives basic information all couples need to understand to fully utilize the elements. In the second section, I outline the nine essential elements. Finally, I address the questions couples have regarding the end of the course. Far from being a one-time experience, the information, tools and solutions this book offers can be put into practice for a lifetime so your relationship continues to grow and deepen.

How to Use This Book

Read a chapter each week and do the accompanying Bedwork that same week. Many people find it helpful to read the chapter in one day (on Sunday night, for example) and then use the rest of the week to do their Bedwork. As such, you will be able to complete the book in thirteen weeks – a perfect time frame to implement genuine and lasting change in your relationship.

Bedwork

You may have some intellectual knowledge as to why things are the way they are in your marriage, but this isn't going to lead to much change. If you want things to be different, you have to begin new behaviors. You will have to put this book down, get off the couch and *do* something different.

To assist you in this endeavor, there is Bedwork at the end of each chapter. These exercises are designed to motivate action and change. Bedwork is your opportunity to try new behaviors. At the end of the book, you will have a list of things that were effective for your relationship, as well as exercises you tried that were not as helpful. This is normal. In fact, it is also normal that, if you are working through the book together as a couple, some of the Bedwork will be highly effective for one person, but not the other. Doing the Bedwork is not about perfection – it is about learning and growing together.

When you find something that works, practice it until it replaces old, unproductive patterns in your sex life. When something does not seem as effective, make a note and move on. It may not fit your personality type, it might not suit your season in life, or it might stretch you further than you are currently comfortable. Set it aside and move on to something more productive. You might come back to the question later in life or completely disregard it altogether.

Here are the guidelines:

1. Pick a minimum of two exercises to do each week. (If you and your spouse are doing this book together, you each get to pick two.) Here's the catch: Pick the exercise that thrills you as well as the one you most despise. Your strong emotional reaction is probably an indicator that spending a bit more time on this topic is prudent and will benefit your relationship. Often we resist what brings us the greatest growth. Naturally, we like our comfort zones because they are, well, comfortable. While working through this book, resist comfort and experiment with change. How will you know the difference? Your reactions will tell you, so listen to them.

2. If you do not have strong emotional reactions to the exercises, pick the two you think your spouse would most appreciate. I call this giving them the home field advantage (more on that later). So men, if your wife is verbal, focus on one of the exercises that uses words and language. Women, if your husband is more of an action type of guy, focus on the action Bedwork. The key here is that you recognize the different strengths you each bring to the bedroom, and then you practice the areas of each other's strengths.

Personal Satisfaction Assessment

As part of your Bedwork each week, you will be asked to rank your personal satisfaction assessment of your sex life on a scale of 1-10.

(1) **Your sex life this week was horrible.** You didn't feel connected to your spouse, you struggled to communicate and/or sex was nonexistent due to *non-logistical* reasons. (Examples of logistical reasons include one spouse is out of town, the wife has her period, etc.)

(10) **Your sex life this week was phenomenal.** The two of you are really connecting, communicating about sex very well and enjoying it together.

The trick to this assessment is that you don't over think or rationalize it too much. Usually the first number that jumps into your brain is the truthful number. Once you have decided what your PSA is, write it on your Bedwork page (in the upper right-hand corner), and then dog-ear the page so it is private. This information is for you and your own personal growth.

You are free to chat about this with your spouse as long as you aren't bludgeoning him/her with this information. For example, it is *not* effective to turn to your husband and say, "Honey, you were a *three* this week. What do you have to say about that?!" However, learning to communicate about sex is an essential component to this workbook, so opening up about your PSAs can be a helpful tool in assessing how each of you is feeling about your sex life.

You might use your PSAs as a conversation starter with questions such as:

- If there is a difference in numbers we have each chosen, why are they different?
- What was I thinking, feeling and experiencing this week that led to my number?
- What needs to be done to close the gap between our numbers?
- How can we improve both numbers together?

Don't tell each other what you have written down as your PSA until you finish the chapter on Communication. By that time, you will hopefully have enough of a skill set under your belt to communicate effectively about this sensitive topic.

Final Thoughts

As you work through this book over the coming weeks, do so with Hebrews 10:24 (NIV) in mind: "And let us consider how we may spur one another on toward love and good deeds." My prayer for you is that this book spurs you to love your spouse more deeply, and to put that love into action so the effects reverberate through your relationship, family, church, community and world.

Part I: Laying the Foundation

Myth-Busting

"I drag my myth around with me."
Orson Welles – Writer, Actor, Director and Producer

Jacqueline is a beautiful, confident and articulate woman. As she tells me her story, she does so striving to be as compassionate and balanced as possible, despite the fact she is relaying a horrific ordeal.

She and her husband moved in esteemed Christian circles. He was a professor at a Bible college, and she was a youth pastor. They waited to have sexual intercourse until they got married. They faithfully attended premarital counseling. Statistically speaking, they were the ideal age to marry. They had phenomenal relationships within their church community. They did everything *right*.

And within three and a half years, they were divorced. Why? They had never consummated their relationship.

In the infancy of their marriage, Jacqueline's doctor failed to recognize she had a physiological impediment that made penetration impossible. For years, she blamed herself for not being able to "suck it up" when it came to the excruciating pain she felt every time she and her husband attempted to have intercourse.

When Jacqueline finally found a doctor who diagnosed her properly, and told her surgery was the only way to correct the problem, Jacqueline's husband already had one foot out the door. Years of misunderstanding, lack of communication, and frustration had worn away at the foundation of their relationship to the point he no longer believed they had a real marriage.

If Jacqueline's story doesn't scare you, it should. We are facing an epidemic of Christian divorce. And the dirty little secret is these marriages are falling apart because we are woefully unprepared for the most taboo aspect of our relationship – sex.

While the inability to consummate a marriage might seem like an extreme example to you – although from my professional experience I can assure you it is not – it highlights our secret assumptions that we can just figure out this thorny and complex issue on our own. The problem with this assumption is we are culturally inundated with myths about sexual intimacy that have no basis in fact, research or even Scripture. We then drag those myths into our marriages and rely upon them as we form our expectations of each other.

If we are going to have a truly thriving sexual intimacy with our spouses, we have to begin by cutting loose the myths we have been dragging around.

Myth 1: I can have a great marriage without sex.

Most of us start out believing that in order to have a great marriage, we need to have sex. We believe this, that is, until life gets in the way. Then, all of a sudden, we move from being advocates of sex to experts on the realities of life, armed with a fistful of excuses. "We sleep in different beds because he snores." "I fall asleep on the couch because I can't go to sleep without watching the *Late*

Show." "I am too tired." "I am too busy." "We'll have better sex when the kids get older." "I don't feel emotionally close right now."

We quickly forget (or ignore) the importance of sex when it stops being easy. But just because it takes more work now does not mean it ceases to be essential. If we are going to have a good marriage, we need to have the Three Cs.

The Three Cs

I was first introduced to the concept of the Three Cs when I was eighteen years old. I was studying law in Scotland, far away from family. My father, sensing I might be homesick, introduced me to a pastor and his wife who lived in London. When I got lonely for family, I would jump on a train for a visit. Eleanor would put on endless pots of tea, talk for hours, and mother me for the weekend.

Since I was seriously dating a man at the time, our conversations inevitably touched on the topic of marriage. It was during one of these talks she introduced me to the cornerstones upon which solid relationships are built, and that make a marriage work – commitment, communication and consummation. If you are missing one, or if any of the three are out of balance, the relationship will be in jeopardy.

When I was eighteen, I had no idea how deeply this bit of wisdom would sustain me in life. It was, for me, a complete paradigm shift that changed my understanding of marital interactions. It has guided me in my own marriage, and has been the cornerstone of my coaching philosophy with couples regarding theirs.

Here's a shot of reality. In North America, we have about a 50:50 chance at making our marriages last. The Canadian divorce rate is lower than the U.S., but not by much. It doesn't matter if we are Christians. In fact, some researchers believe Christians have worse divorce rates than atheists and agnostics.[1] How can this be so? How can it be that our God created marriage, and yet those who profess to follow Him are splitting up at alarming rates?

The reason lies in what we refuse to discuss. We talk about commitment. We excel at extolling the value of marriage. The communication industry is a multibillion dollar a year business. If we need booster shots on communication, we can turn on *Dr. Phil* or select from dozens of self-help books that discuss this subject matter. But consummation is still taboo. If we are lucky, our pastor talks about it once a year or so, but he rarely get into the nitty-gritties.

When everything is shrouded in secrecy, it is very easy to slide into a sexless marriage without anyone else knowing.

Sexless Marriages

Experts tell us couples that have sex ten times or less a year qualify as sexless marriages. It is estimated one in five couples in North America falls into this category. However, a couple rarely goes from having lots of sex to having none overnight. It is a gradual progression. Usually, when couples fail to make sex a priority, there is a slow erosion of physical contact. Couples stop touching, sitting close on the couch, holding hands, brushing up against each other as they pass in the home, hugging or kissing. All physical contact – even non-sexual contact – dissipates.

However, sex is one of the most important parts of your relationship. It is what sets your relationship with your spouse apart from any other relationship in your life. You can have companionship with your friends, be deeply committed to your children, fight with your relatives and even co-parent with your ex.

But you save sex for your spouse. It is the one thing that sets you apart from simply being roommates. It creates bonds on physical, emotional and spiritual levels. It gives you intense pleasure, it draws you closer together, it smoothes out the bumps in your relationship, and it gives you something to look forward to. It makes you laugh. It may be short and quick, or long and luxurious.

At least, it can be all those things. It can also be the most painful, awful thing about your relationship. In fact, issues surrounding sex consistently rank in the top two reasons couples divorce.

Studies tell us that when marriage is good, sex only accounts for 15 to 20 percent of the focus. However, when marriage is bad, it balloons to 50 to 70 percent of the focus.[2] Scott Haltzman, co-author of *The Secrets of Happily Married Men*, makes the point, "This tells us that although sex is one of many factors in a relationship, if you have problems in your marriage, you will have problems with sex."[3]

Myth 2: A healthy marriage means we both want sex at the same time.

It is estimated that one in three married couples struggles with a desire gap in their relationship.[4] Simply put, one person (the High Desire Spouse) wants sex more consistently than the other (the Low Desire Spouse).

In my experience, most couples have a desire gap, but how they navigate it differs from couple to couple. For some, the gap might be small and manageable. For others, it seems like a giant chasm that keeps them from experiencing intimacy together.

Regardless of who gets labeled the "horny" person in the marriage, one thing is always constant – the person who gets to set the frequency in the sexual relationship is the Low Desire Spouse.[5] Logically, this makes sense. You cannot force your spouse to want to have sex. You can try to guilt him into it. You can strike a bargain so she says yes. But ultimately, it is the spouse who needs convincing who gets to make the final choice.

If both parties are communicating effectively and accept this arrangement, it is usually smooth sailing. However, problems develop when:

- there is a large gap between what the High Desire Spouse wants and the Low Desire Spouse wants
- the gap grows because the Low Desire Spouse begins to avoid all physical touch for fear it will lead to sex
- the High Desire Spouse begins to push harder for sex in response to the Low Desire Spouse's pulling away

- communication about the subject becomes acrimonious or nonexistent
- one or both spouses begin to feel misunderstood or unloved by the other.

If the couple does not understand the dynamics of the gap and learn how to bridge it, it can lead to a cycle of misunderstanding, communication breakdown and lack of physical connection. Sadly, if this is allowed to perpetuate in the relationship, the marriage is at high risk for infidelity and/or divorce.

Why Don't the Same Sex Drive People Marry?

One of my greatest joys is to do Passion Salons. At these Salons, I give an educational talk based on questions the ladies have sent me beforehand, and then I open the floor for discussion. During one of these sessions, a young woman spoke up and said, "The people who want it all the time should get married, and those who don't should get married!" She had made a very astute observation. Wouldn't it be wonderful if there were a test so the "once-a-week people" could marry each other and the "every-day people" could marry each other?

Unfortunately, it is not that easy. In the initial "falling in love" phase,[6] our brains are flooded with a cocktail of chemicals designed to bring us together. During this stage of infatuation, we have a spike of epinephrine, norepinephrine, dopamine, serotonin and phenylethylamine. When this happens, we have more energy (even if we have been up until 4am talking to each other), lower inhibitions (we will try things we always swore we wouldn't), and a higher-than-usual libido (we struggle to keep our hands off each other).

Neuroscientists believe somewhere between six to twenty-four months into our relationship, this powerful hormonal cocktail subsides, and we move past the infatuation phase into the bonding or attachment phase.[7] The good news is in this new phase, we have altered levels of oxytocin and vasopressin that are instrumental in creating deeper love and commitment to each other. The bad news is there was no way to anticipate we would have a desire gap in our relationship because it simply did not exist when we were falling in love.

If you are blaming your spouse for "deceiving" you before you got married, stop. It is useless. It might help you to think of those early days in these terms: Back then, your spouse was just high.

When the Roles Reverse

The desire gap can be a daunting challenge in and of itself, but can become even more so if the spouses switch roles. This might be due to stress, illness, exhaustion, children, hormonal fluctuations and a host of other life circumstances. A woman might be the High Desire Spouse before the couple has children, and all of a sudden realizes she has become the Low Desire Spouse. A man might be the High Desire Spouse until he is put on heart medication that affects his libido, and he is no longer as interested in sex as he once was.

When the roles reverse, this can be a source of tension for the couple because all the patterns they had in their relationship up to this point have been disrupted. Even though the husband was the Low Desire Spouse, he enjoyed the fact his wife pursued him for sex. All of a sudden, she is paying all her attention to the kids and has no energy left over for him. Or the wife may have loved the sex life she had with her husband, even though she was the Low Desire Spouse, and now the side effects of his medication have stolen that from her.

This issue becomes even more magnified when the woman becomes the High Desire Spouse after years of being the Low Desire Spouse. I have seen this happen numerous times after teaching a series to groups of women. Suddenly, they are given permission to enjoy sex. When that switch moves from off to on, their husbands are baffled by the change in their wives.

Some men are ecstatic. One morning at church, a man approached my husband. "Thank you. Thank you," was all he said as he shook Eric's hand. "I had this crazy comment from a guy at church today," Eric said on the way home. I simply smiled. "Ah. He must be the husband of one of your clients." Enough said.

Unfortunately, other men feel threatened. When you have been with the same person for years and have always known what to expect, change can be scary – especially when what has always worked for you is no longer working for your wife.

One of the primary reasons this can be a shock is we do not give a lot of credence to the idea of a man who has a "headache."

Myth 3: He Is always the High Desire Spouse.

Can you imagine a guy having beer and wings with his friends, complaining, "My wife is after me all the time. She just can't get enough. She is driving me crazy! I have to go to bed ahead of her and pretend to fall asleep just to get her off my back!"

No. We have a cultural expectation of a man who is in hot pursuit of his disinterested wife. But many, many women are the High Desire Spouses in their relationships. Women who fall into this category often feel a deep sense of shame. Usually, they blame themselves. "If only I could lose this weight." "If only I could learn better techniques in the bedroom." "If only I were more attractive."

As the situation persists, they begin to have even darker fears. "What if he is having an affair?" "What if he is secretly gay?" "What if he is not attracted to me?" "What if we made a mistake getting married?"

To make matters worse, these women also have a profound sense of isolation. Often their girlfriends fall into the category of stereotypically disinterested wives, and this exacerbates the feeling something is wrong with them. "I just get really quiet when my friends talk," one lady confided in me. "I wish my husband would be more like theirs."

The truth is there are many reasons why a man might be the Low Desire Spouse in his relationship:

- The main sex hormone for men is testosterone, and when it comes to this hormone, not all men are made equally. Some men naturally have higher levels in their systems than others. Men who have lower levels of testosterone usually have a lower sex drive. Remember, this lower sex drive might have been disguised during the early days of the relationship because of the high both of you were experiencing from falling in love.

- He might be in the midst of a personal situation that has caused his libido to be lower than normal. Women are often surprised to learn the sex drives of men – just like women – can be effected by stress, financial pressures, work expectations and interpersonal conflict.
- He might be on a medication that impairs his libido. Many prescriptions given to resolve medical conditions such as depression, heart disease, epilepsy and so forth can interfere with the hormones responsible for a man's sex drive.
- He could have a physical issue which impedes his ability and/or desire to have sex. For instance, if he is unable to get or sustain an erection, or if he suffers from premature ejaculation, the idea of jumping into the sack might be fraught with anxiety for him.
- He could be a Cycle Two person who needs a better understanding of how different people become aroused. (See the Myth 4 for a full explanation.)

Regardless whether it is a season where the man is the Low Desire Spouse or whether it will be this way for the entirety of your marriage, the ramifications are important to address. According to a survey done by *Redbook* in which over 1,000 wives responded, 60 percent felt they were "as interested in sex as their husbands – or more so." Furthermore, a startling number of women who are the High Desire Spouse in their relationship felt they were at risk of having an affair because of their loneliness and frustration.[8] Dealing with this issue is essential to the health of your marriage.

Building the Bridge

No matter whether you are the Low Desire or High Desire Spouse in your relationship, the goal here is not to help you eradicate the desire gap. The gap in your relationship might always remain the same as it is today. However, as you gain a deeper understanding about each other and learn about the desire gap in your relationship, you will find ways to reach across the divide.

For some, the divide might simply be caused by the way you each get aroused.

Myth 4: You always experience desire before arousal.

A client once told me when her husband asks if she wants to have sex, she often responds by saying, "I don't know. Why don't you kiss me and we will find out?" She went on to explain it sometimes takes several minutes to figure out whether she really does want to have sex. Whether or not she knew it, she was reflecting what new research is telling us about the sexual response cycle.

The Traditional Sexual Response Cycle – Cycle One

Back in 1966, sex researchers Masters and Johnson published their findings on the sexual response cycle.[9] And for years we have been taught there is only one way we all become aroused. According to this half-truth, the desire light bulb in our brain goes off and says, "I am in the mood!" If we act upon this impulse and begin to engage in activities that feed this desire, our bodies become aroused. Simply put:

Desire = brain (our cognitive recognition we want to have sex).
Arousal = body (our body begins to go through a physiological chain of events which prepares us for orgasm).

Therefore, the traditional sexual response cycle looks like this:

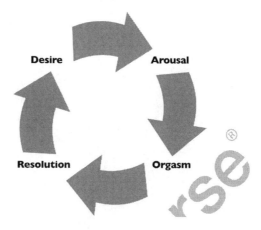

This cycle is easy to understand. It is what we see on TV and in Hollywood. Think back to the most recent sex scene you saw:

Two people lock eyes. They instantly know they want to have sex. They cannot beat back the irresistible desire to jump into bed (or other such place to quench their passion), and they begin to have sex.

There is a scene in the movie *Knight and Day* that brilliantly illustrates this perspective. At one point in this action-packed spy movie, Tom Cruise and Cameron Diaz are trying to escape from a terrorist's house. Diaz' character, who is under the influence of a truth serum and therefore being a bit more honest than usual, suddenly announces, "I think I feel like having sex!" Bullets are whizzing around her head and her brain twigs, *sex.*

You can see how our culture perpetuates the Masters and Johnson sexual response cycle built on the premise our brains recognize we want to have sex before we begin to take action to fulfill our desires. But why doesn't this line up with the experiences of so many married couples?

It turns out Masters and Johnson only got the equation partially correct. While it is true many people do enjoy the sexual response cycle they outlined, there is a significant portion who do not.

The Revised Sexual Response Cycle – Cycle Two

Dr. Rosemary Basson, a psychiatrist at the University of British Columbia, has done extensive research on what makes women tick, and discovered at least a third of her subjects have a different sexual response cycle.[10] The order of their desire and arousal is switched. Therefore, if we were to draw a diagram, it would look like this:

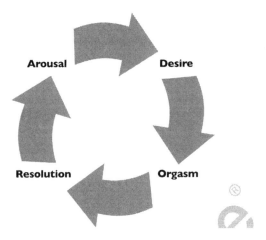

For these Cycle Two people, they have to be physically involved in the act of sex, and get their bodies sufficiently aroused before their brains realize they actually want to have sex. In essence, their desire is actually a *result* of their sexual activity, rather than the *cause* of it.[11]

How do these people end up having sex at all?

According to Basson, Cycle Two people feel "sexually neutral" when they begin to have a sexual experience, even though they are "positively motivated."[12] For example, they may want to have sex so they can connect with their spouse, give and receive pleasure or even avoid an argument. But regardless of their reasons, their desire light bulb comes on only *after* they are engaged in the act. They usually have a great time having sex once they get started – they just start a bit differently.

If you are a Cycle One person (the traditional sexual response cycle), married to a Cycle Two person (Dr. Basson's sexual response cycle), you will need to do two things. First, do some research to find out what arouses your spouse sufficiently enough to feel that twinge of desire.

Second, if you are one of those people who thinks, "Well, if she doesn't really *want* it, then I am not going to *make* her," you need to adopt a new perspective. It's not that your spouse doesn't want it at *all* – you just have to do a bit of convincing first because that is how she is wired.

And if you are a Cycle Two person, my encouragement to you is to take the advice of my client. Instead of saying, "I'm not in the mood," say, "Kiss me and we will find out."

Myth 5: Sex Is something that comes "naturally."

Luke and Olivia were newlyweds who came to me for help. They had been married less than a year and were having significant issues in their sex life. They had made it to the marriage bed as virgins, but not without difficulty. Physical attraction was high with these two. It took everything in their self-control arsenal to not have sex before marriage.

However, almost as soon as the honeymoon was over, they began to find problems creeping into the bedroom. Olivia began to become disappointed they could not achieve simultaneous, face-to-face orgasms. At the time, she didn't know researchers believe only about 25 percent of women can achieve orgasm through penetration alone, making simultaneous, face-to-face orgasms very difficult for most couples to experience. Her mindset was based on artificial expectations based on Hollywood and myth, and she became more and more disillusioned as they failed to live up to her expectations.

By the time they spoke to me, Olivia believed Luke must be doing something wrong, and even let it slip that maybe if he didn't orgasm so quickly, things would work better. Luke was more than willing to do whatever it took to pleasure his wife (and indeed she had achieved orgasm through manual stimulation), but Olivia became convinced their inability to reach this "normal" point in their lovemaking had to be his fault.

This is a classic case of low sexual IQ creating unrealistic expectations that, in turn, cause resentment in the infancy of a couple's sexual relationship. The unfortunate truth is that when couples stumble out of the blocks in this way, it is very easy for them to fall into the misconception that some people are just naturally gifted at sex and, by extension, some aren't.

Allow me to dispel that myth. God did not stand in heaven and naturally endow some of us with the gift of sex while others were left to wander the earth as sexually inept beings. Sex is a skill set developed and perfected over time. Good sex doesn't just happen. It is made.

Sex Is Like Typing

Remember when you learned to type for the first time? You learned where the home keys were so you could begin to hit the correct keys in the correct sequence. You were trained to watch the monitor or the paper (rather than your hands) so you could instantly tell when you had made a mistake. And when this happened – because mistakes are inevitable when you are learning something new – you erased the error, slowed down and made sure your hands were positioned properly again. It took time, practice and feedback to learn how to hit the right keys at the right time to get the correct outcome.

Sex is a lot like typing. There are certain "home keys" on your spouse. These are the areas of her body that are particularly stimulating, arousing and erotic. While these might be the traditional areas you learned in your sexual education course at school, your spouse might have some home keys unique to him. If you have been in other sexual relationships, do not assume your spouse is like your other lovers. What might have made you a superstar in the past might be a complete turn-off now. To become "good in bed," you need to figure out where those areas are on your spouse, and when and how you need to use them.

To develop this skill set, you must get feedback. In a perfect world, all couples would be able to talk about what turns them on and gets them to the place of orgasmic pleasure. There is no doubt verbal feedback is extraordinarily helpful. Wouldn't you love it if your spouse could put into words *exactly* what drives her wild?

But for many couples, giving specific verbal feedback is difficult. Feeling awkward talking about sex is quite common. So common, in fact, that we will discuss ways to open the lines of communication later in the book.

In the meantime, do not neglect the importance of nonverbal feedback. Watch your lover's face when you are touching him. Even if her eyes are closed, you will be able to tell a lot about how she is feeling. Does he look caught up in the experience? Does she look frustrated? Does he look like he is drifting off to sleep? Is she on the verge of orgasm? Also pay attention to other parts of her body. Is he breathing quickly? Is her skin flushed?

Practice Sex

Finally, you must also practice. I don't just mean have sex more often. I mean have times in which you consciously lower your expectations of each other. I find we put enormous expectations on our sexual relationships. They have to be good, all the time. There is very little room for "practice sex."

In practice sex, the two of you decide you want to get more skilled in a particular area. Perhaps she has never had multiple orgasms before, and you want to see what it takes to get her there. Perhaps he would like oral sex as part of your foreplay, and you are completely intimidated by this concept.

Set aside time when the two of you agree you are going to practice. By agreeing ahead of time, you ease the pressure of performance. Then, allow for "mistakes" and "mediocre" sex during this time. To get really good at sex, you have to go through the awkward learning stage. So be patient with each other and enjoy it as much as possible.

When Changes Happen

Unfortunately (or fortunately, depending how you look at it), our bodies are not as simplistic as a keyboard. They are in a constant state of change. Scientists tell us our cells are constantly maturing and then dying off and new cells are being created. From a cellular perspective, the body you have today will be completely different from the body you have in seven years.

If we go back to the typing analogy, it is as though the keyboard changes. Sometimes only a couple of keys are out of place. If they are keys we don't use often (such a "q" or "x"), it will probably take us a while to notice. But if the "a" or "t" suddenly moved places, we take heed immediately.

In our sex lives, we need to realize change is inevitable. What worked in your sex life when you got married might not work after you have kids, and will most likely not work after menopause. Throw in a chronic illness or job loss or depression and you are getting calls from a different playbook altogether.

When you come to a season in your life where the home keys seem to be changing, you might be tempted to let this cause you a great deal of frustration. Allow yourself some time to feel the frustration and grieve the loss of how things used to be.

Then take action. Think of all the new things you will get to try over the years. Shore up your communication skills with your spouse so you can better navigate the changes together. The very fact change is inevitable forces us to get out of the rut we have fallen in, look at our spouses through new lenses, and learn about them in a deeper way. This process, when done well, builds incredible intimacy.

But as you navigate these changes and build your skill set, beware of perfectionism.

Be a High Achiever, Not a Perfectionist

Whenever I talk about developing the skill set of sex, all the perfectionists come out of the woodwork. I meet a lot of them in my line of work. Perhaps there is an unusually high correlation between perfectionism and sexual hang-ups. I've never heard of a study being done on the subject, but would love to see one.

Perfectionists do not like mistakes. They like to be correct all the time. There is no tolerance for error in a perfectionist's world.

However, when it comes to sex, this is a problem because good sex takes practice. Inherent in the concept of practice is the understanding there is room to make mistakes. When you are practicing, mistakes are acceptable, permissible and even expected.

I have noticed when perfectionists become extremely fearful of making mistakes they give up altogether. Perhaps they try a few times, realize they are not living up to their own internal standards, and then quit. The worst culprits give up without even trying. They are terrified of mediocre and so twist the old adage of "If it's worth doing, it's worth doing well" to justify their inaction. And in doing so, they completely miss the value of battling through the awkward learning stage.

As one of my strategies to combat the threat of perfectionism in our own household, I have a saying for my young daughter. "We learn more from our failures than our successes." Our failures are not just a vivid reminder we are not perfect (which, as it turns out, is really ok). They also give us valuable clues to the areas we need to adjust, change, and grow in our lives so we can be successful.

People who can grab on to this concept are high achievers. Like perfectionists, high achievers have very high standards of what they want to accomplish in their lives. But unlike perfectionists, they embrace mistakes and failures as part of the normal learning process they must endure to get to greatness. They elicit and heed feedback because they can use the information to move past the awkward learning stage and into the skilled phase.

I met a high achiever one weekend at a Passion Salon. This woman shared she wanted to become better at oral sex. Now, I have met many women who realized they were not very good at oral sex and just gave up. Instead, this woman asked her husband for feedback. "What do you like? Is this working? What can I do to get better?"

Unfortunately, her husband wasn't particularly skilled at giving her the feedback she needed. Maybe he was embarrassed, preoccupied in the moment, or perhaps didn't know how to answer her questions. Perhaps she did not ask the right questions or catch him at the right time. Regardless, she wanted more information, so she bought a book and practiced her new knowledge on her husband. He was thrilled. And when I met her, she had a confidence that emanated from her.

Remember, when you are developing your skill set, cut yourself some slack. And cut your spouse some too. Aim to be high achievers, not perfectionists. As you work to develop your sex skill set, do so with the understanding there are seasons that are inevitable in every sex life.

Myth 6: This Is Just a Phase.

I once had a pastor's wife tell me, "I used to think that sex would get better when the kids got beyond the toddler years. I later thought it would get better when they got their driver's licenses. Then, I thought it would get better when they moved out of the house. But by the time all of that happened, I went through menopause. I have come to the conclusion that the best sex happens at sixteen in the back seat of a car!"

Now, morally she didn't agree with her own statement, but it reflected the frustration she felt for years in her sex life. She had spent her entire life expecting change was around the corner and constantly out of reach.

I call this the Phase Trap. It is deadly for your relationship because it assumes things will change due to *time* and *circumstances* rather than *action*. In this trap, we pin our satisfaction levels to external forces we cannot control, rather than our own choices we can. Your sex life will not become everything you dream it to be because everything around you changes. It will only become the sex life of your dreams because *you* change.

It is true that despite all your best intentions, there will be periods of time in your marriage where your sex life will be strained and difficult. All couples go through these times. However, if you are not aware this is an expected season in your sex life, and if you do not deliberately tend to it during these times, a pattern of sexlessness can become the new normal in your relationship. The longer this pattern continues, the more difficult it becomes to jump-start your sex life again.

Instead of allowing your understanding of the seasons to excuse you to inaction, use it as knowledge so you can be intentional about taking *more* action. During the seasons in life when sex is difficult, set goals so you can communicate better, and ensure sex occurs frequently enough so both parties feel understood and loved. The skill set you are building during the difficult season is going to make the easy seasons so much more fun. You will hit the ground running, and won't have that awkward, "How do we get started again?" phase.

During your relationship, you need to be on the lookout for three primary seasons of stress and a number of challenging times.

Primary Seasons of Stress

Given decades of sex together, these are difficult phases that most couples will go through.

The Beginning of the Sexual Journey

Just as Luke and Olivia were experiencing a completely unexpected start to their sexual journey, many couples find they get off on the wrong foot. For some, this might be because their lack of sexual IQ and understanding causes hurt and resentment that can build layer upon layer if not quickly addressed.

For other couples, the spouses are carrying baggage from past experiences or beliefs that hinder their ability to connect with each other. These might be messages taught during childhood that now conflict with their sexual experience. For example, my clients who believe pleasurable touch is wrong, or sex is dirty, or virginity is the ultimate status in life have far more to learn than simple techniques to increase intimacy in their sex lives. They are battling with psychological issues that must be addressed before the physiological ones.

Another significant hurdle that can present early in a sexual relationship is past abuse. If there has been sexual abuse in either or both spouses' history, especially abuse which has been hidden and not dealt with, there is a high chance it will impact their sexual relationship. For some couples, this might manifest itself as lack of trust, a profound dislike of sex, inability to orgasm, or refusal to be creative in their lovemaking.

The Birth of Children

There is no doubt the addition of children can be one of the most significant steps that a couple takes together. It can also put incredible stress on all aspects of their relationship, especially their sexual relationship.

Many couples having their first child operate under the flawed perception that sex will automatically get back to normal after the six to eight week restriction period after childbirth. Nothing could be further from the truth. Most mothers (and usually the fathers too) are sleep deprived, stressed from the mammoth task of parenting, and simply too "touched out" to fall passionately into each other's arms at the end of a long day. Basic survival is the primary goal of many young parents.

One lady wrote me and asked, "My feeling and assumption is that it is fairly common to have a mismatch in libido between a husband and wife that is even more pronounced during the years that you have small kids. Are there any stats that might encourage us about when this might improve? Like 50 percent of women notice an improvement in their libido once their youngest child has started school, or something like that?! Just looking for something that might provide a bit of hope!"[13]

When I responded to this lady, I let her know it is true libido can return when the children get older but this, of course, depends on whether you have crammed in new activities to all the free time you are experiencing. Furthermore, if you put sex on the back burner with the best of intentions of moving it back up the priority list after the kids go to school, you are looking at four to five years if you only have one child. If you have more children, it could be ten-plus years before you choose to make sex a priority again. That is a very, very long time to go without sex as a priority.

Even though some issues become easier as the kids grow up (they begin to sleep better, go off to school, etc.), if you fall into the Phase Trap, you will make the subsequent challenges in life into excuses as well.

Menopause and Andropause

While menopause can be extremely challenging to a couple's sex life, more and more experts are now speaking openly about the pitfalls (sexual and otherwise) women face when their estrogen levels drop and they journey through perimenopause, menopause and then post-menopause. Women are finding a host of options they can choose to suit their own experiences and preferences as they go through this phase in life.

Culturally, we are further behind when discussing this phase in men. Andropause is the time in life when testosterone levels begin to drop in men. While the decline in hormones is usually less abrupt in men than women, it nevertheless has a huge impact on their outlook on life. Men going through this season often feel declining energy levels and low libido. This is often accompanied by an acute sense of isolation because if men are unaware this is a normal part of the aging process, they feel they alone are grappling with these issues. And of course, if their wives are unaware this change will take place, they may be baffled as well. Thankfully, we are beginning to see more information on this ambiguous area, and treatments are becoming available for men.

Other Challenging Times

While the primary stressful seasons are periods in their lives that the majority of couples will navigate together, there are also other times that have a profound impact on the sex lives of those who experience them. While the numbers of couples that experience these particular issues are fewer, they nevertheless put extreme stress on their sex lives.

Infertility

There are few things more debilitating to your sex life than doctor-prescribed sex. When you desperately want a baby and the doctor tells you to have sex on days eight, ten, twelve, fourteen, sixteen and eighteen, it is difficult to drudge up sufficient romance to get the deed done with any amount of excitement. If you throw in fertility drugs (which will inevitably turn you into a raving lunatic), or procedures such as in vitro fertilization or a lengthy adoption process, then your relationship is in for a bumpy ride.

Illness

When the doctor diagnoses an illness, your whole world changes. If the illness is life threatening, you immediately begin the process of gathering the information and then taking the actions that you will need to survive. If the illness is chronic but not life threatening, you will most likely have to adjust the way you have been living so you can function in this new reality. During the initial stage of diagnosis, sex may not be high on your priority list. However, as the worst subsides and your new life normalizes, you will need to find fresh ways to communicate about sex, express intimacy with each other, and bridge the desire gap.

High Stress

Amongst other circumstances, these times might include a job loss, death of a family member, moving, building a house or career change.

I had one client who experienced the last three situations all at once. After describing the dismal state of their sex life, she cried, "I don't know how we got to this terrible place in our relationship!"

"I do," I responded. "In the past year, you have moved to a new state, completely renovated a house, and your husband started his own business. I would be shocked if your relationship hadn't deteriorated during this time!" Realizing the state of her marriage was expected and normal, given her life's circumstances, infused her with the hope she needed to hold on and hunker down.

Hunker Down

I spent years living in the South, and down there we have an expression I am particularly fond of: *hunker down*. The Oxford English Dictionary defines the term this way: "To squat, with the haunches, knees, and ankles acutely bent, so as to bring the hams near the heels, and throw the whole weight upon the fore part of the feet." Essentially, when you hunker down, you keep yourself as small as possible while simultaneously being ready to move quickly.

In all these stressful seasons, whether they are inevitable or you experience them by the luck of the draw, you must actively choose to hunker down together. If it is helpful to get a picture in your mind, view the two of you in a trench together, protecting each other as you are bombarded by ammunition. Your spouse is not your enemy – you are facing the enemy together.

During these times, lower your expectations of each other (because no one behaves their best during stressful times), be intentional about clear and effective communication, add extra tools to your relational tool belt, and fight for the best sex possible during these seasons.

When things ease up – because they will – you will have a solid foundation to enjoy the easier times. In fact, the skill set you developed will make for a fabulous sex life when the bombardment ceases.

Myth 7: I have to feel emotionally connected before I have sex.

How many times have these words been uttered in your relationship? I am going to pick on women here, because this is the complaint I hear from them time and time again. Women need to feel emotionally connected to men to have sex, and men need to feel sexually connected to be emotionally available. As couples become dissatisfied with their relationship, they can slide into a subtle resentment of each other that goes something like this:

> Wife: "If he could just talk to me, I would be more open to letting him get some."
> Husband: "If I could just get laid, I could endure her endless chatter better."

This gets to be a game of chicken couples play with each other, waiting to see who will be the first to give in as they both become more and more entrenched in their own positions because of their refusal to see things from their partner's perspective. It is usually the marriage that is the casualty of this deadly game, slowly dying as the layers of resentment between them build, each becoming more and more resolved to "win," rather than focusing on resolving the problem.

But scientists are learning more and more about what happens in the brain when we feel emotionally close to each other. That feeling of contentment and bonding has a lot to do with the hormone oxytocin. Oxytocin helps ease our fear and increase our trust levels. It has a way of making us forget negative things and feel closer to others.

This bonding hormone also plays a significant role during intercourse. Under normal circumstances, a woman has more oxytocin in her body. There is, however, one time when a man's levels rival that of his wife's – orgasm. At this moment, the oxytocin in a man's system can surge as much as five hundred times his normal amounts.[14]

Why is this significant? Because that feeling of emotional closeness you so deeply desire could very well be just on the other side of orgasm![15]

I have challenged countless women to begin having sex with their husbands on a consistent basis. "Try it as an experiment for two weeks and see what happens," I encourage. These women come back to their coaching sessions completely baffled. "What happened over the past couple of weeks?" I ask.

"He kissed me when he came in the door."
"He did what?!" I say.
"He was more attentive to the kids too."
"I can hardly believe it!" I enthuse.
"He even did the dishes!"
"No way!" I shout.

All of a sudden, the men were more attentive to their needs, helped more around the house, and were more responsive to requests these women made. The oxytocin bonding had done its work.

There is no doubt having sex on a regular basis will increase the bonding in your relationship. However, do not discount the importance of carving out time for each other as well.

Making Time to Connect

In our frantic pace of life, the relationships with our spouses are often the last thing in which we choose to invest. It is so easy to get caught up in the immediacy of the demands of life. The kids need to be taxied around to their various activities, the Smartphone never gets turned off so the boss can be kept happy (or so we can feed our own personal addiction to email and Facebook), and we have a myriad of social responsibilities outside work and home.

All these duties can be either the *source* of our lack of intimacy or our *excuse* so we don't have to be intimate. It is pretty easy to hide behind the kids as a way to avoid intimacy. After all, if you are making all those sacrifices for your kids, you are being a good parent, right? Or if you are pouring yourself into your work, it is very easy to justify it as a sacrifice so your family can have the better things in life.

However, if a couple is not spending time together, they are not investing in their relationship as a twosome. More often than not, their relationship existed before the children came along, and yet most couples find little to talk about outside work and kids. They no longer spend hours talking about life, the universe and everything. As a result, their relationship deteriorates into function instead of intimacy.

Time alone as a couple includes time exploring intimacy. If you are struggling to find time to spend with each other because of the innumerable responsibilities you both have, you need to do an honest assessment of what activities eat up your time, and what value you actually place on them. Ask yourself:

- What do I need to delegate or outsource?
- What do I need to give up?
- What do I need to ask for help with?

As you clear your schedule, don't get caught in the numbers game.

Myth 8: We are failing if we aren't having sex two to three times a week.

When I was a senior in high school, I took a psychology class. At one point, the teacher happened to mention most couples have goals for how many times a week they had sex. This made me curious, and so I went home and asked my mom what my parents' goal was. I realize that might seem odd, but I grew up in a household where sex was openly discussed, and it was quite natural for me to ask for perspective from my parents.

"Every day," my mother answered without missing a beat. "Of course, it doesn't always happen because sometimes we are tired. But that is our goal."

I have lost track of how many times I have been asked, "How much sex is normal?" The difficulty with this question is there is no such thing as "normal." If you were to believe my parents, normal was every day. For other couples, normal might be once a month.

We could look at some of the studies that have been done on the average number of times a couple has sex. We used to believe it was two to three times a week. However, new studies show this frequency is declining. Researchers say couples in North America have sex just a bit more than once a week.[16] In fact, the 1950s housewife had more sex than her modern-day counterpart![17]

When addressing the issue of how much sex is enough, most sex therapists believe in quality rather than quantity. Healthy sex lives do not have a particular number of times per week. A healthy sex life develops when both spouses are communicating openly and honestly about their needs and desires, and making a way for sex to happen so they can connect on this very intimate level.

Final Thoughts

Scripture tells us "The truth will set you free,"[18] and debunking the myths we have about sexual intimacy is the first step to that freedom. I cannot count the number of times that learning about the truth behind one of the myths has started a chain reaction of growth in a couple's relationship. Couples begin to feel hope. Hope for true change. Hope for genuine intimacy. Hope for a sex life filled with excitement, enjoyment and anticipation.

Take time to work through your Bedwork this week to recognize and truly dig to the bottom of any deception you have believed, so you can experience the full freedom of truth. When you are finished reflecting on your Bedwork, we will move towards setting goals so you begin to take those small, steady steps (or even leaps and bounds) towards dynamic, lasting change in your relationship that will continue for a lifetime.

Bedwork: Myth-Busting

This week, answer question number one and then choose at least two other questions to answer. If you have a strong emotional reaction to the questions, pick the one you love and the one you hate. If you do not have a strong reaction, pick an exercise that your spouse will appreciate. Don't forget to record your PSA.

1. **Goal.** What is your goal for your sex life with your spouse during the time it takes you to read this book?

2. **Myths.** What myth have you allowed yourself to believe and what impact has that had on your relationship?

3. **Priorities.** Think about your sex life during the course of your marriage. How would you respond to this statement: Our sex life is an important part of our marriage.

   a. Strongly disagree
   b. Disagree
   c. Agree
   d. Strongly agree

   How do you think your spouse would answer this same question? Do you have different answers?

4. **The Sexual Response Cycle.** Think about these questions:
   * Are you a Cycle One (desire, arousal, orgasm, resolution) or Cycle Two (arousal, desire, orgasm, resolution) person?
   * Which one is your spouse?
   * Are you in a mixed-cycle marriage?
   * If you are a Cycle Two person, what type of lovemaking sufficiently arouses you so you feel the spark of desire? Get specific. What can you do ahead of time to jump-start the process of arousal?
   * If you are a Cycle One person married to a Cycle Two person, what do you need to do to ensure desire sparks? If you are not sure, ask your spouse for specific things you can do.

5. **High Desire and Low Desire Spouses.**
   • Who falls into what category in your marriage?
   • Has it always been that way? Or has it changed over the years?
   • Take a moment to look at your relationship through your lover's eyes. Ask yourself:
   • High Desire Spouses: How does it make him/her feel when I initiate sex? What am I noticing about him/her before I initiate? What makes my spouse feel loved and respected, and how can I do those things for him/her?
   • Low Desire Spouses: How does it make him/her feel when I say no? How does s/he interpret my refusal to give a hug or a kiss? What would I be communicating to him/her if I said yes, even if I am not totally in the mood?

6. **Sex As a Skill Set.** Have you been the type of person who thinks you weren't given the natural talent for good sex and are doomed to bad sex for the rest of your relationship? What little changes can you make this week to build your sex skill set? Do you need to read a book on the subject? Talk to an expert? Ask your spouse what s/he really enjoys so you know what you can work on? Have you allowed perfectionism to get in the way of making these changes? If so, how are you going to change your thinking so perfectionism doesn't impede your ability to get better and better as the years go by?

7. **Emotional Connection.** If you are someone who wants to feel emotionally connected before having sex, what does that look like? What do you want your spouse to do (be *very* specific) that will make you feel closer to him/her? Then reflect on the way s/he feels connected to you. What does this look like in your relationship? What specific thing can you do to connect with him/her this week?

8. **Time to Connect.**
   • Sit down and write a list of all the activities you do on a daily basis (work, child care, making meals, tidying house, etc.).
   • Then write down the activities you do on a weekly basis or a few times a week (grocery shopping, coffee with friends, sporting activities, cleaning house, etc.).
   • Reflect on each of these activities individually and ask yourself: Is this activity stealing time away from my spouse? Do I have a healthy balance between activities and time with my spouse? What would my spouse say?
   • Consider this: What you do during the day uses up energy? Would you be better reallocating some of that energy so you have more left over at the end of the day?
   • Think about some things you can eliminate from your schedule, delegate to someone else, or ask for help with so you can make space in your life for greater intimacy.

Hint: This is a good exercise for your spouse to do as well. Once s/he has done this exercise on their own, sit down and talk about the answers you each gave.

Define Your Direction

"I find it fascinating that most people plan their vacations with better care than they plan their lives. Perhaps it's because escape is easier than change."

Jim Rohn – Motivational Speaker

Somewhere between the "this food is awesome" appetizer and the "I am so full I could puke" course of our fondue meal on New Year's Eve, one of our friends broached the topic of resolutions. There were a few smirks, a few comments mentioning the same old, same old. *Lose weight. Make more money. Blah, blah.* After a bit of awkwardness due to the lack of enthusiasm for the subject, my husband finally put an end to the discussion when he announced that in 1992 (the year we met, ironically enough) he made a New Year's resolution to never make a resolution again. In all his years, it is the only one he has successfully kept.

Fortunately, or unfortunately depending on your view, not everyone makes resolutions like my husband. For the vast majority of us, at the beginning of each year there is an innate desire to start fresh, and an overwhelming desire to commit to that fresh start. For some of us, we let go of the past year with a tinge of regret, for it was good to us. For others, we look to the New Year with a bit of desperation. "Thank God that year is over! This year has to be better!" we mutter as we clink our glasses of champagne at midnight. There is something slightly magical about that hour. It's as if we can turn the page on the divorce or house fire or grief that marred the year. We can begin a new chapter.

But just as we begin to feel hopeful and excited, cynicism sets in. If you resolve to make a change in your life, how long can it actually last? In North America, the average New Year's resolution lasts three weeks. Culturally, we can't even cut it for a month. Perhaps we are lazy. Perhaps we get distracted. Perhaps we feel overwhelmed. Perhaps we set our sights too high. Perhaps we don't have a clue what it takes to make true change.

And yet, I firmly believe if you are reading this book, it is not so things can remain the same in your sex life. You are reading because you want to see change, to deepen your sexual intimacy, and to make your sex life better than it is today. And I want to see you succeed. To do so, you need to grab hold of the concept of true change.

Fortunately, there has been an inordinate amount of research in this area. From weight loss to addiction to intense shopping habits, researchers are working tirelessly to figure out how we can make a change in an area of our life, and get that change to stick. Here is some of what they have discovered.

True Change Needs a Well-Defined Target

My husband and I love to take road trips in the car. There have been many times we have hired a babysitter and gotten in the car just to drive. We put on some good music, set the cruise control and go. We have no destination in mind – the journey is paramount.

And yet there are other times we travel with the intent of going somewhere. Perhaps we are going to visit friends or family, or simply getting out of town for a vacation. In those times, we have clearly defined where we are going, how long it will take us to get there, and the milestones along the way. Both types of road trips bring value to our lives, but our purpose defines which type we will take.

When you want to see true change in your relationship, you need the latter type of road trip. To see success, you need to clearly know where you are going, how you are going to get there, and what your timeline is.

When creating a well-defined target, I teach my clients to use the PASS technique.

P – Positive

Since my early childhood, my aunt has had a saying, "What you focus on will grow." The concept is borne of the biblical wisdom – "Seek, and you will find."[1] If you are diligently looking for something, you are going to find it. You will see it in every situation and circumstance. Therefore, deliberately choosing your focus is a crucial part of the goal-setting process.

Let's say you created the goal "I want to stop having boring sex." What are you going to be focused on? Boring sex! You will be counting the number of times you were bored this week, and comparing them to your boredom quotient from last week. The problem with this focus is that you turn your full attention to what you want to *stop* doing. But in neglecting to define this goal in a positive manner, you have merely created a vacuum that exists when the boring sex disappears. When you stop doing a prohibited activity, it leaves you with a lot of spare time on your hands.

If you want to deepen sexual intimacy, it is much more effective to define it by what you *are* going to be doing when you make a change in your relationship. You can apply this principle when defining all sorts of new intimacy-building behaviors:

- When you decrease the number of activities in your life to make more time, what are you going to do with your spouse?
- When you set aside the computer, video games or Smartphone, what will you do with your hands instead?
- When you stop watching porn, what are you going to do with all your free time?
- When you stop fantasizing about the neighbor down the street, what is going to fill your thoughts instead?
- What are you going to do instead of saying no the next time your spouse initiates sex?

To achieve change in your relationship, you are going to have to define what goes in that vacuum when the undesirable activity is removed. So, to return to the example above, ask yourself:

- When you stop having boring sex, what are you going to be doing instead?
- What will make it not boring?
- Where will you be?

- What activities will you be engaging in?
- How will your spouse respond?
- Do you need to learn anything new to make all this possible?
- What type of communication will be most effective in communicating your desires to your spouse?
- What do you think would qualify as not boring to your spouse, and how can you implement that response into your goal?

As you answer these questions, your focus will change to the positive actions you are taking. You will do something constructive to take the place of the destructive activity you used to do. Once you begin to put your plans into action and then review your progress, you will focus on all the productive things you did for your relationship.

A – Action-Oriented

Many people mistakenly make a goal that revolves around their feelings. They want to "be happier" or "feel less guilty" or "feel more love" for their spouse. Obviously, we all strive for positive emotions in life, but defining your goals around your feelings is at best ambiguous and at worst a completely frustrating endeavor. Instead focus on actions you can take. Having consistently taken those actions, feelings and emotions will be the rewards that follow.

For example, some people resolve "to love their spouse more." This is an admirable goal, but what does that mean in real terms? It is true we feel love, but this emotion also flows from the deliberate actions we take to nurture it. When creating a goal to feel love, think about the actions you take when you are feeling love. What are you doing? What are you saying? What are you thinking? How are you acting?

You could define your goal by deciding:

- I will leave a love note for my spouse to discover at least once a week.
- I will kiss my spouse when we meet at the end of the day.
- I will ask how my spouse's day was and then listen to the answer without interrupting.
- I will encourage my spouse to pursue _____ since it is something s/he has dreamed of doing for years.
- I will take on the chore of doing _____ because I know how much it will mean to my spouse.
- I will pay attention to the things that are important to my spouse, and actively engage when s/he talks about them.
- I will put higher priority on our sex life (by doing _____) since I know it is important to my spouse.

Those are specific, quantifiable things you can measure. You will know whether you have success in your goal or not because the actions were either taken or they weren't. The feelings of loving your spouse more will flow out of your intentional actions – because what you focus on grows!

S – Short-Term

If you have a huge goal, I applaud you. Around our household, we call these BHAGs (BEE-hags) for Big Hairy Audacious Goals.[2] I love big hopes and dreams and goals. I think all of us need to have BHAGs we are working towards because they take our eyes off the immediate and give us hope for something big. Couples and families should have BHAGs. Teaching your children about big dreams you are working towards is an incredible gift to give them that will pay off for the rest of their lives.

However, when we are setting BHAGs, we need to recognize every large goal has to be broken down into small, bite-sized pieces. To achieve success, you are going to have a myriad of short-term goals. You need to break your goals into one-month, one-week, and one-day goals to get you there. After all, "A journey of a thousand miles begins with one small step."

The benefit of these shorter-term goals is twofold. First, once you taste success, you are motivated to have more. People working to lose weight will often shriek and yell when they see the first pounds drop off the scale. They see success and they like it. It motivates them to keep doing whatever they did to lose that weight so they can lose more.

Second, consistency will propel you towards your overall goal. It's the old tortoise versus the hare story – as you plug away faithfully, you will eventually get there. When people groan to me about a long-term goal, "It will take _years_!" I say, "You are going to be living those years anyway. Why not be chipping away at your goal?" In our instant gratification culture, we pay too little heed to the value of working slowly and consistently towards a long-term goal. The little steps matter greatly and will eventually lead you exactly where you want to go.

If you want to see change in your relationship, I recommend a goal you can reach by the end of this book. If you read a chapter a week, you have about twelve more weeks. Set a goal with that time frame. It is long enough to ingrain a new habit, but short enough to taste success. Once you have determined what you want to do over the next twelve weeks, break that goal down into chunks of one-week goals, one-day goals and so forth.

S – Specific

It is imperative your goal identifies a specific action to be done a specific number of times in a specific period. If you have decided that you want to have more sex with your spouse as the two of you read through this book, you need to decide what this "more" looks like specifically. Is that two times over the next twelve weeks? Six? Twelve? Twenty-four? Forty-eight?

Believe it or not, specificity is usually the most difficult thing for couples to articulate. We get caught up in the belief that, since we are speaking the same language, we mean the same thing. We are using the same words, but meaning radically different things. Let me give you an example.

One of the biggest complaints I see in my coaching practice is the couple who comes to me and one person – usually the wife – wants to "make love" rather than just having sex. The husband usually hears the wife articulate her need to make love, and he immediately thinks to himself, "I can do that. I know exactly what she needs!" He will set about the task of doing everything he thinks she needs to fulfill the criteria of "making love." They are both using the same terminology, but can mean vastly different things.

Without knowing specifically what "make love" means to his wife, the husband will be doing back flips to make her happy, and could still be way off target. He could be diligently doing everything that falls within his definition of "making love," but completely missing what she wants and needs. Unless she can specifically define what "make love" means to her, they are both going to be extremely frustrated.

When I encounter this type of situation, I usually begin with a series of questions:

- What is "making love" to you?
- Is it longer foreplay? If so, for how many minutes?
- Deep kissing? With tongue or without?
- How long does he need to be touching you before he can "go for the goods"?
- How much attention does he need to give you during the day (before sex is ever initiated)?
- What does that look like? Is it a phone call? A flirtatious text message?
- Do you need to sit down with a cup of coffee when you both get home and debrief about your day before you begin to have sex?
- Does he need to look deep into your eyes?
- How long does sex last when you are "making love"?
- Does "making love" mean you get to achieve orgasm, no matter how long that might take?

You get the idea. I continue to ask questions until both the husband and wife have a crystal clear picture of what "making love" entails. When a couple defines specifically what they want to change in their relationship, it sets them both up for success. He knows exactly what he needs to do to make his wife feel connected to him sexually. And because she has clearly identified what she is truly looking for, she will be able to recognize it when it happens. As such, the odds of actually succeeding in making love have just gone up exponentially.

Putting PASS Together

Let's take a look at all the elements of a PASS goal.

To stop having an infrequent and boring sex life.

- Is it positive? No, it focuses on what this couple wants to stop doing.
- Is it action-oriented? No, it gives no actions that they should undertake to reach their goal.
- Is it short-term? No, it has no defined time limit.
- Is it specific? Not at all.

Here is a way this couple could redefine their goal:

Over the next six months, we are going to increase the frequency and creativity in our sex life by having sex at least once a week (Mondays and Thursdays are the best for our schedules), and trying something new at least once a month (we will read a book together to learn about different options for "new").

This couple has now clearly defined what they are going to do to implement change in their sex life, and given themselves a solid chance at achieving the change they want to see. Clearly articulating your goal is only the first step. Once you have defined it, you need to write it down.

Write Down Your Goal

Research has shown that people who write their goals down are more successful in accomplishing them than those who do not.[3] So, once you have defined what you want to accomplish using the PASS test as your guide, write your goal down on an index card and put it in a place where you will frequently see it. Taping it to your bathroom mirror is a great place to guarantee you will view it several times each day (three or more is best). Of course, if you have children who can read and your goal is explicitly sexual in nature, this might not be the best place!

You might also want to put the goal:

- on your bedside table
- in your wallet next to your primary form of payment (credit card, debit card, cash)
- as a bookmark in a book that you read daily
- taped to your computer monitor.

Regardless of where you choose to put it, the important part is you will see it frequently. Every time you see the card, read it to yourself and reflect on it for about one minute. This will ensure your goal remains part of your focus for your day. As such, every time you see your goal, it will be reinforced.

After you have your goal clearly defined and written down, take the next step in enacting true change in your relationship.

True Change Needs Accountability

I find North America's obsession with the TV show "Biggest Loser" completely fascinating. Here is a group of people who would typically be ostracized in society because of their weight, and yet they become international heroes. And yet, at its heart, the story has very little to do with pounds on a scale. The hook that lures us in is the desire to see ordinary people face magnificent odds and win the battle week after week. Regardless of whether you are a size twenty-two or a size two, the story will spark your imagination and give you hope.

I happened to catch an episode in which Bob Harper, one of the trainers, was talking about his concern for the contestants when they returned home. The show was in its ninth season, and they had already noticed a disturbing trend of people who lose a tremendous amount of weight only to go home and gain it back again. It is tragic to see those who worked so hard lose all that ground.

To combat this trend, the show decided to send the contestants home for a two-week challenge to see how they did. It gave them the chance to practice life in the "real world" while still competing for the title of Biggest Loser.

One contestant, Koli Palu, realized the depth of the challenge of being in a house with a bunch of buddies who cared little about healthy lifestyles. In one scene, the pizza boxes were littered across the floor as all the guys camped around the TV. It seemed Palu looked a bit lonely as he sat off to the side and ate his fish and veggies for dinner.[4] What the contestants realized during this at-home challenge is true change needs accountability. On the ranch (their home while on the show), they have numerous forms of accountability. They have trainers who are watching their every move and breathing down their necks – literally and figuratively. They have full access to a gym with all the exercise equipment they could possibly imagine. They have other contestants who are their competition, their teammates and their friends. And, of course, they have the very public weigh-in every week. Accountability is everywhere.

But if they want to stay on track at home, they have to recreate their own accountability systems. Doing so begins with a good accountability partner.

Find an Accountability Partner

In one study, researchers found that when people found an accountability partner to check in with weekly, a whopping 76 percent achieved their goals. (Study participants who did not have accountability partners trailed behind significantly as only 43 percent achieved their goals.)[5] If you are working through this book with your spouse, you might want to be accountable to each other. Setting up a weekly routine where you talk about your goals together, how you succeeded and where you failed, gives you the opportunity to increase your intimacy, practice the skill set of talking about sex with one another, while moving you towards your goals.

However, it could also put you on a fast track to failure if the two of you have a pattern of enabling each other, or if one of you will simply feel nagged by the other in the midst of this process. If this is the case, you will both need to find a friend to whom you can be accountable. I have seen couples go through The Essential Elements of Sex course that chose to be accountable to another couple. The women met to talk about their goals and the men did the same. Obviously, given the sensitive nature of what you are trying to accomplish in your marriage, confidentiality is key to making this relationship successful.

Using wisdom to choose your accountability partner is crucial. A good one will cheer you on and promote healthy relationships to others around you. A poor one will suck you into destructive patterns of perfectionism, and will not be empathetic in the moments when your goal feels ridiculously far away. It might be helpful to see this person as a cheerleader.

I went to high school in Texas where Friday night football is not just a pastime, it is a religion. And if I learned anything through this experience, I learned everyone needs a good cheerleader.

The guys on the team need to know there are people whose only job is to encourage them. But the people in the stands need cheerleaders too. The cheerleaders rally community support for the players on the field. And, the cheerleaders support and encourage whether the team is winning or if they are behind by twenty-one points. Their job is to believe you can win. When you lose, their job is to believe you can do better next time.

However, you not only need to have a partner who can cheer you on and hold you accountable, you also need to take a look at the environment you have around you.

Create Environmental Accountability

Experts on addiction have long known if you want to stay sober, you have to change your environment. You can be determined to change, and even have a sponsor to talk to, but have all your best intentions undermined by the environment in which you live. Therefore, if you are an alcoholic, you will no longer be able to hang out with your buddy Joe who loves to get drunk every weekend. If you are a drug addict, you will no longer be able to drive down the same street where your dealer lives. You will no longer be able to go to the same parties. You might have to change your phone number. You might even have to change the route you take home from work because you are accustomed to swinging by the liquor store along the way.

But even outside the field of addiction, researchers are also realizing the significance of triggers that set off these habits we want to change. For instance, a person who is trying to eat healthy foods should go to a different grocery store – a new location or chain altogether. The act of being in a different environment sends a signal to your brain that this is new, and there will be no junk food purchases at this store.

If your sex life has been stymied with bad patterns, you will need to figure out what triggers those behaviors, and change your environment accordingly so you can set yourself up for success:

- At night, you flop on the bed and immediately turn on the TV. By the time your shows are over, you are too tired to have sex. Environmental change: Get the TV out of the bedroom. Put a bedtime on yourself and set it one hour before you are too tired to do anything else so you have time and energy for sex. Then follow that bedtime.
- Your bedroom is a complete disaster and so you avoid it for all activities except sleeping. Environmental change: Clean it up. Spruce things up with a new coat of paint and maybe some new bedding. Move around the furniture. Add some plants or fresh flowers.
- You go to bed at a different time than your spouse. Environmental change: Go to bed together. If the night owl needs to sneak away after his/her spouse is asleep, then do it. Alternatively, set the alarm a half hour earlier and wake up to have sex in the morning.
- You never have time together without the kids. Environmental change: Find a babysitter and get out together. If the idea of having a teenager watch your children causes too much anxiety, form a babysitting co-op with friends and take turns watching each other's kids, or recruit Grandma.

- You hang out with friends or family members who constantly criticize your spouse, believe marriage is a burden, or think sex is a nuisance. Environmental change: Limit your time with those people or phase them out of your life completely. Find new friends who believe marriage is fabulous and sex is amazing.

After you get a clear picture of what change you want to see, and surround yourself with people and an environment that will support your new patterns, begin to build consistency.

True Change Needs Consistency

In 2008, I attended a convention in which Jack Canfield, co-author of the *Chicken Soup for the Soul*[6] series and co-author of *The Success Principles: How to Get From Where You Are to Where You Want to Be,*[7] was the keynote speaker. During his talk, Canfield told the story of a NASA experiment in which a group of astronauts wore convex goggles so the world looked upside down to them. After twenty-five to thirty days of wearing the goggles, the astronauts reported their world looked right side up again. Neurologically, when we create new habits, we are forming new pathways in the brain, and are actually replacing our old habits with new ones. Their brains had created a workaround that made the world normal again.

But does it take twenty-five to thirty days of *continuous* change to enable the brain to form new pathways? NASA anticipated this question as well.

There was a second group of astronauts who were told to take off their goggles on day fifteen and take a break. After twenty-four hours, they were told to put the glasses on again. Guess what? They had to start from scratch. For this group, it took an additional twenty-five to thirty days before the world readjusted itself. The takeaway is it takes a minimum of twenty-five days *in a row* to create a new habit. It may sound long, but it takes time for the brain to create new pathways. As we practice new behaviors, we overlay the old ones, like treading down the same horse trail over and over until the new behavior eventually becomes the habit.

This is the tragic aspect of our New Year's resolutions. Most of us are unable to stick it out long enough to allow the new habit to form. If we are not constantly reinforcing the new actions (and yes, that means every single day without fail), the old habits are going to remain dominant. People are giving up just as their new habits are beginning to take root.

Now, I am not suggesting you must have sex each and every day with your spouse. Rather, you need to be consistent with achieving your goal each and every week. Do not skip, telling yourself you will catch up next week. Do not allow a week to go by without achieving your goal. This consistency will create new neuropathways in your brain that will soon become your new "normal."

To keep yourself on track, you will need some incentives along the way.

True Change Needs Rewards

When my daughter was in kindergarten, she decided she wanted to take horseback riding lessons, which are quite expensive. Riley is privileged enough to have dance and music classes, but horses are in a price point of their own. But she persisted in asking. It was really a big deal to her.

At that time, her reading skills were a priority to Eric and me. Since there was something we wanted her to deliberately develop in her life, and there was something that she really wanted, we decided to strike a deal. If she read one hundred books by the end of kindergarten (five months), we would put her in horseback riding lessons during the summer.

Very quickly, Eric and I realized it was going to be exceedingly difficult for a five-year-old to stay motivated for that long without tangible signs of success and smaller benchmarks along the way. So, Riley and I made a chart with the numbers one to one hundred and places for stickers. She would give herself a star every time she read a book. But there were a lot of stickers between her and her goal. She needed a few more incentives to keep going.

We therefore declared we should celebrate every time she completed twenty-five books. Riley decided she would like to go have sushi (her favorite food) for dinner every time she met this benchmark. These times usually turned into a mini party, as she would often invite close friends to join us for dinner. The final goal, of course, was rewarded by horseback riding lessons.

Her goal was broken into small, measurable steps with celebrations along the way. She had:

- immediate rewards (stars)
- mid-term rewards (sushi dinners)
- long-term reward (horseback riding lessons).

Because her success was so tangible and there was always some reward within reach, she accomplished her ultimate goal a whole month early.

Why Do We Need Rewards?

It is very easy to grasp the concept of rewards when talking about a child. But so often we grow up and forget how important these principles are.

Remember the NASA experiment? It was pretty straightforward for those astronauts. Once they signed up for the study, they didn't have a choice but to keep the goggles on for as long as they were told. But what happens when we aren't being told what to do? What happens when it is not our job?

Scientists are discovering if we set up goals in our lives without rewards, it will be extraordinarily difficult to accomplish them.[8] This isn't because we are childish and need a star to stay motivated. It is not because we lack focus and determination. It is because our brains are wired to respond to hormonal rushes that give us pleasure.

One of the primary hormones responsible for rewards and motivation in the brain is dopamine. When we find pleasure in an activity (eating food, having sex, shopping for shoes, etc.), our brain is flooded with dopamine. The next time we are presented with the opportunity to do that activity again, our brain reminds us it was pleasurable and we *should* do it again. While this is not so great when feeding an addiction (such as drugs and alcohol), dopamine is wonderful when reinforcing an activity that is healthy and productive in our life, such as great sex with our spouse.

This is one of the reasons why most couples agree that when they are having a lot of sex, they want more. The more they have, the more they want. The rush of dopamine (in addition to oxytocin and other hormones) is reinforced in closer intervals, allowing the reward center of the brain to light up more consistently around the act of sex.

Since goal accomplishing is all about rewiring the pathways in our brains, we have to understand how the current pathways work so we can choose our rewards wisely.

Choosing Your Rewards

A friend once told me she decided to implement an exercise plan. She had done some reading on osteoporosis, and realized one of the best defenses was to build up muscle strength. She bought herself a bicycle and set a goal of how often she would go riding.

But she took this plan one step further. She realized there would be days when it would rain, and she would be sorely tempted to skip her ride. Since she lived in a climate where rain was frequent, the weather was going to be a significant deterrent to her goal. So, she decided that she needed an incentive for those days. When she went riding in the rain, therefore, she would come home and download a song off iTunes. It cost her less than a dollar, but it was both sufficiently *large enough* and *rewarding enough* for my friend to persist when she did not want to go riding.

There will be times when you will, very simply, not feel like pursuing your goal. Maybe you have decided to set your alarm half an hour earlier each day so you and your spouse can find time to connect before the chaos of the day begins – but when it begins blaring in the early morning, all you want to do is hit the snooze button. Perhaps you have decided not to say no during the weeks of this book, and yet when your spouse initiates, all you really want to do is watch the game on TV. Perhaps you and your spouse have decided to try a new position once a month, but you never seem to make time to get to the bookstore for that book on positions you promised to buy.

When we seek to make true change in our life, there will be times when we just don't feel like doing what we promised. This is completely normal and expected. However, you need to anticipate those times and set up a pay-off for your diligence. In those situations, you need to have a reward large enough and rewarding enough to push through.

What motivates you? A monetary coupon (you decide the amount – $1, $5, $10, etc.) towards an outfit? Going to the golf range to hit a bucket of balls? A square of fine chocolate? A monetary coupon for a spa appointment? A night out with the guys? Saving up for that flat-screen plasma TV you have been wanting? Flying lessons?

Figure out what works for you, and then clearly define together under what circumstances you will earn your rewards.

Keep in mind, in your marriage one of you might not need any extra motivation to accomplish the new goal for your sex life. The act of sex alone might be enough. It alone motivates you and rewards you sufficiently to follow through. If you are this type of person, do not begrudge your spouse a reward system. This does not mean s/he is weaker, less motivated, or less dedicated to your marriage than you. It simply means s/he operates differently. Respect this difference and work with your spouse to set up rewards that work. You will ultimately benefit.

A Note of Caution

If you feel you are becoming trapped by your goals, you need to reevaluate them. One of my friends, a pastor, shared with me that at one point in his life, he actually had a breakdown because of his goals. He was driving himself so hard to reach new heights in his ministry, he felt he could no longer keep up the pace and stopped, utterly exhausted.

Perfectionists are particularly prone to this form of burnout. Their drive to fulfill their goals is fueled by their deep-seeded desire to be *good enough* rather than out of a genuine longing to make *improvements* in their lives. If you feel you are being driven by your goals, rather than driving them, take a step back.

It is at these points I find the advice of psychologist and professor Dr. Paddy Ducklow particularly helpful for my clients. "Seventy is my new one hundred," he says. "Perfectionism does not help [you] do the job better, it only ensures that [you] will enjoy the success less."[9] Often our obsession to be perfect makes us too focused on our perceived failures. If, however, we consciously choose to succeed with 70 percent of our goals for ourselves, we give ourselves permission to relax a bit. Think about it in this context – 70 percent is still a long way down the road from where you began. And long-term growth (as opposed to obsessive behavior which leads to burnout for us and those around us) is really what we need to be aiming for in our lives.

Final Thoughts

As a coach, I want to see you succeed. I don't want you to *talk* about change – I want you to *do* it. However, change is difficult. If it were easy, we would all be skinny, wealthy and free from addictions. Unfortunately, many of us are still a long way off from where we want to be. As you set about making changes in your sexual relationship, ensure the best possible success. Harness the discoveries scientists have made about how our brains were created to work for you during this process.

Bedwork: Define Your Direction

PSA: _____

*This week, answer **all** the questions so you have the best chance of achieving your goal as you work through this book. Don't forget to record your PSA.*

1. **PASS Test.** Look at the goal you developed in your Bedwork during the last chapter. Does it meet the PASS test (Positive, Action-Oriented, Short-Term, Specific)? If it doesn't, then redefine it this week. Write it on an index card and put it in a place where you will frequently see it. Every time you do, read it to yourself and reflect on it for one to two minutes. This will ensure your goal remains part of your focus that day.

2. **Accountability.** Who can you choose as an accountability partner to keep you on track and be your cheerleader? Is it your spouse? Is it another (same gender) friend? Another (same gender) person reading this book with you? Check in with this person each week to let them know how you are doing with your goal. Understand that any accountability relationship grows in trust over time, so if this concept is a big step for you, start small.

3. **Environment.** What changes do you need to make in your environment to support the new habits you are developing?

4. **Rewards.** What rewards do you think will be large enough and rewarding enough to keep pursuing your goal? Clearly define your reward system and share with your spouse.

Faith

"Sex. God. They're connected. And they can't be separated.
Where the one is, you will always find the other."
Rob Bell – Pastor and Author

Back in 2009, I attended a fundraiser and the keynote speaker was Brian Stewart, one of Canada's most renowned journalists. In his talk "Faith on the Frontlines," he spoke about his own journey to Christ, which was greatly impacted by what he saw on the ground as he traveled the world in pursuit of the latest story. In trip after trip, he noticed Christians were always there first. This was not just his observation. One of the conversations the reporters frequently had amongst themselves was the fact the Christians were always in the beleaguered areas where the devastation was happening.

On one of his trips, he flew into a small village in Africa during a humanitarian disaster. He looked at his cameraman and they both agreed, this time, they would beat the Christians to the punch and arrive first. And yet, as their plane touched down, a Dutch pastor met them on the tarmac and welcomed them with a pot of tea. He was already there in the midst of the disaster.

Stewart said this was a powerful part of his conversion process because, slowly over the years, he began to perceive Christians as courageous men and women. When everyone else was evacuating, Christians stayed to take care of those who were stranded and alone. They shared the burden of war, famine and other horrors alongside the local people.

Christianity has a rich history of normal, everyday believers taking a stand for the principles laid out for us by Christ. We have been known for caring for our neighbors, loving the unloved, feeding the hungry, clothing the naked and giving a cup of cold water in Christ's name. And that's hardy an exhaustive list.

And yet, with very few exceptions, we have not earned this reputation in the area of sexual intimacy. Instead, Christians are seen as hypocritical, judgmental, guilt-plagued, fearful, angry, silent, frigid and – in my opinion, this next one is worst of all – research-adverse.

This boggles me because our God created sex. In fact, He designed our bodies with sex in mind. Sex was not just an add-on, like an upgrade on a car. *Why yes, I would like to have power windows, alloy wheels and the optional sex package, please.* No. When God was creating us in His image, He wove sex into the design. Now, obviously, He put the proper plumbing in. You need to have the genitals fit together properly for the act to take place. But He did even more.

Did you know studies have shown semen causes women to be less depressed?[1] Or that men, when kissing their wives, transfer testosterone in their saliva so help boost her libido?[2] What an amazing God we serve who took such care in the details so we could experience the richness of sexual intimacy.

Because of this, sexual intimacy should be one of the things we do best. It could be an evangelism tool. *Oh, you know those Christians – they know how to get it <u>on</u>!* And yet something has gone terribly wrong in how we communicate this message.

Stories from the Front Lines

When I met Bethany, her marriage was on the verge of divorce. Sex had ceased to be a priority, and the communication between her and her husband had grown steadily more and more toxic. She explained she and Paul had sought counseling from their pastor, but once he realized the source of their issues was sexual, he escorted them out of his office. I was dumbfounded.

"What did he say?" I prompted her.

"He just said that he wasn't comfortable discussing it." She replied.

"But surely he gave you a reference for someone who *was* comfortable with talking about it." I simply could not believe she was telling me the whole story.

She looked a bit confused. "Why, no, he didn't."

Laura was another woman who shared with me a deeply traumatic experience she had during her years in a Christian high school. She wore a long skirt to school and it had a slit up the back, presumably so she could walk with ease. A boy from the school told his mother later that evening the skirt made him feel tempted. The mother called the principal and unleashed her fury on him. Consequently, the principal decided to have a whole school assembly to talk about the importance of wearing "appropriate" clothing.

When Laura was informed that she was the center of the brouhaha (because she was completely oblivious to the fact that she had done anything wrong until the principal called her into his office and spelled it out for her), she was mortified because being seductive was the furthest thing from her mind.

Bethany felt completely shamed that her issue was so terrible even the pastor didn't want to talk about it. In reality, what she and her husband were facing really wasn't a big issue. In fact, it was one of the fastest fixes I have ever seen in my practice. But it was still taboo.

Laura's experience in high school caused her to make an inner vow that to be godly, she would never allow herself to be sexual. You can understand a teenager coming to this conclusion, trying so hard to be faithful to God. But it had massive ramifications when it was expected she be sexual with her husband. It took months of talking through the freedom God gives us within the context of a marital relationship before she was able to see strides in this very intimate part of her relationship with her husband.

Our History

Unfortunately, we have a rich history of misunderstanding the nature of sexual intimacy in our Christian heritage. Here are a few examples:

- Augustine believed sex was good unless you paired it with passion and desire. If you had these things, you were no better than an adulterer, even though you were with your spouse.[3]
- Martin Luther said, "Intercourse is never without sin, but God excuses it by His grace" for the greater good of marriage.[4]

- More recently, a popular marriage book describes the penis as a "tumor" and the vagina an "open wound." In essence, the author took some of the most precious of creations and reduced them to terms of disease and pain.[5]

Now, I don't want to spend a lot of time disparaging Christian leaders and authors. It is not my goal to make good-meaning people look bad. But I do think these stories are important because they represent the reasons people end up in my practice. These are Christian couples, going to church, loving the Lord, trying to be faithful to God and each other, and yet they carry baggage into their marriage that is a result of how sexual intimacy was represented to them by spiritual leaders.

These people are in your church. They hide out, with all their myths and assumptions and secret pains. They have these lies they have been told, and they sit down in the pews or the pastor's office. And they desperately want better marriages. They desperately want sexual intimacy with their spouses. Instead of having Stewart's experience, where Christians are on the front lines courageously working with the hurting, the lost and the lonely, people struggling for sexual intimacy have felt more and more alone.

We can change this situation. Our God has given us all the tools we need in the Scriptures and in the clues He has left us right on these bodies He created. But if we are to understand what God intended for us, we must begin with how His ultimate plan was distorted. To do so, we must expose one of the most insidious and terrifying monsters in the history of our faith.

Shame

As both Bethany and Laura's stories illustrated, there are few subjects in the Christian faith that make us feel more unsafe, fearful, anxious or trigger our shame buttons faster than the area of sexuality.

This should not be surprising because the issues of sexuality and shame have been entwined since the dawn of time. Genesis 2:25 (NLT) tells us when God created man and woman, "Now the man and his wife were both naked, but they felt no shame."

Skip ahead a few verses, after Adam and Eve eat of the Tree of Knowledge of Good and Evil, and this is what happens in Genesis 3:7-13:

At that moment their eyes were opened, and they suddenly felt shame at their nakedness. So they sewed fig leaves together to cover themselves. When the cool evening breezes were blowing, the man and his wife heard the LORD God walking about in the garden. So they hid from the LORD God among the trees. Then the LORD God called to the man, "Where are you?" He replied, "I heard you walking in the garden, so I hid. I was afraid because I was naked." "Who told you that you were naked?" the LORD God asked. "Have you eaten from the tree whose fruit I commanded you not to eat?" The man replied, "It was the woman you gave me who gave me the fruit, and I ate it." Then the LORD God asked the woman, "What have you done?" "The serpent deceived me," she replied. "That's why I ate it."

What Is Shame?

Dr. Brené Brown, a professor at the University of Houston who has spent the past decade researching shame, contends shame is universal. Unlike personality disorders or medical illnesses, we cannot distance ourselves from this unsightly attribute by sorting ourselves into "us and them" categories. Everyone has it. You have it. Your pastor has it. Your counselor/therapist has it. Your teachers have it. Your parents have it. Your spouse has it. Your kids have it. I have it. We all have it.

The only types of people who do not feel shame are those who are unable to connect with others. If you are a human who can, you have shame. Dr. Brown goes on to explain that not only do we all have shame, but we don't want to talk about it. Furthermore, the less we want to talk about it, the more we have it.

This is a huge problem, because shame is the trigger that deactivates the effectiveness of Christians in the area of sexual intimacy. We, as a faith culture, are completely undone by shame.

What Are Its Attributes?

If we are going to combat shame, we need to understand it. Starting with some definitions is helpful.

Simply put, shame is the fear of disconnection. As we dig a bit deeper, we realize we fear disconnection when we, in a deep, dark part of ourselves, believe we are not worthy of love and connection. Since we were created to have relationship with God and others, the fear of being cut off evokes a raw, instinctive reaction in us. This is shame.

Research also shows shame is different from guilt, humiliation and embarrassment. This chart illustrates those differences:[6]

Name	Belief	Examples of Self-Talk
Embarrassment	Lots of people have done this before.	"I bet I looked silly tripping on the sidewalk, but I know I am not the only one who has done it."
Humiliation	I did not deserve the treatment I received.	"I didn't do what the teacher accused me of, and so I don't deserve to be sitting in the principal's office right now."
Guilt	I am a good person, but I made a bad mistake.	"I deeply care about people and their feelings, but I was really cruel to Marie in that email I sent."
Shame	I am a bad person, and I am alone.	"I can't believe I did that. I am such an awful person. No one else has this problem."

You might realize how people react to their circumstances varies depending on each individual and his/her life experience. So, what might be embarrassing for one person is shameful for another. What might trigger guilt in one will evoke shame in another.

Bethany could have walked out of her pastor's office and said to herself, "That guy doesn't have a clue what he is talking about. Of course we have to talk about the issues of sex in our marriage. I'll go find someone who isn't so fearful about talking about sex, and get this issue sorted once and for all." Instead, the pastor was able to trigger her shame button. There was something in the way she was raised, or something in the way she related to her husband, that made her think, "I am worthless because I can't get my act together in this area."

Likewise, Laura could have reacted with humiliation to her school situation. She might have said to herself, "I was dressed appropriately that day, and I am not responsible for the out-of-control hormones of a teenage boy or his mother's fear." Instead, she believed the message she was a temptress who was a danger to good Christian boys. She was the bad one. And this belief almost undid her marriage years later.

Common Examples

Bethany and Laura are not the only ones who have shared stories of shame with me. Here are some other examples I have seen over the years:

- You were told that sex is wrong for years, and your thirty-minute wedding ceremony was not sufficient enough to undo all those messages.
- You and your spouse crossed all the boundaries you set before you got married, and even though now sex is permissible, you cannot let go of your shame.
- Your parents slapped your hands away from your genitals when you were a young child leading you to believe pleasure is wrong, and you do not know how to change this belief in your marriage.
- No one gave you any instructions on the nitty-gritties of sex, so you and your spouse stumble along, not really knowing what you are doing or where to go for help.
- You were molested as a child and so all sexual touch is fraught with anxiety, fear and vulnerability.
- You are infertile and the act of sex is a constant reminder of your inability to bear children, so you avoid it at all costs.
- You indulge in pornography when no one else is looking, and are not sure how to get free without doing further damage to your relationship.
- You have had increasingly lustful thoughts about your co-worker and you don't know how to stop.
- You cannot stand the way your body looks and cannot bear to have your spouse see you naked with the lights on.
- You were pushed beyond your personal boundaries in an earlier abusive relationship and now anytime your spouse begs for sex, you feel threatened and exposed.
- You don't believe you are any good at sex, so it is easier to just avoid it altogether.

- You experience pain during sex, but your doctor says there is nothing physically wrong with you so it must be "in your head."
- You believe sex is not to be enjoyed – it is only for procreation.
- You get turned on by something you are not sure is normal, acceptable or right.

Every person who told me their story believed it was too awful and horrible to talk about, and that no one else had these thoughts or feelings. They were able to clearly identify shame in their life because of their reactions.

How Do We React When We Feel Shame?

Shame completely undoes us. Neuroscientists tell us when we feel shame, our bodies react like they have gone through physical trauma. We are stunned, we feel numb, our hearts beat faster, and our mouths go dry. It's as though our limbic centers (the fight, flight or freeze parts of our brains) have just been whacked with a big stick.

It is helpful to understand that when you first feel your shame button triggered, your prefrontal cortex (the thinking, processing part of your brain) goes offline. There is no rational thought in this moment. In fact, it could take a good ten to fifteen minutes to get your prefrontal cortex back online. Furthermore, during that time period, you are extremely vulnerable to having a reaction to your own shame – a reaction that could be incredibly damaging to those around you.

Dr. Linda Hartling and others at The Stone Center at Wellesley College have outlined three ways people tend to react in these circumstances:[7]

1. We move away and isolate ourselves.
2. We move towards the person who shamed us and try to please him/her.
3. We move against the person and lash out in rage and blame.

Reaction Style 1: Adam and Eve initially employed this tactic when they felt the shame of their nakedness in the Garden of Eden. When they realized what they had done, they hid from God.

My client Bethany also reacted this way. When her pastor cut off any conversation that pertained to sexual intimacy, she withdrew and didn't say another word to anyone until she met me. It was only after several meetings with her that she able to tell me her story and share how hurtful the pastor's response was to her and her husband.

The destructiveness of this reaction style is that sexual intimacy entails building connection with your spouse. When your reaction to shame is to withdraw and isolate, you move away from your spouse, creating disconnection. If you draw further into yourself, you also remove yourself from the community of friends and family who could be your support network.

Reaction Style 2: Laura's story is a classic example of someone, who has been shamed by another, trying to please her shamer. Laura spent the rest of her years in high school taking extreme care she was dressed properly, and behaved the a way "good Christian girl" should so she would meet the approval of the high school staff.

This is the most insidious reaction style because it looks like a good Christian response on the surface. It might appear to be holding yourself accountable to authority, or working towards reconciliation, or even taking responsibility for your own actions. However, it is actually just a cover-up to look good so no one will shame you again. At the root, the shame still festers.

Reaction Style 3: Once Adam and Eve realized hiding from God was a futile course of action, they shifted gears into Reaction Style 3. When God asked why they were clothed, Adam quickly blamed Eve. "It was the woman."

What did Eve do? She blamed the serpent. "The serpent deceived me."

My mother used to call this "passing the emotional hot potato." When we feel the pain of shame, we try to get rid of it as quickly as possible, and often do this by dumping it on the people closest to us. Sadly, passing the hot potato is a common reaction in Christian circles.

- There was the worship leader who was called into her pastor's office and scolded for sharing insights from her own sex life with younger women who had questions. (Blame her for speaking out.)
- There was the pastor who railed on a newlywed who had been given a bedroom toy at one of her bridal showers by saying, "Any marriage that needs that is no marriage at all." (Blame her for asking a question about her wedding gift.)
- There was the elder board that fired a pastor because he came forward to admit he had an emotional entanglement with a woman on his staff and needed help. (Blame him for straying and asking for help.)

And these are just to name a few. You can see how shame can have a chain effect. In the first example, something in the pastor made him very uncomfortable when he found out his worship leader had been sharing about sex, so he ordered her to stop. The worship leader responded to being shamed by isolating herself and doing everything she could to please her pastor.

When you are carrying your own messages of shame regarding sexual intimacy, you will most likely heap shame on the person who (perhaps inadvertently) pushes that button. As the chain of shame continues, the message is clear – this is not an area we can discuss. It must be kept secret.

Being a leader (pastor, counselor, therapist, small-group facilitator, etc.) does not exempt you from issues of shame. In fact, if you have not done your own homework in this area, there are few other issues that will pull you down faster and make you more inept in dealing with people. Despite all your best intentions, you will thwart the healing and forward movement of the couple who shows up in your office.

Here is a tip: If you are not inviting people into a conversation and genuinely listening to their perspectives, inner thoughts, and secret fears and doubts about sexual intimacy, you need to do a self-check to see if your own shame button has been pushed. Your reaction might have more to do with your own issues around shame than with what that person let you see.

Where Does Shame Thrive?

Shame loves secrecy. Silence is its sustenance. One of the hallmark traits of shame is that it makes its victim feel completely alone and cut off from all possibility of connection with the people s/he loves and respects. People living in shame feel worthless because they convince themselves no one else deals with this issue.

If you feel you carry a horrible secret no one else will ever understand, you are going to be highly resistant to the idea of opening up and sharing with others. And yet, the problem with silence is it is the exact environment shame needs to thrive. When shame comes out into the open, the healing process begins. As James 5:16 (NIV) encourages us, "Confess your sins to each other and pray for each other so that you might be healed."

How Do We Heal Shame?

When I talk about shame, it triggers the Texan part of me that says, "Ok, it's big and it's ugly. So how can I smash it in the head so it never comes back?!"

Current research tells us that while we can never eradicate shame (in doing so, we would eradicate our ability to connect with others), we can become adept at healing it. Here are some of the keys as laid out by Dr. Brown:[8]

1. We must believe we are ***worthy*** of love and belonging.
2. We must develop the ***courage*** to tell our stories because shame cannot survive in the open.
3. We must show ***compassion and empathy*** to those around us struggling with their own shame.
4. We must choose ***connection*** rather than cut-offs.

The Prodigal Son

The parable of the prodigal son in Luke 15:11-31 beautifully illustrates these steps. It is the story of a young man who totally and completely messes up. The modern equivalent would be a teenager who runs away from home, gets hooked on drugs, alcohol and women, and parties incessantly until he hits bottom as a homeless guy eating at the soup kitchen downtown. To put it mildly, he makes some bad choices.

To his credit, he comes to a place in which he realizes, even if he is not worthy to be a son, he is qualified to be his father's hired servant. He has an inkling that he is worthy of belonging. It was a small concept at that point, but he took action.

The Father's Reaction

When his father saw him coming down the road, he had a choice to make. Culturally speaking, he would have had a tremendous amount of shame because of his son's actions. Scholars contend the younger son's actions were paramount to saying to his father, "I wish you were dead." The father's friends and respected members of his community would have known what his son had done. They might have talked about the situation behind his back – or perhaps had lengthy discussions with the father about his parenting skills.

With this as the background to his son's approach, the father could have very easily greeted his son by saying, "Shame on you for your sinful behavior! What were you thinking? Do you realize how much flak I have taken because of your actions?!" The son would have been further shamed, and would have responded with one of the reaction styles. He might have run away again. He might have thrown himself before his father and begged to be a servant. He might have lashed out with "If you hadn't been so focused on your business, I wouldn't have left in the first place!"

Thankfully, none of that happened because the father responded to his wayward son with compassion. He ran to him, celebrated him and welcomed him home. He refused the title of servant and accepted him as son. He made his compassion public by throwing a huge welcome home party. The father and son were able to reconcile because of the father's choices. In essence, he created space for his son's shame to be healed and restoration to take place in their relationship.

The Older Son's Reaction

The older son's reaction is also worth noting. He was seriously ticked off. He was the good kid who had done everything right and his younger brother – the family "screw-up" – got a feast. The sin of the older brother was he could not see the larger picture of grace and redemption because he was too mired in his own issues.

Perhaps he was afraid he would have to split the remaining portion of the inheritance with the brother who had already blown his half. Perhaps he was offended his good deeds were not celebrated sufficiently. Or, perhaps the younger brother had always been his father's favorite son even though the older son was the faithful one. Whatever offence he was carrying clouded and compromised his ability to reach out in empathy to his brother.

His reaction reflects the darker, uglier side in all of us. We need to carefully heed our reactions to those who show compassion and extend a hand of healing to those struggling under the weight of shame. I have seen the older son reaction when working with clients recovering from an affair in their relationship.

One woman, who took her husband back after he cheated on her, told me her Christian friends no longer wanted to spend time with him. "They say they have forgiven him, but they haven't, really. They told him he was the 'scum of the earth.' People are incredibly judgmental," she said.

When we are tempted to react like the older brother, we must remember Jesus had ridiculous amounts of patience and compassion for society's "screw-ups." He regularly hung out with the "scum of the earth." He saved His wrath for the religious people who thought they had it all together – those who magnified people's shame rather than empathizing and healing it.

Moving Beyond Shame to Freedom

Shame holds us back from sexual freedom and expression. But once we identify our shame and move towards healing it, we realize the Bible is full of encouraging teaching on sexual intimacy.

What Is Our Scriptural Foundation?

God addressed the issue of the desire gap thousands of years ago in the words of Paul in I Corinthians 7:3-5 (NLT): "The husband should fulfill his wife's sexual needs, and the wife should fulfill her husband's needs. The wife gives authority over her body to her husband, and the husband gives authority over his body to his wife. Do not deprive each other of sexual relations, unless you both agree to refrain from sexual intimacy for a limited time so you can give yourselves more completely to prayer. Afterward, you should come together again so that Satan won't be able to tempt you because of your lack of self-control."

These verses set up an interesting dynamic. As opposed to other religions and cultures that made sexual satisfaction completely dependent on the male perspective, Paul's admonition to the Corinthians outlines a beautiful principle of reciprocity. Sexual expression is expected and incumbent on both parties. Both spouses are to give and receive sexual intimacy freely. Their bodies are not their own, but belong also to the other person.

Following Paul's teaching helps us eliminate lust in our relationship. Lust and desire look very similar on the surface. In fact, the way they are manifested can look identical. However, as you investigate deeper, you realize the motivations are very different. Lust is driven by the compulsion to objectify the other person – to use them for your own ends. You secretly think:

- I've got to get my needs met.
- I have to orgasm.
- I don't care what you are thinking.
- Just go along with it.
- Why can't you be more like _____ (a specific person, personality or body type, etc.)?

Desire, on the other hand, is borne of yearning for connection – to reach out and join with the other person. It is important to carefully distinguish between the two. I have seen many husbands hurt when their wives assume they are just trying to get their needs met, when in truth, sexual expression is the way these men genuinely connect with their wives. The reciprocity in Paul's teaching creates a checks-and-balances system to promote desire and extinguish lust from the sexual relationship.

However, this concept of reciprocity also evokes a lot of questions. One of the most common I receive is "If our bodies do not belong to us alone, then where are the boundaries of sexual propriety? When can I say no?"

Where Are the Boundaries?

When I was a child, I was profoundly affected when my mother told me of the boundaries Billy Graham set for himself. Concerned he could be placed in situations where he would be exposed to temptation, he designed a strict code of conduct when he was with women.[9] For example, he would not ride in a car or dine alone with a woman other than his wife. These boundaries were an acknowledgement that all men and women are vulnerable to temptation, and one of the best solutions was to prevent the circumstances in which temptation arose.

Since Graham set these guidelines in the 1940s, the term "boundaries" has become part of the common vernacular in Christian life. We have lengthy discussions about what is prohibited and how we can create limitations for our own protection. This is crucial. There is tremendous pain that comes with crossing into sexual sin. I work with couples healing from affairs and sexless marriages. I work with men and women who were sexually abused as children and now struggle to connect sexually with their spouses. I see their pain.

However, we tend to use the term "boundaries" exclusively for what is forbidden. This is a limiting definition. Dr. Henry Cloud and Dr. John Townsend contend a boundary, in its most simple of senses, is a "property line."[10] Within that property line is the land you own. It is yours. You can enjoy long walks on it, make sure it is fertilized properly, and plant wildflowers if you please. You can also completely neglect it and allow weeds to grow. But it is still your property.

Outside that property line is ground that does not belong to you. Someone else owns it. You get in a lot of trouble if you start treating that land as your own. Once you cross that property line, you are no longer planting flowers to beautify the world. You are trespassing.

When it comes to our sexual relationships, the question should be "What is boundaried-out and what is boundaried-in?" To answer this question, let's take a look at what Scripture outlines as the boundaried-out activities because that is by far the shortest list.

Boundaried-Out

The Bible outlines the following as sinful behavior:

- Unmarried sex (Galatians 5:19, I Corinthians 7:2, 36). The term "fornication" is usually used to describe sex between people who are unmarried.
- Adultery (Exodus 20:14, Matthew 5:27). Once a man or woman has made a marriage vow to another, s/he may not have sex with another person.
- Bestiality (Leviticus 18:23, 20:15-16). Fido is off limits.
- Prostitution (Leviticus 19:29, Deuteronomy 23:17, Proverbs 23:27, I Corinthians 6:15-16). Do not pay a woman or man for sex or be paid for those services.
- Incest (Leviticus 18:6). Sex with close relatives is forbidden.

Most of the verses and categories are self-explanatory, but allow me to comment on the point of prostitution. While I do meet people who have hired prostitutes, the more common form of prostitution I see is couples who have paid women (and men) to have sex in front of them with other men or women. They do not venture into the streets or wife-swapping clubs to get these services. They find them in the comfort of their own homes.

Porn has become the new trendy prostitution. It offers many advantages over the traditional "world's oldest profession." It is virtually impossible to contract a sexually transmitted infection (STI) while masturbating to porn. It is much more secretive because there is a plethora of ways to pay for it to come into your home without ever leaving the house and being seen in public with it.

Many people even couch porn in terms of "marriage enhancement" since they watch it with their spouse and use the images to increase the eroticism in their relationship.

However, you might not be having intercourse physically with the porn star, but you are still paying her to get you to orgasm. If this does not adhere to the *letter of law* regarding prostitution, it certainly does fall within the *spirit of the law*. The letter is the list of sexual sins we cannot engage in during our lives. However, if you only pay attention to the letter of the law, and neglect the spirit, you will find ways to break the letter. The sprit of the law, however, addresses the fact we should have sexual intimacy with our spouses that grows and deepens as the years go by.

Other than this note, the list of boundaried-out items is surprisingly short and straightforward. And yet, we see people stumble all the time in the area of sexual morality. This is because, even though boundaried-out guidelines are good and necessary, they are not *enough*. They keep you from straying onto someone else's land, but do nothing to make your own property thrive. They will not protect you from the consequences of sexual atrophy and emaciation. The best defense to sexual sin is a thriving sex life at home with your spouse. And that takes us into the realm of what is boundaried-in.

Boundaried-In

It is amazing that Solomon's Song of Songs survived the canonization process. It is a story of incredible passion, eroticism and sexual desire. Augustine must have skipped over it because he would have seen the whole book from start to finish as sinful. In fact, it is pretty graphic. If you read what scholars say the metaphors mean, it is pretty heady stuff.

But it is important for us to understand because it is a story of what our relationships should look like. Through this expressive love story, we are given a clear example of a marital relationship that is pure and passionate.

Tim Day, senior pastor of The Meeting House in Oakville, Ontario says, "The reason this song is in the Bible is that it affirms that the Garden of Eden love affair between man and woman is at the center of God's heart. It reminds us that God delights in true intimacy between man and woman and that He values it first and foremost…It reminds us that covenant love that is inflamed with sexual intimacy is the most beautiful of all God's creation. It is the return to the Garden of Eden."[11]

So, what does "covenant love inflamed with sexual intimacy" look like?

- The term "Lover" is used to describe the man. Culturally speaking, we often think of a lover as someone outside the marriage covenant. For example, a man might have a wife and a lover. Rarely do we use this term to refer to our spouse, which is sad. In our marriages, we play many roles – life partners, co-parents, companions, friends and lovers. We are very often comfortable with speaking every role except the one that sets us apart from any other relationship. It is important to remember our sexual connection with each other and verbalize it.
- The Beloved and the Lover speak highly and frequently of each other's physical attributes. They spend lots of time itemizing the features they love about each other –

from the hair, to the eyes, to her breasts, to the lips, the arms and legs, and even the teeth. When was the last time you looked at your spouse and said, "Well, hello there. Your teeth are looking mighty white. That new toothpaste you are using is fabulous!" It might seem a bit silly to us in this day and age, but the take-away is the couple does not hesitate to compliment each other graphically and profusely. It gives us a model to emulate in our marriages.

- When away from each other, the Beloved and Lover hunt each other down because they desperately want to be with each other. At one point, the Lover reaches through the gate trying to get to his Beloved. Later in the book, the Beloved risks her own safety to go out in the middle of the night to find her Lover. Throughout, they are constantly seeking opportunities to spend time with each other. This stands in stark contrast to the majority of modern marriages. One of the greatest threats to our marriages today is time. We simply do not spend enough time with each other. Many of us are in dual-income families, and so we rush the kids to school, head off to work, rush home, help with homework, tuck the kids into bed, and stumble into the bedroom utterly exhausted. If we want our sexual expression to flourish, we must follow the example of the Beloved and Lover and carve out time for each other.

- Both the Lover and his Beloved are highly responsive to each other. They do not hesitate to express passion in their love for each other. The Scriptures speak of them "grabbing a hold" of each other. They are unashamed of their desire to touch each other and hold on. Interestingly, modern studies show when we hug and hold on to each other, our oxytocin levels (our bonding hormone) go up and our cortisol levels (our stress hormones) go down.[12] God designed our bodies to *feel* better when we touch.

- The Lover and Beloved liken kissing to wine. One of the saddest things I see in marriages today is that couples stop kissing. Perhaps they give each other a peck here and there, but they have long since forgotten how to kiss deeply and passionately. This is the type of kissing the biblical couple is describing – kissing so deep it is intoxicating. It makes you dizzy and light-headed. It moves you to a place that transcends logic and taps into something deeply sensual.

- The Lover and Beloved speak candidly of sexual acts with each other. Scholars tell us oral sex, manual stimulation, and foreplay are all alluded to in the book. For example, the word "browse" is used frequently to describe the leisurely pace of exploration the couple employs when touching each other's bodies. They take time to discover every nuance, every curve and every angle. This is not a quickie. They are not rushing the process. Their language denotes taking time to explore, linger and pleasure each other.

- They talk about a fierce, exclusive love that is never surrendered. The study notes on my NIV Bible say "Marital love is the strongest, most unyielding and invincible force in human experience."

One of your Bedwork assignments this week is to read the Song of Songs for yourself. I challenge you to do so, and discover for yourself other aspects of it.

Final Thoughts

Some of you reading this book are overwhelmed by the state of your marriage right now. You feel like you have hit a brick wall or run into a mountain. And yet, Christ tells us, "I tell you the truth, if you have faith as small as a mustard seed, you can say to this mountain, 'Move from here to there' and it will move. Nothing will be impossible for you."[13] As Christ followers, we are ordinary people called to extraordinary things. This extends to our relationships.

God designed sexual intimacy to be a frequent, desirous, sought-after, fiercely exclusive, seductive, deeply vulnerable, frisky, fun and expressive connection between a husband and wife. How couples manifest this connection is as unique to them as fingerprints are to each person. As you continue to read this book, you will see what your relationship looks like now, what you want it to be, and what steps you need to take to get it there.

Bedwork: Faith

PSA: _____

This week, answer at least two questions. If you have a strong emotional reaction to the questions, pick the one you love and the one you hate. If you do not have a strong reaction, pick an exercise your spouse will appreciate. Don't forget to record your PSA.

1. **Shame.**
   - What does shame feel like to you? How do you know when your shame button has been triggered?
   - What triggers your shame button? (Think about things in your past that have caused a shame reaction within you for clues.)
   - What is your typical reaction style? Do you move away, move towards or move against?
   - How can you combat and reality-check the lie that shame tells you? Are you *really* the only one who deals with this secret? Does this secret *really* make you unworthy of love and belonging?
   - Who can you go to in moments of shame to safely share your story? Who will listen to your story with compassion?
   - You might want to read Dr. Brené Brown's book *I Thought It Was Just Me (but It Isn't)*[14] on shame for further insight.

2. **Read Song of Songs.** After you have read it through once (it is short), go back through it again and write down all the aspects of the Beloved and Lover's relationship that were boundaried-in. How did they react to each other? What did they think about each other? What did they say to each other as well as to their friends? How did they view their love for each other? If you were writing a love sonnet to your spouse, could you find the words to do so? What would they be?

3. **Old Messages.** Think back on the things you were taught about sexuality during your childhood.
   - Write out messages communicated to you verbally or nonverbally.
   - How did you interpret those messages as a child? (What did you tell yourself about sex?)
   - Do you have distinct memories around this subject? What feelings do you remember having? What role do they still play in your marriage?
   - What do you want to believe now about sexual intimacy in your marriage? What does Scripture say? What feelings do you want the subject to invoke in you now?
   - Write out those current beliefs in as much detail as possible.

- Prayer. At this point in the process, I offer a sample prayer for people to say, but you can change it to better suit your own wording if you wish.

  Father God, I realize that for my entire life, I have been operating under the assumption that sex is _____. I realize now these beliefs have undermined what you designed sexual intimacy to be in my marriage. Through examination of your Word, I now realize intimacy with my spouse should be _____. Please remind me of your truth every day so I can have freedom in this area of my marriage.

4. **Read I Corinthians 7:3-4.** What does that mean in your marriage? Have you been acting upon one of those verses but neglecting the other? How would your relationship, actions and belief system change if you truly believed your body belonged to your spouse and vice versa? What would you do differently? Be as specific as possible.

5. **Sex in Scripture.** Search through the Bible. Find a verse that speaks to desire, passion, eroticism or sexual intimacy that you particularly like. Write it on the bottom of the index card with your goal on it. This way, not only will you be looking at your goal every day, you will see your favorite verse as well.

Part II: The Essential Elements

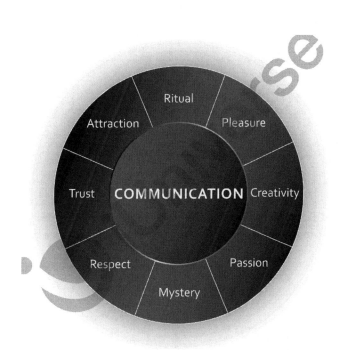

Element 1: Communication

"Everyone communicates; few connect."
John Maxell – Author and Speaker

A number of years ago, I was at a bridal shower and they asked me to share some advice. As I was giving tips on communication, I said, "Just because your husband isn't talking, it doesn't mean he has stopped communicating." During my talk, I noticed one of the ladies was smiling and nodding, so I invited her to share with the others.

One day, while she was at work, her husband made some changes to their bedroom. When she arrived home, she saw he had installed a dimmer switch to add some mood lighting in the room. Furthermore, he had laid out the remote to the dimmer, a condom and a bedroom toy in the middle of the bed. She said, "I guess he was talking to me!"

The most cynical of women would snidely say, "He just wanted to get you in the sack." It is true. It seemed pretty obvious he wanted to have sex that night. But to only see that and disregard all the other things he was communicating would be incredibly unfortunate.

According to the woman, her husband is an electrician, and a very good one at that. He works eight to ten-hour days honing his craft out in the world. But on this particular night, he wanted to use one of his greatest assets to create a romantic setting for his wife and woo her. As if this were not enough, he added something he knew would bring his wife pleasure – the toy she enjoys. Was he inviting her to have sex? Yes. But he was also telling her that he wanted to romance her and bring her pleasure. That is pretty powerful stuff.

Communication is the metaphorical lubricant in our sex lives. The amount of effective communication we have will determine our levels of friction on the subject, the amount of pain we experience as a couple, and the chance of infection spreading throughout the rest of our relationship. If you can learn to communicate about the subject of sexual intimacy, the eight other essential elements will become much easier to implement. It is the hub that holds them all together.

It is vital, though, to point out there are huge differences in the ways that men and women communicate. You have probably heard that *Men Are from Mars and Women Are from Venus,*[1] or that *Men Are Like Waffles and Women Are Like Spaghetti.*[2] Dr. Helen Fisher, a renowned anthropologist with Rutgers University who specializes in romantic love, spoke about the different ways men and women communicate and bond in her TED (Technology, Entertainment, Design) Talk in February 2008:

> Women tend to get intimacy differently than men do. Women get intimacy from face-to-face talking. We swivel towards each other; we do what we call the anchoring gaze, and we talk. This is intimacy to women. I think it comes from millions of years of holding that baby in front of your face and cajoling it, reprimanding it, educating it with words.

Men tend to get intimacy from side-by-side doing. As soon as one guy looks up, the other guy will look away. I think it comes from millions of years of standing behind that bush, sitting behind that bush, looking straight ahead trying to hit that buffalo in the head with a rock. I think for millions of years, men faced their enemies as they sat side by side with friends.[3]

For centuries, men and women accepted the proposition that there were differences in the genders. However, because the understanding of differences was so heavily entwined with inequality for women, we had a cultural backlash that began in the 1960s. Since you cannot change culture without some extremism, we entered a period where the pendulum swung from one side to the other. In our pursuit to equalize the genders, we neutralized the differences between men and women.

Thankfully, due to the work of Dr. Fisher and many others, we are slowly coming to a place where we can recognize and honor the differences between the genders without treating one as inferior. This is the birthplace of genuine and intimate communication between men and women.

Gender Differences

Effective communication begins with understanding our differences. To fully appreciate why and how men and women are different, we must have a bit of a science lesson. In this chapter, we will merely dip our big toes into this pool of knowledge, but this is important information to understand as it greatly impacts our relationships.[4] (Please note: When I speak of gender differences, I speak in generalities. There are always men and women who are exceptions to the rule.) These differences start with the male and female brains.

The Basics of the Brain

- Your brain is made of two halves. The right side is the center of creativity, emotions, music and art. The left side controls your sense of logic, understanding, analytical thought, language and orderliness.
- Bridging the divide between these two sides is a bundle of fibers called the corpus callosum. These fibers allow us to move from using one side of our brain to the other.
- The limbic region of your brain plays an essential role in emotional attachment. It is where your memory, emotion, reward and fear centers are located. The biology behind how we bond and connect is wrapped up in this portion of our brain.
- Inside the limbic region of your brain, you have an almond-shaped cluster of neurons called the amygdala that acts as the brain's alarm center. It governs your intense emotional reactions (either pleasant or unpleasant) and, if it senses danger, it triggers your fight, flight or freeze responses.[5] When one of these responses is activated,

the thinking part of the brain, the prefrontal cortex, shuts down so your body can instinctively respond in the fastest way possible.

- Situated close to the amygdala is the hippocampus, another cluster of neurons. This is the region that stores your memories. Not only do you remember the facts about what happened, you also remember the emotions you felt at the time, the various sensations in your body, and what you were thinking about the event.
- The hypothalamus (by way of the pituitary gland) is the portion of the limbic region responsible for the hormones you experience including, but not limited to, oxytocin (bonding), cortisol (stress) and vasopressin (protection). This area also controls your sex pursuit instincts.
- The prefrontal cortex is the "executive part of the brain,"[6] allowing you to judge, think through your actions, bring your impulses under control, and step outside yourself to decide a wise course of action.
- When there is a size difference between regions in the male and female brains (for example, the amygdala is larger in men than women), they exist in areas where there is a high concentration of sex hormone receptors. Researchers believe this is because male and female hormones influence the way the brain forms in the uterus.[7]
- Within ten to twelve weeks of conception, a male fetus' brain receives a rush of testosterone his female counterparts do not get.[8] This "marinating" in testosterone continues until the boy is about a year old, discontinues for a few years, and then begins again when he is about ten.[9]

Those are the bare-bones basics, and believe it or not, they make a tremendous impact on our relationships.

How We Approach Sex

How we approach the act of sex is a combination of our hormones, the wiring of our brains, and how we were brought up. Although I am not going to delve into the issues and complexities of family of origins here, it is safe to say when you engage in sexual activity, there is more than just you and your spouse in the bed. Unwittingly, you bring in both sets of parents as well. Your parent's perceptions about the act of sex have a tremendous impact on the decisions and attitudes you have with your spouse. But since that is a book in itself, let's take a look at the biological aspect of sex.

Sexual Pursuit and Appetite

Research has indicated the areas of a man's brain that stimulate sexual pursuit (the hypothalamus) and sexual appetite (the amygdala), are larger than those areas in women. Studies on the amygdala also show men are far more affected by visual stimuli than women.[10]

It might well be the infusion of testosterone a boy's brain received in the womb that accounts for the difference in size between the genders.[11] Between the extra testosterone and these larger regions of the brain, it is no wonder men think about sex more frequently than women. They literally have sex on the brain.

Focusing on the Act

Not only do men have an easier time wanting and pursuing sex, but once they engage in the act, they focus much faster than women. Women are superb multitaskers. They can juggle multiple thoughts, activities and agendas at once. This is fabulous when a woman is making sure the kids get to their various activities and scheduling a run to the grocery store, while simultaneously putting together the finer points of her presentation for work. It is not so great when she is trying to have sex with her husband. Too easily, her mind can drift from the intimacy they are beginning to have to the fact she forgot to buy milk earlier in the day.

One of the greatest deterrents to entering the moment for a woman is her pesky amygdala. If she has any sense of fear or anxiety during sexual activity with her husband, it will be impossible for her to orgasm. Researchers have done brain scans on women during sexual arousal and orgasm and, during this process, took note of which areas of their brains became active or "lit up." They have shown while nearly eighty regions of the female brain light up, one area goes dark – the amygdala.[12] It is only when women fully relax – usually because they feel safe and secure – that they can fully enter the sexual experience.

However, they have yet another biological hurdle to getting there. A woman has a larger hippocampus than a man,[13] and this is the region of the brain that stores emotional memories. If her experience with sex has been fraught with pain, discomfort or emotional turmoil, this is locked in her experience and it becomes very difficult for her to enter the moment without dragging in her past baggage. This is why a man probably is not going to get lucky if he ticks his wife off earlier in the day and doesn't get around to resolving the issue before they hit the sheets that night. It is also why women who come from past abuse struggle in the pursuit of intimacy with their husbands.

The good news about the hippocampus is this: If she can retain negative memories, she has an amazing capacity to retain positive ones as well. As you build in the richness of your intimacy together, as you layer positive experiences upon positive experiences, her body retains this information in vivid detail. And, she can give her husband the directions on how to do so.

Taking Directions

Researchers believe men have a thicker cerebral cortex in the area of the brain that controls spatial skills. This means they are particularly adept at measuring, map reading, working with objects and perceiving directions. If you are struggling as a couple to figure out anatomy, get a "map."[14]

How We Make Eye Contact

Remember when Dr. Helen Fisher said women get intimacy through the "anchoring gaze" and men get it from "side-by-side doing?" These instincts are hard-wired into our brains and have been further developed during childhood.

Nature

Studies done on young infants have shown from the moment they are born, female babies gaze longer at the human face.[15] This ability to hold eye contact increases exponentially during the first year of a baby's life,[16] and so by twelve months old, girls are leaps and bounds ahead of their male counterparts in the ability to hold eye contact.[17] Some researchers have suggested this inability to maintain eye contact in males is not a lack of interest, but a propensity to hyperarousal in boys and men.

As scientists delve into the mysteries of the brain, they have realized most men have larger amygdalas than women.[18] In this situation, size truly matters. "Bigger" sets men up for hyperarousal because they receive greater stimuli in this region of the brain. When they hold eye contact, there is the distinct possibility men will instinctively interpret this as aggressive, and therefore feel a rush of the stress hormone cortisol.

Scientists believe men were designed like this because for years, they were the warriors and protectors of their families. As Fisher said, "They faced their enemies and sat side-by-side with their friends." Their larger amygdalas also give them the ability to move into fight or flight mode faster than women. While it was a life-saving tool during the hunter-gatherer years, it can be deeply disconcerting for a couple trying to have a conversation today, and the wife is expecting her husband to look into her eyes.

Nurture

However, the level of eye contact men can maintain is not merely an issue of how their brains are constructed. Studies show caregivers sustain 50 percent more eye contact with girl babies than boys. When a parent looks into the eyes of a baby girl and she gazes back, this consistency of contact encourages the parent to continue to maintain eye contact. However, when a parent looks at a baby boy and he looks away, the parent will often interpret his lack of eye contact as *disinterest*, and will therefore move on to some new activity. Dr. Patricia Love and Dr. Stephen Stosny, in their book *How to Improve Your Marriage Without Talking About It*, suggest that when this happens, the baby boy interprets the situation as his own inability to "do relationships right."[19]

Putting This Information to Use

When I am teaching couples how to communicate about sex – which can be a very stressful endeavor for them – I encourage them to harness this information about eye contact and make it work for them. Creating an environment in which you both have the best chance of a highly successfully conversation might mean limiting the amount of eye contact you maintain.

Women, when the only form of communication you find acceptable from your husbands is sitting down, eye to eye, you are actually demanding a very aggressive form of conversation with your husbands. Naturally, instinctively, this is going to cause him to be more assertive or action-oriented. If, however, you want to come to agreement in a friendly and peaceful manner, then set him up for success by communicating side by side.

This strategy is incredibly effective in the lives of my clients. I was once discussing this tactic with a client and she suddenly gasped and said, "Oh! That must be why we communicate so much better when we are on the phone!" Seizing this solution to help this couple in their current state of crisis, we decided whenever she began to feel her conversation with her husband was headed for a fight, they would get on their phones. One of them picked up the landline while the other went outside on the cell phone. They were able to continue their conversation without the eye contact, and their discussions immediately became less heated and more productive.

How We Deal with Emotions

In modern marriage, how we interpret and express our emotions with each other is given supreme importance.

Sensing

Many researchers have suggested women have a deeper limbic system (the emotional attachment center) than men. Their ability and desire to connect and bond with others is hard-wired and they have the biological functions to facilitate this desire. For example, in one study coordinated by Dr. Simon Baron-Cohen, a professor of developmental psychopathology at the University of Cambridge, researchers found that "When asked to judge when someone might have said something potentially hurtful, girls score higher from at least seven years old. Women are also more sensitive to facial expressions. They are better at decoding nonverbal communication, picking up subtle nuances from tone of voice or facial expression, or judging a person's character."[20]

These findings might not seem like rocket science to anyone who has stumbled on a group of women consoling a lady who is emotionally distressed. Women naturally console each other through touch, eye contact and language.

However, far too often we compare women's style of empathy with that of men, and we come to an erroneous conclusion that men don't feel emotions. The fact that men tend to show less expression on their faces when dealing with negative emotions reinforces this fallacy.[21] When women are experiencing crisis with their husbands, one of their chief complaints is that they are in agony and he appears to be totally unaffected.

But the assumption men feel less than women is simply not true. Men feel very deeply. Remember the boy baby who had to look away from your gaze? This is not due to a lack of emotion, but an overwhelming amount of emotion that floods his senses.

In one study, researchers studying the amygdala found men had very high levels of response when presented with sad images.[22] Their brains were clearly taking in the emotion they felt and registering their sad moods. However, it seems that how men and women process this emotion differs significantly.

Processing

When men feel a rush of emotion, their amygdalas flood with hormones. They feel, and they feel deeply. However, instead of lingering in that place, their brains are very adept at redirecting all that emotion to the cortex – the part of the brain responsible for logic.[23] Instead of dwelling on the emotion, they quickly go into an analytical, reasoning place.

This is why, when a woman tells her husband she had a bad day, he tries to fix it. His emotional response most likely induces a rush of vasopressin – the "I need to protect my wife" hormone – and his logical brain immediately begins to create a plan to take care of her. The very act of proposing a strategy to deal with her bad day is his way of communicating how deeply he cares for her.

Women's brains, on the other hand, do not go into "fix-it" mode quite as quickly. Eric and I were speaking at a marriage conference recently, and had the privilege of listening to another presenting couple speak on communication. Early on in this couple's marriage, when the wife was teaching her husband what form of communication she found most helpful, she told him to rub her back and tell her he understood. Women need greater time to feel the emotions they are experiencing before they move into a place of being able to access the issue logically.

And they want to talk about it.

Verbalizing

There is no doubt that women like to talk more than men. In fact, when scientists study infants as young as eighteen to twenty-four months, the girls are already far ahead of the boys in their ability to verbalize.[24] It seems the wash of testosterone that floods a boy baby's brain in the womb has a direct impact on his verbal expressiveness later in life. Even in adulthood, women, on average, speak about seven thousand words a day.[25] Men, on the other hand, speak about two thousand.

However, the innate ability in women to be more verbally expressive than men might also have to do with the size of the corpus callosum. In some studies, it has been shown women have a thicker corpus callosum than men.[26] Since it is this bundle of fibers that helps us navigate between the two hemispheres of our brain, women can do it more quickly than men.

For example, this thicker corpus callosum enables women to flip more rapidly between the emotion hemisphere of her brain (the right side) and the language hemisphere (the left side), which makes her a superb verbal communicator. One of the reasons women are so chatty is they have an easier time putting their emotions into words.

Putting This Information to Use

We live in a world in which a higher and higher emphasis is being placed on the ability to communicate verbally. We spend an inordinate amount of time teaching men how to verbalize their feelings. It is usually one of the first things couples are asked to do in therapy and marriage seminars. It has become our gold standard of communication. When we use the word "communicate," everyone assumes we are talking about flapping our gums.

But what happens to the guys who do not put their feelings into words as easily as their wives? What happens when men just don't want to talk as much?

It is easy for men to feel a bit behind in this department. Even worse, women can fall into the trap of feeling superior because of their highly tuned verbal skills. It is crucial we recognize the strengths we bring to the relationship, and leverage them for the overall health of our marriage. Women – you need to recognize your husbands *do* feel – but they may not *verbalize* these feelings as fluently as you.

But here's the deal. Men have no difficulty communicating. They just don't tend to do it like women.

How We Prefer to Communicate

A number of years ago, my husband illustrated this point very clearly when he went to play golf with a buddy. Both guys were going through a taxing time at work and needed to get out of the house and blow off some stress. Knocking the heck out of a bunch of innocent little golf balls seemed to be the perfect solution.

When he got home, I asked him how he enjoyed his day. "It was amazing. We played golf all day." Looking for more information, I asked, "So, what did you talk about?" Eric had a great smile on his face. "That's the best part. We didn't talk at all!"

Had he built relationship with his friend? Yes. Had they emotionally bonded? Yes. Had they communicated effectively? Absolutely.

One of the greatest threats to communication in marriage occurs when a wife or husband (or both) decide his/her way of communication is superior to that of his/her spouse. It is extremely easy to slip into an attitude of believing your spouse needs to change for your relationship to improve. This attitude can rapidly devolve into condescension and contempt. Furthermore, if you are hanging out with friends who can only see things from your perspective, your attitude is not likely to change.

The only way we can implement change in our relationships and get the closeness we so deeply desire is if we take a long hard look at our own patterns and ruts, truthfully assess whether they are working or not, and make changes when necessary. It is possible – and foundationally important – to learn our spouse's communication techniques.

Active Communication Techniques

Our relationships are like a dance. They have rhythm. They have patterns. They have steps that each of us takes as we respond to the movement of the dance.

My husband and I fell in love on the dance floor of Billy Bob's in Fort Worth, Texas. It boasts to be "The World's Largest Honky Tonk." Really. I could not make that up. Twenty years later, we are still dancing. When my husband and I dance, he makes one move, and I respond with another. He puts his feet in one place, and I place my feet in the next position.

As with partners on the dance floor who have practiced for years, our marriages can run on autopilot. He makes the dinner, she cleans up. He makes the first move in bed, she responds. She tidies the house, he does the yard work. He tells her how beautiful she is, she writes notes for him to find around the house. If both parties are happy with this arrangement and it is working for their marriage, then it is a wonderful benefit of being married. Sometimes being on autopilot is efficient – it saves time from negotiating each and every task or interpersonal exchange.

Inevitably though, things change over time. Perhaps a child comes along, and so the person in charge of initiating sex rolls over and falls asleep instead. Perhaps a new, more time-consuming job comes along, and so the house doesn't get tidied as often. Maybe someone gets sick, and so the dinner routine becomes ordering take out. Sometimes the compliments and little notes become casualties of the immediacy of life. If couples are able to negotiate these changes in life with open communication about their expectations and needs, and find there is compromise (at the very least) on these expectations and needs, then usually things proceed well.

However, when couples become disappointed with each other because of lack of or ineffective communication, the dance can change from something fun to watch and be a part of to one which is jarring and uncomfortable. No longer do the steps flow, but now he steps on her foot and she jerks back, and he lurches forward to catch her and she moves her feet out of the way to avoid getting stepped on again. And yet, if the couple doesn't stop and take stock of what is off course, it is easy to fall into a new, awkward (if not painful) dance pattern.

It might look like this: He doesn't seem happy anymore so she is cautious when he walks through the door. He sees she is not exuberant to see him, and so brushes past her to go see the kids. She feels ignored, and so doesn't ask him about his day. He feels insignificant, so after dinner, he withdraws to watch TV. She follows him into the TV room and complains he never talks to her anymore. He feels nagged and responds by withdrawing further, maybe even to the guest room for the night. And on and on. Many times we have our own "dances" we fall into – patterns that are highly predictable when we actually break them down into their individual steps.

The advantage of recognizing these patterns is it empowers us to do something different. And we don't *both* have to recognize the pattern – *one* of us will do. This is the power of active communication. We are not using our mouths. Instead, we are *doing* things differently. And one small change in that old familiar pattern can affect a whole new chain of events. Very often, this is far more powerful than words.

So, in the words of the country singer Toby Keith, we are going to try "a little less talk and a lot more action."

Act "As If"

Many of the couples that come to me do so because they believe – they hope – things can change in their sexual relationship. While there is nothing that might indicate that is even close to reality, they have faith.

Faith believes in things we cannot yet see.[27] It might look like:

- having faith your spouse will come back home
- believing your sex life will indeed get better
- trusting your marriage does not have to be dull, boring and monotonous
- believing you can truly have your needs met within the context of your current relationship.

When we act as if, we are putting this faith into action. The basic concept is when we act as if everything we want is about to happen, has already happened, or is in the process of happening, people's attitudes and actions change around us. Because we are responding differently to the same set of circumstances, they cannot help but respond differently as well.

Acting as if is a powerful tool in changing patterns. So, in the previous example of the couple that reacted to each other and devolved into a state of hostility, what if the wife's reaction to her husband's unhappiness had been to greet him at the door with a warm "Welcome home, honey," as if he were walking through the door as happy as could be? Or he had seen her cautious behavior and gave her a big hug anyways? Either action could have circumvented the other steps that led to his sleeping in the guest room. When we act as if, our demeanor, attitude and requests change, and this has a domino effect in the lives around us. It is not being inauthentic, untrue to ourselves or play-acting – it is making a choice to see things through the eyes of faith and behave differently as a result.

Acting as if is easier when you are focused on the positive parts of your relationship.

What You Focus On Will Grow

As you begin to deliberately cultivate active communication, you need to begin by changing your own perceptions. Back in 1965, researchers studied and developed a concept now known as the Pygmalion Effect.[28] According to this phenomenon, a teacher who expects a certain student to do well in her class will give that student more feedback, smile at him more often, and nonverbally reinforce the expectation that this student will succeed. Often, these students go on to meet all expectations and rise to the top of their classes. It is, in essence, a self-fulfilling prophecy.

Nearly two decades later, Doctors Eden and Ravid tested the concept of the Pygmalion Effect in their Israeli Defense Forces' experiment.[29] Members of the Israeli military were brought into a command combat course for training. Four days before the training began, the researchers told the instructors that they had assessed each trainee and given them a "regular," "high" or "unknown" command potential (CP). The instructors were to study all the soldiers' files and their accompanying CP scores before classes began.

Unbeknownst to the instructors, these command potentials were not based on testing done on the soldiers, but instead randomly assigned. Roughly a third of the soldiers fell into each category of command potential. Soldiers in all three command potential groups were then evenly distributed amongst the classes and instructors.

In as little as a week, researchers noticed a difference between soldiers who had been designated with a high command potential and the others. They were at the top of their class, having rapidly excelled past the others. By the end of the training period, not only had they outperformed the other soldiers in their coursework and exercises, but they also reported they had a much more positive attitude towards future training, and evaluated their instructors much higher than the other soldiers.

What CP have you assigned your spouse? Is it high? Regular? Unknown? People rise or fall to the level of expectation around them. Whether you realize it or not, you send out nonverbal messages of anticipation to your colleagues, friends, children and even your spouse. They respond to these messages in how they behave around you.

How is this a communication technique? If you are constantly expecting, perceiving and thinking of your spouse's failure, you are going to see it. You will miss all the times your spouse does well because you will subconsciously toss out any exception to the rule and look for instances that confirm your belief of him/her. More importantly, your spouse will fail because s/he is not getting the subliminal reassurances that you expect her/him to succeed.

The great news is the Pygmalion Effect works both negatively and positively. You can change your levels of expectation with your spouse. When you begin to focus on the positive aspects of your relationship, this allows her space to change and grow. It allows him to be appreciated for his efforts. It allows her to respond warmly to you. The fact you have shifted your attention to the successful encourages him to keep up the good work.

Stop Doing "More of the Same"

My husband calls this the "quit being crazy" principle. Do you know the definition of insanity? Albert Einstein claimed it was "doing the same thing over and over again and expecting different results." As creatures of habit, we often fall into the trap of repeating our actions, but believing something different will magically happen next time. I realized I was guilty of more of the same behavior as I tried to get my daughter out the door on time each morning.

Let me give you some insight on my daughter. She is *intensely* verbal. From the moment her eyes open until the moment they close at night, she is engaging people in conversation. She habitually goes to the school office during recess with some made-up excuse just so she can have a discussion with an adult. So when she wakes up, she wanders into my bathroom while I am putting on my makeup so she can consult about her outfit for the day, or relay something funny she read the night before, or even test out her latest joke.

The child loves to talk. I love to be on time. And these two loves are on a direct collision course at 7am.

My reaction used to be something like this:

"Riley, hurry up and get dressed. We are going to be late." No response.
Louder: "Riley, hurry up and get dressed. We are going to be late." No response.
Even louder: **"Riley! Hurry up and get dressed. Don't you know we are going to be late?!"**

I would do the same thing, over and over again, deluding myself by thinking changing my volume would make my words more effective. We spent morning after morning going to school frustrated with each other, and usually both of us were in tears. Then, I realized I needed to quit being crazy.

So, I thought about who my daughter is as a person. Not only is she social, but she also likes games and is extremely competitive. I began to set a timer and told her if she got all her chores done before the timer buzzed, she could get a reward after school. All of a sudden, I no longer had to tell her to get ready. She did it all on her own. I never dreamed the child could move so quickly. And who knew she could close her mouth for a bit when a competition was on the line? Now our household is significantly more peaceful in the mornings simply because I stopped doing more of the same.

We all have patterns in our sex lives of doing more of the same, and they undermine the health of our relationship. He initiates and she says no more out of instinct than actually thinking it through. She tunes out during sex and thinks about anything other than what is going on. He spends so much time on the computer watching fake sex, that the real thing disappoints him. She would rather go shopping than pick up a book to learn about new techniques in the bedroom.

Unless we recognize the pattern we have fallen into and make a change, we cannot hope to achieve the sex life of our dreams.

Do a 180

This is a great way to stop being crazy. Through working this principle, you choose to do something completely opposite to what you normally do. If this seems strange, try this technique as an experiment for a couple weeks or so. As you do, pay close attention to the results.

I have a girlfriend who is the Low Desire Spouse in her household. A number of years ago, she got sick and tired of her husband bugging her for sex all the time. She told me the nagging was driving her nuts. She lived in constant anxiety he was going to ask and she would have to tell him no – again.

After some self-reflection, she decided to do a 180 – something radically different than anything she had tried before. She determined he would never initiate with her again because she was always going to beat him to the punch. She was going to decide when *she* wanted to have sex, and he wouldn't have a chance to ask anymore.

The results were instantaneous and extraordinary. He was stunned and ecstatic – that part is probably no surprise. But she was astonished by how much she enjoyed the sense of empowerment she got from initiating. She began to get excited about planning the next time she would initiate. The creativity levels in their relationship increased. They had sex more often. Their communication about sex deepened. And most importantly, they were both extremely happy. Her decision to do a 180 radically changed the dynamic of their sex life.

A 180 in your relationship might look like:

- yes instead of no
- initiating sex in the morning instead of at night
- making a choice to have sex while the kids are asleep next door
- having loud sex (please do not combine this point with the previous point)
- changing the spouse who gets to experience orgasm first
- blocking off an hour for sex instead of having a quickie.

If things are not working in your sex life, it might be a matter of changing the way you do things. Try a 180 and see what happens. You won't know until you try.

Laughter

From post-traumatic stress syndrome to depression, psychologists are turning to humor therapy to help their clients get unstuck. Laughter is often the glue of our relationship when we first get together (how many times have you heard a single person say s/he is looking for someone with a "good sense of humor?"), and yet it is one of the first things that falls to the wayside when we hit bumps in our relationships. When we have times of crisis, we often forget how healing laughter can be.

When we laugh, we release endorphins in the brain. When this happens, we have a feeling of light-heartedness. We get the feeling we can succeed. But laughter does so much more as well. It:

- releases a host of feel-good hormones such as dopamine and oxytocin
- reduces anxiety, stress and pain
- lowers blood pressure
- helps us feel good about ourselves
- boosts our immune systems
- helps us deal with our emotions
- breaks us out of a painful cycle
- relaxes tense muscles.

Dr. Paddy Ducklow, a psychologist who has spent decades working with families and marriages, has witnessed the benefits first-hand and says, "I get people to laugh all day long. I come home happy and they go home changed."

Never underestimate the value of laughter in your marriage. If you are struggling to connect, remember what it is like to laugh. Rent some funny movies. Go to a comedy show. Watch your kids get up to crazy antics. Take a break from the talking and carve out time to be together and laugh. Laugh long, hard and loudly.

Furthermore, do not be afraid of laughter in the bedroom. Obviously, you want to be laughing *with* your spouse rather than *at* your spouse. Please be very clear on that distinction. But often I will have couples report that one person got the giggles and it undermined their time of intimacy together.

I'm going to be really frank here. Sometimes funny stuff happens when we are having sex. Sometimes someone farts. Sometimes a caress tickles. Sometimes air gets trapped in the vagina and sounds really odd when it comes out. Sometimes someone falls asleep. That's just life.

We can choose to let those moments distance us or allow them to draw us closer. When we laugh, we enter the moment with each other and acknowledge those are rare moments we alone share. It's really ok – you can finish up later or some other time. But do not neglect the opportunity to laugh together, both inside and outside the bedroom.

Learn Your Spouse's Love Language

Everyone communicates differently. There is nothing better about one form of communication over another. The trick is to learn how to hear what the other is saying. Gary Chapman wrote the groundbreaking book entitled *The Five Love Languages*.[30] Chapman explains there are five primary ways we communicate and receive love:

- words of affirmation (verbalizing your appreciation for your spouse)
- quality time (creating time to connect with one another)

- receiving gifts (physical tokens of appreciation such as flowers, lingerie, etc.)
- acts of service (helping out with chores and errands)
- physical touch (this extends to all touch including sex).

You can see quite quickly only one innately involves verbalization – words of affirmation. The rest rely on action. If you have not yet read Chapman's book, put it on your reading list. It is a simple and yet profound way to expand your understanding of active communication techniques.

Verbal Communication

Couples who become experts in active communication techniques will decrease the amount of time they will have discussions – particularly acrimonious discussions – about their relationships. It is inevitable, however, that there will be times when you actually need to talk. The principles here are communication techniques that have helped couples experience breakthroughs when talking about their sex lives.

The Setting

Choose Your Timing Wisely

When you are asking to have a conversation with your spouse about sex, particularly if you want a change in this department, it is crucial you choose your timing wisely. Nothing will derail your conversation faster than launching into a discussion when your husband is settled in front of game seven of the Stanley Cup. Or when your wife is trying to decorate the two dozen cupcakes she volunteered to bring to the school fundraiser. When you decide to have a conversation about your sex lives, set yourselves up for success by ensuring you are both able to give the discussion the amount of concentration it deserves.

Think back to times when you have had successful conversations about other aspects of your marriage. Where were you? What time of day was it? What were the two of you doing at the time? What did you ask each other? How did you phrase your exchanges? The answers to those questions will give you clues as to what a "wise time" looks like in your household.

Once when I was speaking to a group of breast cancer survivors about timing, one lady told the rest of the group she and her husband had a breakthrough conversation about sex while they were taking a road trip. They had miles to go, nothing else was demanding their attention, and they talked and talked. Some of the solutions they brainstormed together in that car were instrumental in putting their sex life back on track after her cancer treatments. I think every woman that night mentally made a note to book a road trip when she got home.

Beginning a habit of asking each other, "Is this a good time to chat?" is a good practice to instill in your relationship as well. If it is *not* a good time, your spouse can let you know, and this will avert unnecessary frustration and anger. In that moment, talking about this subject might be the most important thing in the world to you. However, if your spouse is not in the place to hear and respond well, you are not going to get the results you want. So, set yourselves up for success.

Take a Couple of Minutes to Prepare

Jason Mitchell, an associate professor in the department of psychology at Harvard University suggests that taking one to two minutes to think about the impending discussion from the other person's perspective will change the outcome of your conversation.[31] People who take the time to reflect before they begin are more likely to be altruistic and share resources. In essence, when you take the time to get inside your spouse's head before you talk, you are more likely to be solution focused because you are more open to his/her perspective.

Men and women I have coached find this exercise particularly helpful as they try to bridge the desire gap. When they begin to think about who gets stuck with the task of initiating sex or receiving an offer from their partners' perspectives, they walk away with tremendous empathy.

After one of my speaking engagements, a woman wrote to me and said, "When you wondered what it might be like to be the spouse always denied, it was exactly what I needed to be reminded of, and elicited a new compassion and softness for [my husband] in a place that has been hard and angry for a long time."[32] We have scriptural foundation for this concept too. In Philippians 2:3-4 (NIV), Paul put it this way: "Do nothing out of selfish ambition or vain conceit, but in humility consider others better than yourselves. Each of you should look not only to your own interests, but also to the interests of others." When we consider others, we clear the path to intimacy.

Don't Discuss Sex In the Bedroom When You Are Getting Started

It never ceases to amaze me how a man and woman can live together for years, raise children, weather financial ups and downs, dream of retirement and never speak of sex. It's almost as if they remain stuck in prepubescent embarrassment about the subject, even though they have moved on with such maturity in the other areas of their lives.

If this is the first time you have had a serious conversation about sex, talking about it in the bedroom is a bad plan. It could seriously backfire. There are few other places where we feel as vulnerable as when we are naked in front of each other. This is not the time and place to point out she takes too long to come to orgasm, or his fingers are making the situation worse instead of better. Have these discussions outside the bedroom first.

Go for coffee together, take a walk in the park, or have a nice dinner with the express purpose of talking about sex. Always begin the discussion with the things you love about your sex life together. If you are nervous about the conversation, jot down some notes beforehand so you can read them to your spouse or give them the paper to read. Better yet, both of you can write out lists and then switch them over dinner.

Only once you establish a solid foundation of communication about your sex life together outside the bedroom, should you move the conversation inside.

The Conversation

Here are some basic guidelines as you begin to talk about sex.

When You Are Looking for Information, Ask Open-Ended Questions

Simply put, open-ended questions cannot be answered with a simple yes or no. In this situation, your goal is not to direct the conversation, but to elicit information. For example, if you are interested in discovering what place enables your wife to feel most comfortable having sex expressively, you might want to ask her, "Where is your favorite place to have sex?" Or, you could ask, "When do you feel the most freedom to cut loose when we have sex?"

Asking the question this way (rather than "The bed is your favorite place to have sex, right?") opens the door for her to give you answers you wouldn't have guessed. Far too often we put our spouses in neat, tidy little boxes with labels on them. Consequently, we struggle to see them in different categories. Your wife might surprise you with the answer, "On the beach at 2am." Trust me – this is good information to have. When we begin the process of asking open-ended questions, we can discover new delights in each other.

When is your favorite time of the day or night to have sex? What is your Top Five List for best sex together? What is the most pleasurable way to orgasm? All of these questions (and more in the Bedwork section) are designed to get you to start talking, but you don't have to worry about answering them all at once. Take one or two questions at a time, and consider the remaining questions opportunity to have multiple dates with your spouse.

When You Are Expressing Your Needs, Be Assertive and Direct

One of the greatest gifts you can give each other is a road map to success. The more you can communicate what you need and desire, the better the odds your lover can meet those needs and desires. This entails being assertive and direct.

As you are practicing your communication skills, ask each other what is working in your sexual relationship. Give all the details you can on what is good, pleasurable, exciting and intimate in the bedroom. Elaborate as much as possible. As you clearly identify what is working, both of you can expand on it.

After you establish warmth, rapport and success in this area, move on to questions that invite suggestions for ways you can improve as a lover. "What is one thing I can do to bring you more pleasure?" Or, "What can I do to help you so we can enjoy alone time later tonight?" If you are on the receiving end, give specific answers. Remember the discussion around "making love" in the Define Your Direction chapter? The same holds true here. You will not give your spouse a road map to success if you use ambiguous terms. What brings you pleasure? Be as precise as possible. If you honestly don't know the answer to the question, let your spouse know that this is something the two of you will have to discover together, and set up time to do so.

Often we fall into the trap of believing our spouses should be mind readers. I frequently hear clients express, "If s/he loved me, s/he would just know what I need." This is ridiculous. No one can ever truly know what you need without you communicating those needs. Forcing them to guess what you are thinking is borderline manipulative – criticizing them when they are wrong is nothing short of abusive. Too often I find this behavior is used to mask personal embarrassment or shame. Don't allow it to sabotage your relationship.

Practice Participative Listening

Dr. Stephen Covey, author of numerous books including *7 Habits of Highly Effective People*, said, "Most people do not listen with the intent to understand. They listen with the intent to reply."[33] If you want to truly understand your spouse, then be quiet and listen. That's right. Don't open your mouth until your spouse is done. (If you have a spouse who is prone to verbal diarrhea, then set time limits for each person to talk. Once the time is up, the listening spouse can respond.) Allow your spouse to speak without interruption, and focus on what she is saying without "flowing" your next argument.

Anyone who has taken debate will understand the concept of flowing. Debates are won and lost on how well the debaters can track and then refute arguments. During the speech, the other team writes copious notes on the various lines of reasoning put forth by the speaker so he can address each and every argument. If he fails to respond to each point, no matter how ridiculous it might seem, he will lose the debate. The skill to which each debater records his opponent's speech and then rebuts it determines the winner.

In marriage, if you are looking to win by flowing your spouse's talking points, you will both lose. Instead of formulating your next argument as your spouse is talking, listen for the heart of what your spouse is saying. Pay attention to the emotion in the words. Watch the expression in the face, the hands and the rest of the body. Listen with an open heart and mind.

Clarify to Ensure You Have Understood Your Spouse Correctly

There is nothing more frustrating than working to make your spouse happy only to find you aren't doing what s/he asked. So, once you have listened to your spouse, it is extremely helpful to repeat what you heard. This practice helps eliminate confusion and misunderstanding that can often occur when discussing difficult topics. You might want to begin with the statement, "What I heard you say was…" to ensure you did hear accurately, and give your spouse the opportunity to correct you in the moment, if needed.

As the two of you become more comfortable with speaking about your sex life, you will most likely get more creative in how you reflect your understanding to your spouse and no longer need the crutch "What I heard was…" The essential tool to develop, however, is the ability to walk away from the conversation with an accurate understanding of what your spouse wants and needs from you.

After The Conversation

Put It Into Action

Once you get the suggestions from your lover, make sure you incorporate them into your sex life. Does your husband love deep kissing? Then remember back to the line from K.T. Oslin's song "Hold Me." "Don't kiss me like we're married / Kiss me like we're lovers." Put it into practice.

Does your wife want variety in the bedroom? Then surprise her with something new. Research a new position, put new lighting in the room or pick a new place to have sex. Even if this is not what you chose for improvement, try it out of respect for them.

Be Grateful

When your spouse listens to your desires, be on the lookout for change. But beware: It is probably going to take your spouse some time to build her skill set in this new area. Be patient and praise his attempts. Change takes place when we celebrate successes – even if they are mere baby steps. As your spouse becomes more confident in this new area, as you continue to praise and encourage, she will get better until it is everything you hope and dream.

Final Thoughts

It is inevitable as you work through this book, there will be times you need to communicate with your spouse about change you want to see happen. When asking for change, give your spouse home field advantage.

Why do professional sports teams fight for home field advantage in the playoffs? It is where they practice day in and day out. They hone their skills on their home field. Their fans come to games at their home field. They know all the nuances of the field and how the light hits the stadium at different times of the day. It is their comfort zone.

As you communicate about sexual intimacy, choose a communication style that gives your spouse the best chance of success. So, if your husband is not a big talker, quit griping to your girlfriends and take action. If your wife needs to talk, turn off the TV and listen. Intimate communication only happens when we give up our own entrenched positions and create space for spouses to express themselves wholly and completely.

Bedwork: Communication

This week, answer at least two questions. If you have a strong emotional reaction to the questions, pick the one you love and the one you hate. If you do not have a strong reaction, pick an exercise your spouse will appreciate, or give them home field advantage. Don't forget to record your PSA.

1. **Gender Differences.**
    *   What new insights did you get while reading the section on the differences between men and women?
    *   How does this new knowledge change your perspective of your spouse?
    *   What specific actions can you take to improve your relationship with this new knowledge?
    *   What changes can you make to your communication style based on this new knowledge?

2. **Preferred Methods of Communication.**
    *   Do you and your spouse fall into the stereotypes of how men and women like to communicate (he likes action and she likes to talk)?
    *   If not, how would you describe each of your preferred methods of communication? Do you have the same methods?
    *   Will this understanding of your preferred methods change how you communicate with your spouse? If so, what are you going to do differently?

3. **Choosing Your Timing Wisely.** Think back to times when you have had successful conversations about other aspects of your marriage and ask yourself:
    *   Where were you? What time of day was it? What were the two of you doing at the time? What did you ask each other? How did you phrase your exchanges?
    *   Once you have answered these questions, arrange these circumstances and have a conversation with your spouse.
    *   Afterwards, answer these questions. How did the conversation go? Were you more successful in having open lines of communication? If so, write down what was helpful so you can remember next time. If not, write down what you need to change next time for a more favorable outcome.

4. **What You Focus On Grows.** Begin to shift your focus from what *doesn't* work in your sexual relationship to what *does*. For example, if one of you has a higher sex drive than the other, talk about the times you had sex and detail what was pleasurable, enjoyable and intimate about those times. Talk about what attracted you to each other in the first place.

List all the aspects of your sex life you love. The more you focus on the positive aspects, the more likely you are to recognize those things in your spouse.

5. **What You Focus On Grows.** What were the circumstances around the last time you had great sex (or even sex at all)? Who initiated? Was there something special that happened? How were you feeling emotionally before you had sex? Did you feel empowered? Or less tired? Or deeply connected to your spouse? Did something different go through your mind beforehand? Once you have a clear picture of what it was that made that last encounter great, duplicate it!

6. **Act As If.** What do you have faith for? What are you holding on to believing even though you cannot yet see the results? How can you act as if those results are already here? If everything were going the way you wanted it, how would you be acting differently? Let's say your spouse has a lousy attitude lately. Perhaps you even know *why* his/her attitude stinks – s/he is stressed at work, worried about finances, etc. – but it still doesn't change the fact his/her attitude stinks. Has this changed your reaction to him/her? Have you stopped doing the little things (that are actually large things in a loving relationship) you normally would do? Think about implementing them regardless of his/her attitude right now.

7. **More of the Same.** What are some of the doing more of the same patterns in your life? What do you do (over and over) that is completely unproductive in your relationship? Try something new instead this week and see what happens. If giving your spouse the cold shoulder, or talking until you are blue in the face, or moping around the house is not producing the changes you want to see in your spouse, stop. Try something new.

8. **Do a 180.** What are your more of the same patterns in your sex life? Write each one down and brainstorm some creative ways to do a 180 in each. Change the time or location of your sexual encounters, learn a new sexual technique, make the choice to say yes no matter when the next request comes, etc. Monitor the results and see how your spouse responds. Was it effective? Did it make a difference to the outcome?

9. **Memorize Philippians 2:3-4 (NIV):** "Do nothing out of selfish ambition or vain conceit, but in humility consider others better than yourselves. Each of you should look not only to your own interests, but also to the interests of others." Then, begin to practice thinking through things from your spouse's perspective before you begin conversations.

10. **Open-Ended Questions.** Here is a list of questions you can ask on your dates together:
    - When is your favorite time of the day or night to have sex?
    - Where is your favorite place to have sex?
    - What is your Top Five List for best sex together?

- What is the most pleasurable way to orgasm?
- What do you enjoy me doing the most?
- What body part do you enjoy me touching?
- Do you have any fantasies about sex? If so, what are they?
- What makes you feel most connected to me?
- What makes you aroused, interested in sex or horny?
- What is one thing I can do to make our sex life better?

Element 2: Ritual

"The key to growing a marriage that is personal, and not just logistical,
is to be intentional about the connection rituals of everyday life."
Dr. William Doherty – Author and Therapist

When I was working in Kelowna, I had the pleasure of meeting Todd and Grace. They were both intent on making their relationship more intimate and fulfilling, but having come from conservative backgrounds where sex was simply not discussed, they had never been taught how to make their intimacy grow over the years. They were very much in love and yet thoroughly ready to try something new to liven up their sex life.

I originally met Grace at an in-home party. She gravitated to the bath and body products that contain pheromones. She shared with me a bit of her conservative background, and her desire to move slowly into bedroom accoutrements so she could first ensure Todd was on board with her decisions.

As is the nature of in-home parties, I met up with Grace again at another party, and asked her how her aromatherapy products were working out. She lit up like a Christmas tree. She explained Todd realized how much she responded to the effects of the pheromones in her new products, and so he had taken to drawing her a bath in the evenings. This was significant to her because she owned a hair salon and would spend long hours on her feet, talking to clients and managing her staff. After a particularly long day, she would arrive home to a drawn bath full of sensual bath salts and other pampering products. When she emerged from the bathroom, she felt rejuvenated and refreshed, ready to be intimate with her husband.

Of course, once Todd realized this was an effective way to help Grace make the transition from hardworking entrepreneur to sexy wife, he made it a priority that her bath products were fully stocked and her bath was run after a long day. After fourteen years of marriage, they had found new ways to demonstrate their love to each other, and rediscovered a passion in their marriage that had long lay dormant.

Unbeknownst to them, they had stumbled across the importance of ritual.

What Are Rituals?

Anthropologists who want to learn about a new culture study its rituals as insight into what the people group holds dear and precious. When I lived overseas, one of the first things I tried to understand was the greeting ritual of the country. In Nepal, for example, I learned to hold the palms of my hands together (as if uttering a prayer), and say, "Namaste." Literally translated, this means "the spirit in me greets the spirit in you."[1]

Furthermore, the placement of my hands was crucially important. When I greeted someone of high stature in the community, I would place my hands above my nose indicating I acknowledged their superior status. In contrast, when I greeted a child, my hands would be below my nose communicating my position as their elder. Since I sought understanding of the various aspects of the greeting, I was able to quickly gain insight into the importance of both religion and status in Nepali culture – knowledge that made my stay in their country much more pleasant and effective.

Just like different cultures, each family has its own rituals. The Johnsons sit down to the dinner table at 6pm each night. The Browns have busy teenagers, but they make it a point to have Taco Night together as a family every Tuesday evening. Mr. and Mrs. Tang connect by doing the dishes together after the meal. Mr. and Mrs. Taylor delegate the dishes to their kids so they can have a cup of tea together in the living room. Regardless of the logistics of our activities, the rituals we choose bring meaning and identity as a family unit.

Rituals also provide the foundation of stability and consistency in your sex lives. Perhaps it is the date night that allows you to connect each week so your need for quality time together is met. Perhaps it is the routine you choose for putting your kids to bed. Perhaps it is your unspoken agreement that she orgasms first so he can roll over and fall asleep after sex with little (or at least less) guilt. All of these are rituals you have that underpin your sex life. They are unique to you as a couple – special and shared just between the two of you.

Paving Rituals

Many couples I meet dream of having better sex lives, but the desire quickly gets drowned in the busy details of life. They might have had the best of intentions to connect sexually, but then the business meeting went later than planned, or the dinner got burned, or the neighbor stopped by, or the baby pooped in the tub, or there was a special on TV that could not be missed. Sex has a way of sliding to the bottom of the priority list when we are bombarded with the realities of life.

Paving rituals pave the way for sex to be possible. They create time and space. They smooth the path. They eradicate the excuses. Couples who create paving rituals make their lives conform to their needs and desires rather than allowing the craziness to dictate fulfillment in their relationships. They realize that in order to have the relationships they truly want and deserve, they need to be proactive about protecting them.

One of the primary ways a couple can protect their sex life is by realizing the significant role the brain plays in any paving ritual.

Engaging the Brain

There's an old joke that goes: "What is a wife usually thinking when she is having sex? 'Beige. I should paint the ceiling beige.'"

The brain is the most powerful sex organ we have. If we are not engaged mentally, it is difficult to become engaged sexually. This is why we joke about women being able to decorate the house while having sex. (It appears that women can do more than decide on paint colors. I once had a math teacher tell me she factors polynomials during sex!)

Making the transition from the roles we play during the day to a sexy, engaged spouse at night can be problematic and difficult. Often the details of the day intrude on our time of intimacy together. This is especially difficult when we do not think about sex at all during the day, and then have to rapidly shift gears in the evening.

Thinking about Sex

Men are much better wired for engaging their brains throughout the day. Back in 2004, the ABC News show *Primetime* did an American Sex Survey.[2] The results showed 70 percent of men think about sex each day whereas only 34 percent of women do. Furthermore, 43 percent of men think about sex multiple times a day in contrast to 13 percent of women. This study demonstrates an extremely significant gap between the genders.

Researchers theorize this might have to do with the higher levels of testosterone men have coursing through their bodies. Early in the womb, male babies are flooded with testosterone, and this hormone directs the development of their sexual organs. Once they are born, testosterone plays a significant role in the growth of their bodies as they develop from boys to men. As men, testosterone is one of the key hormones that drives the desire to have sex.

Creating true sexual intimacy with your spouse begins by actually *thinking* about it before you both skid into the bedroom at night. If you are someone who does not think about sex very often (outside of during the act itself), you can train your brain to place it higher on your priority list. Here are some ideas clients have found helpful:

- Put a sticker on your bathroom mirror. The sticker can be of something completely random like a rhinoceros, a castle or a baseball. In fact, the more it makes you laugh, the better. When you look at this sticker, make yourself take thirty seconds to think back to a great sexual encounter with your spouse. Remember it with as much detail as possible. Then, take the time to think of this memory (or memories) each and every time you look at that sticker. If you find you begin to ignore the sticker over time, because you become so accustomed to its presence, move it around your mirror periodically.
- Alternatively, if the sticker idea seems too random for you, find a picture of the two of you when you were feeling particularly amorous. It could be your honeymoon or another vacation you took together. Put the picture in a place you will see frequently, such as on your desk at work or in your wallet. Just like the sticker exercise, use the visual reminder to train your brain to think about sex.

The trick to these exercises being effective is having the discipline to stop for thirty seconds and remember that sexy moment with your spouse. To put this in context, that is the length of a commercial on TV. Advertise your own sex life by training your brain to think about sex.

Flirting

When thinking about your spouse gets you worked up, flirt a little. Send him a text message or email, or leave a message on her phone letting them know you are thinking about her.

I have a friend who likes to say, "My husband treats me like a crock pot. He makes sure I am turned on all day so I will be warmed up at night." Flirting throughout the day (while you are at work, making dinner, watching the game, or attending your children's sporting events) is a fabulous way to connect sexually before the physical act begins. When we fail to connect in this manner, we put our relationship at risk.

One of my clients came to me in tremendous pain because her husband only paid attention to her when he wanted to have sex. They would exist without any touch or flirtatious communication until minutes before he was ready to take off his clothes. She was desperately lonely and contemplating having an affair so *someone* would flirt with her. To her, flirting represented the attempt to woo her, rather than just expecting her to cater to his desires when he wanted.

However, when flirting is standard operating procedure in your relationship, you are paying attention to the embers of passion in your relationship, and making sure they are not completely cold when it comes time to build a fire.

To be an effective flirt, you must find out how your spouse likes to be flirted with. Does she respond to physical touch, such as a brief touch on the lower back or the nape of her neck? Does he prefer verbal flirting, like a phone call or promises of what will come later whispered in his ear? Does she prefer to find notes detailing what you want to do to her later in the day? What language does he like you to use? Does she like you to catch her off guard when you are around the kids or alone in private? Does he like your flirting to be serious and sensual, or playful and fun?

Relaxing

The brain is also the key to relaxation. Remember the amygdala, the alarm center? If you were to take a brain scan of a person when aroused, this portion of the brain would be darkened – no activity would be taking place in this region. The focus has moved from concern about the day to focus on the pleasure of the moment.

For women in particular, it is difficult to deactivate this part of our brain. Women will often go through the motions of sex while thinking something along the lines of:

- I forgot to get milk at the store today. When am I going to find time tomorrow to pick it up?
- Will the kids hear us? What if we wake them up?
- My boss is sure driving me crazy. What is tomorrow going to be like?

When men understand how important the brain is to the sexual process, they can help their wives tremendously by doing things to help them focus on the matters at hand.

One couple I met had a phenomenal ritual when the woman was struggling to fully engage in their lovemaking. The husband would begin to describe a location (usually tropical in nature) in great detail, painting an image for his wife of a far-off place he was taking her. His words would transport her away from the craziness of her life to a vacation, even though she was still in her own bed. This was incredibly effective for her as a way to detach from the concerns of her day, and focus on a seductive encounter with her husband.

Once our brains are primed for sex, there are other paving rituals that need to be heeded as well.

Timing

One couple ran their own photography business. They were passionate about what they did and consequently put in long hours. They would put their kids to bed in the evening and go to work. They put so much creative energy into their work, there was little left over for sex. I made a simple suggestion – put the kids to bed, have sex, and then start work. This change in sequence created a new paving ritual which made having sex when they still had energy much more possible for them as a couple.

It is also important not to get locked into thinking sex only happens at night. You can wake up earlier in the morning, meet at home for "lunch," put your kids in activities at the same time in the early evening so you can have a "date," begin a habit of Sunday afternoon "naps," and so forth. Find a time that really works for you as a couple, and then make sure you plan for it.

And yes, this does mean that you should make it part of your schedule. When I meet creative-type personalities who resist scheduling, timeline and structure, they often complain they want their sex lives to be more spontaneous. I love spontaneous. I think it is fabulous. I think more couples should be spontaneous more often.

However, couples that schedule sex have it more frequently. So, for those creative types, I suggest you create a day, or even a two-day window, in which sex can be "spontaneous." That way, you will know when you have missed an opportunity (because it will be clearly defined) and so you can redress it. Furthermore, when you have narrowed your plan to a window of opportunity, it gives you lots of leeway to be spontaneous in how you act upon your plan to connect sexually.

Clearing the Slate

One female client of mine had to have the kitchen completely clean before she could relax enough for sex. There was nothing she hated more than going to bed with a dirty kitchen waiting for her in the morning. It stressed her out – so much so that she was often grumpy if her husband wanted to have sex.

Once her husband recognized this, his paving ritual became pitching in and helping her get it done. In his mind, cleaning the kitchen became part of foreplay. Not only did she feel grateful for the assistance (and therefore much more amorous), but the task got done faster, leaving more time for fun!

Help your spouse tick off his to-do list so he can focus completely on you. Does she need you to watch the kids while she finishes up a project for her meeting tomorrow? Does he need an hour of quiet to decompress? Does she need you to pick up dinner on the way home because she hasn't had time to get to the grocery store? Does he need time to exercise and work off the stress of the day?

Illness

Chronic illness can greatly impede a couple's ability to have a robust sex life. When one person is not feeling well, usually the last thing they are interested in is sex. If the couple cannot find a way to strike while the iron is hot, so to speak, it is very easy to slide into a sexless marriage.

It is under these circumstances I recommend the couple pays heed to what *does* work, so they can create paving rituals around these solutions. When sex is easier, what is happening with your spouse's body? What kind of day has s/he had? What type of environment was created that day? What went right?

For example, one couple had a strain on their sex life because the wife has severe arthritis. As they looked at the times when their sex life was better than others, they realized when she was warm, she felt better about having sex. So they installed an infrared sauna in their home. Now, when they want to have sex, he makes her favorite drink and sends her to the sauna. As the heat soaks into her bones, she feels less pain and can turn her focus to enjoying her husband. For them, the financial investment in the sauna was minor compared to the breakthrough in their sexual intimacy.

Hygiene

Believe it or not, hygiene is a huge impediment to enjoying sex for many couples. The simple acts of brushing teeth, grooming carefully, or showering can be complete turn-offs to one spouse if the other fails to do so. Men, in particular, need to realize what an impact it makes on their wives when they overlook something that seems fairly minor to them, but is a huge deal to their wives.

One of my clients realized she was often held back from wanting to have sex because she was concerned about her *own* hygiene. Not wanting to smell during sex, she simply turned her husband down. After meeting with me, she began to take a shower in the evenings. She was able to shave her legs if she didn't have a chance to do so earlier in the day (which made her feel much more attractive), spray on a bit of perfume after her shower, and go to bed feeling much more confident. Even if they didn't have sex that night, she felt more feminine and confident.

Keeping the Good Stuff Handy

Other couples make sure they keep a bottle of their favorite lubricant on the bedside table so they can engage at any time. Bedside tables with drawers are particularly helpful for stashing private items. (If you have kids, either teach them not to go into the drawer or put a lock on it.) Alternatively, you can have a box with a lock on it that tucks under the bed. It is a great place to store condoms, lingerie, and any other accoutrements the two of you enjoy.

Kids' Bedtimes

There is one area that comes up over and over in my practice: kids' bedtimes. When I was first pregnant with Riley, I did a lot of reading and research into different parenting styles. I concluded as long as the child was loved and cared for with all of his/her physical needs met, the parenting style was probably less important. The "best" way to raise your children depended on the personality style of the parents.

I believed that, anyway, until I started meeting woman after woman who was having difficulty in her sex life because her kids either stayed up as late as she and her husband, or had an open invitation to climb into bed and sleep with them. After years of seeing these erosive patterns, I have come to the conclusion that, regardless what parenting style you use, bedtimes need to be clearly defined and strictly enforced. Having your kids tucked in their own beds so you have time off the mommy and daddy clock is incredibly important not only to your sex life, but also your relationship as a couple.

Of course, there will be exceptions to this rule – when your baby cries all night because he is teething, your young child needs soothing after a scary dream, or your teenager wants to debrief after her date. But outside these types of exceptions, keeping your bed as sacred space for you and your spouse is a prudent pattern to develop.

For parents of younger children, I suggest they be in their beds with their lights off at least an hour before you retire to bed. Two hours seems to be easier on parents because it gives the children an hour to fall asleep, and then the parents still have an hour to find their own source of entertainment with the secure knowledge they won't be interrupted. So, if you go to bed at 10pm, have your kids in bed by 8pm.[3]

As the children get older, having early bedtimes becomes more problematic due to activities, homework and the desire to connect with friends. You can still set firm boundaries for when you are and are not available. Modeling a relationship where you place a high value on investing in your marriage by carving out time to be alone is a great example to your teenagers for their future relationships.

One of the healthiest gifts you can give your children is the stable foundation of two parents who deeply love and are committed to each other. I hope by this point in the book, I have convinced you sexual intimacy is a crucial component to this connection.

Initiating Rituals

Initiating rituals signal interest in having sex. These rituals may be obvious or incredibly subtle. Some people totally miss their spouses' signs of interest because it is not the way they themselves would express desire. One couple relayed a particularly humorous exchange they had one morning as the woman complained her husband had missed her signals to have sex the previous night.

> Husband: "What do you mean you wanted to have sex? Why didn't you say so?"
> Wife: "I *was* telling you! I was *naked*!"
> Husband: "It's the middle of summer. I thought you were just hot!"

The initiating rituals are especially important to understand when one person is particularly shy talking about sex. Perhaps this person did not grow up in a home where it was an acceptable topic to discuss. Perhaps he has tried to express interest before and has been shot down. (This stops a lot of people from being vulnerable enough to ask again.) Perhaps she hasn't given herself permission to ask for sex because it feels selfish or slutty to do so.

Understanding when your spouse is communicating his/her desire to connect with you is essential to deepening sexual intimacy.

Reading the Cues

There are thousands of ways people can communicate their desire to have sex. The important thing is that you recognize your spouse's own style. Take this as an opportunity to chat about the ways you initiate sex.

Verbal Cues

I love the episode of "Friends" where Joey coined his famous pickup line, "How *you* doin'?" I still hear this line, sometimes in the most obscure of contexts. For my generation, at least, it is an iconic come-on. Of course, there are numerous ways to verbally communicate you are interested.

Here is the key for verbal cues: Make sure you are using language your spouse really likes. Shockingly, he might not be so turned on by the phrase "Do you want to initiate coitus immediately?" Likewise, she might be resentful of hearing "I'm ready!"

Take the time to discuss with your spouse what you like. Do you like fairly straightforward language, or do you prefer something subtler? Do you want your spouse to use proper terminology, or do you like a bit of slang? Obviously, the more you can speak your spouse's language, the better off you will be. Remember, the way you initiate is a huge determining factor in whether you are successful or not.

Physical Cues

These can be subtler than verbal ones, so it is important to understand what your spouse is communicating by their actions. The initiation ritual might look like:

- putting away the reading material earlier than usual
- a kiss that lingers rather than just a peck
- a massage
- taking a shower or brushing teeth at night (!)
- putting on lingerie
- giving *that* look
- a full-on grope.

Environmental Cues

Just like the electrician who installed a dimmer switch in his bedroom, there are ways to communicate desire by setting up the right environment:

- lighting candles
- putting on special music
- turning down the bed
- putting the kids to bed early
- setting the alarm earlier than usual (for no other discernable cause).

The Designated Initiator

Many relationships have one spouse who is, whether by spoken or unspoken agreement, assigned the role of Designated Initiator. It falls to this person to initiate sex the vast majority of the time.

Sometimes the High Desire Spouse assumes the role of Designated Initiator. Sometimes the High Desire Spouse has been rejected so often, s/he will relegate the task to the Low Desire Spouse out of self-protection or even respect for that person's desires and needs. If both parties are happy and content with this arrangement, there is nothing wrong with it. As the saying goes, "If it ain't broke, don't fix it!"

Some couples I meet with, however, are unsatisfied. The Designated Initiator would like to see the other person express interest. Perhaps this spouse would like some space to initiate on his/her own terms. The words "Just back off a bit so I can actually ask you!" have been uttered frequently. Of course, if you haven't taken the time to discuss this as a couple, chances are you are floundering on how to broach the topic, especially if it has been an unspoken agreement for quite some time.

In couples in which the desire gap is quite wide (the Low Desire Spouse and High Desire Spouse have vastly different expectations of what entails a "good" sex life), a compromise will have to be reached. For example, the spouse who wants to have sex every other day might have to accept the bulk of responsibility for initiating in a relationship with a spouse who only wants to have sex every other week. However, this does not excuse the Low Desire Spouse from initiating. The couple could come to an arrangement where the Low Desire Spouse initiates every couple of weeks and the High Desire Spouse initiates in the interim. Each spouse, therefore, is responsible to initiate on his/her own frequency of desire.

The Don't Say No Experiment

No one likes to extend his/her hand only to have it slapped away. No one likes to be rejected. When the person we love most denies us time and time again, it is our nature to withdraw within ourselves or become frantic because our needs are not being met. Neither of these scenarios is particularly healthy or effective if you are aiming to have sexual intimacy for a lifetime with your spouse.

When I meet with a Low Desire Spouse who wants to make a change in his/her sex life, I often recommend that s/he try the Don't Say No Experiment. For a time (perhaps two weeks or so), I tell them to:

- Go home and tell your spouse you are not going to say no. This does not mean you need to begin initiating or even get excited about sex. It simply means you will acknowledge to your spouse you will not reject him/her.
- When your spouse initiates, say yes.
- Use these extra opportunities to further the pleasure and enjoyment you both receive during your times of intimacy.

When you tell your spouse you will no longer say no, it has a powerful effect. First, it takes away his/her fear of rejection. (Yes, if you have been saying no for a long time, expect your spouse to be hesitant and test the waters a few times just to make sure you are for real.) Many Low Desire Spouses radically underestimate the power their no has over their spouses. This rejection is corrosive, eating away at the foundation of sexual intimacy.

Secondly, the psychology of need dictates that when we cannot have what we need, we become more desperate to get it. (Did you know in Maslow's hierarchy of needs, sex is one of the most basic?) When the Low Desire Spouse deactivates that sense of desperation by acknowledging the

High Desire Spouse will be able to have sex, the High Desire Spouse relaxes the intensity to which s/he has been pursuing it.

One lady, who tried the Don't Say No Experiment with her husband, came back to me and reported the results. She said when she told her husband, it was like a weight lifted off his shoulders. He stood up a bit taller and said, "Really?" with a big grin on his face. When she put this promise into action, he felt he could trust her more and more not to shut him down. As this trust grew and sexual encounters became more frequent, the intimacy in all areas of their relationship flourished. She said to me, "I had no clue how much it hurt him when I said no."

Interestingly enough, her husband did not abuse his newfound freedom. I point this out because the deep, dark fear of every Low Desire Spouse is that if s/he says yes all the time, the High Desire Spouse will want sex multiple times a day, every day. With this couple, however, his gratitude and deepening trust manifested itself in respect that she desired sex less than him. Because she acknowledged his needs, he became more respectful of hers.

The goal of this experiment is that you begin a life-long pattern where a no is the exception to the rule in your relationship. Obviously, we can't go through life saying yes each and every time our spouse wants to have sex. However, if we are saying yes most of the time, the no will be rare and put properly in context.

Sex Rituals

Couples in long-term relationships are surprisingly ritualistic about how they actually have sex together. They have a prescribed amount of foreplay that can range from zero to twenty minutes or so. They have the same two to three positions they use. One party typically experiences orgasm before the other person. They prefer the same setting with the same amount of lighting at the same time of the day or night.

When this routine is highly satisfying to both parties, there is no problem. In fact, it can be incredibly efficient because both parties know what the expectations are and they both get their needs met. They are in tune with their spouses' wants and desires and they know how to fulfill these requests. They can complete this dance with incredible proficiency without sacrificing intimacy.

However, if this is a pattern where one (or both) parties are bored, unfulfilled or unsatisfied, then it is time for a change.

Unsustainable Rituals

Here are some of the unsustainable patterns I have seen couples fall into:

- A wife has never had an orgasm. In the beginning, she might not have been too concerned about it or was too intimidated to figure out how they could rectify this issue. Years later, she is caught in a trap of wanting more, but not sure how to express it without offending her husband.
- A husband is bored silly with the positions he and his wife stick to in their sex life. He would like her to be more open to trying something new, but getting her to have sex at all is a stretch, and so he settles for what he can get.

- A wife used to enjoy satisfying amounts of foreplay with her husband, but over time this has been significantly curtailed due to pressures from work and kids. She wants to break out of the rut they are currently in, but is struggling to know how.

I encourage couples to be open with each other if they have fallen into the rut of unsustainable rituals. As our bodies change over the years, as we become open to ideas that might have terrified us when we knew little about each other, as we grow more comfortable within our own skin, we need to give each other to permission change, adapt and ask for something new.

Here are some aspects of the act of sex from which couples create rituals.

Foreplay

The average woman takes between twenty to forty minutes to become aroused enough to enjoy an orgasm or multiple orgasms. I do like to emphasize that this is the average. I have met women who only take ten minutes and those who take sixty minutes. Men, typically, take far less time to become aroused than the average woman. As I mentioned earlier, the brain is a crucial component to arousal for women.

Bill and Pam Farrel have a great way of describing this process. In their book, *Men Are Like Waffles; Women Are Like Spaghetti*,[4] they conclude men have various "boxes" in their brain. "Work" has a box, "Kids" has a box, and "Sex" has a box. When a man is in one box, he is *in* that box, and it takes him a bit of time to transition to the next one. Women, on the other hand, are like spaghetti because all functions of their lives mingle together like a heap of pasta on a plate. Work, kids and sex are not in neat, tidy little boxes – they all affect each other.

The Farrel's description is a great illustration for what we know about the human brain. Since women have a thicker corpus callosum (the bridge between the right and left sides of the brain), this makes them superb multitaskers. While this might be helpful when a woman is juggling twenty items on her to-do list for the day, it greatly interferes with her focus on sex. Unlike men, who can move into the sex box without thinking about anything else, it is very difficult for a woman to turn her brain to sex and stay there.

This is why foreplay is essential. Foreplay is the bridge between his arousal time and hers. It is his opportunity to coax her into the place where all she has on her mind is the connection they are exploring together. As she turns her brain and body to a place where she can focus on what is transpiring – as she fully engages in the act – she comes to the place where her body can let go and experience orgasm. (I talk in further detail about ways to engage in foreplay in the chapter on Pleasure.)

What are the rituals you have regarding foreplay? How long does it last? Is that sufficient? What are you doing for foreplay? Is it enjoyable? Is it boring? Do you need to make a change? What do you love about it?

Orgasm

Sometimes just changing who experiences orgasm first can be groundbreaking in a couple's sex life. I have met with couples that always allowed the husband to experience orgasm first. I have met with those who have a ritual that encourages the wife to go first. I met one couple where the husband would go first, then he would ensure his wife had an orgasm (or more), and then was so aroused, he would orgasm again.

When couples fall into a pattern where the husband orgasms first, but then falls asleep before she experiences orgasm, she is going to feel pretty frustrated over time. Furthermore, if she is the Low Desire Spouse, this ritual is not going to do anything to encourage her to jump at the chance of having sex next time.

We are obsessed with male sexual dysfunctions. We are bombarded by commercials telling us every man should be able to be ready for sex whenever he wants, and will last longer if he uses their product (but not longer than four hours – call your doctor if that happens). Recently, my husband and I were having dinner with a friend who is a therapist, and he commented every man in his sixties has the middle name Ed (for erectile dysfunction).

Premature ejaculation is also a deep concern for many men. What might start with a one-off experience turns into a dread it will happen again, and the psychological pressure makes the situation even worse. The sex therapist, Dr. Ian Kerner, wrote a book called *She Comes First: The Thinking Man's Guide to Pleasuring a Woman*[5] that was borne, in part, from his struggle with premature ejaculation.

Men are terrified of the inability to perform. Women are terrified that if he can't "perform," he will disengage completely. The problem with our cultural perspective, however, is it is wholly based on the presupposition that men must satisfy a woman with long periods of intercourse. And what is wrong with that perspective, moreover, is that research tells us less than 25 percent of women can experience orgasm through intercourse alone. More than 75 percent of women need to have clitoral stimulation to reach orgasm.

When men follow Dr. Kerner's advice and create a ritual of pleasuring their wives first, women are less concerned about how men perform during intercourse. It takes the pressure off the man to live up to ridiculous expectations of how long he should be able to last.

Refractory Period

Every man has a refractory period after sex. It is the time after orgasm in which it is physically impossible for him to become erect again. The refractory period varies widely among men and is based on, amongst other things, age, energy levels, stress, health and fitness. One man might have a refractory period of minutes – another might need a couple of days.

The refractory period will often signal the transition into the couple's resolution rituals.

Resolution Rituals

I once had a couple come to me to chat about ways to increase the desire and frequency in their sex life. As they were sharing, the wife mentioned that every time they finished having sex, the husband would pull out his laptop and get some work done. It was a complete killjoy to her. Just thinking about how sex would end got her so steaming mad, she didn't even want to get started.

Many couples believe once the act of sex is over, sex is done. Not true. The potential to build intimacy does not end when the act of sex does. What you do when you are finished – your resolution rituals – can deepen intimacy or squelch it.

Now, for the guys out there who are groaning right now and thinking, "Is she going to tell me that we have to cuddle and talk after sex?" understand resolution rituals do not have to conform to this stereotypical female expectation. But you do need to have a discussion about what you do when sex is over, and whether that is working for both of you.

When sex is over, what do you do, and how do you react?

- Does one person want to talk and the other wants to fall asleep?
- Do you stay in the same room, or does someone get up and leave?
- Do you roll over and get out the Smartphone, flip on the TV or the laptop?
- Do you want to wait twenty minutes and then go again?
- How do you clean up?

Cleanup

You would not believe how many women I meet who avoid sex because of the cleanup phase. They have a really bad ritual in cleanup, but rather than fix it, they fall into a pattern of avoiding sex altogether. (One woman said it took her an hour to clean up after sex. I can only guess she was doing laundry every time!)

What if you realize you get really annoyed when you get stuck in the wet spot after sex? I met one lady who had this happen all the time. She changed this ritual by beginning to keep a "happy towel" by her bed. Other couples have a stack of hand towels close by them. Some couples plan to jump into the shower together after intercourse is over to extend the period of intimacy while cleaning up.

Bonding Time

What if you want to talk after sex, rather than falling asleep, at least once in a while? Then have sex in the afternoon or early morning for a change so the two of you are less prone to snoozing immediately after you are done.

Final Thoughts

There are no right and wrong rituals as long as you are meeting each other's sexual needs and growing closer together as a couple. The rituals that work for your friends, your parents, or even your ex-spouse may not work for the two of you. This is part of the beauty of rituals – they are special and unique to your relationship. Once you have figured out what rituals you currently have, you can decide as a couple whether they work for you. And once you have identified what you dislike, you can change it.

If, on the other hand, you are thoroughly enjoying a particular ritual, let your spouse know. S/he might not have recognized its importance, and you need to articulate it. Keeping the lines of communication open is vital because what works for you now is not guaranteed to work for the next five or ten years. As our bodies change, as we become more comfortable with our sexuality, as we want new things out of our sex lives, it is important to make tweaks to our rituals to reflect these changes.

Bedwork: Ritual

This week, answer at least two questions. If you have a strong emotional reaction to the questions, pick the one you love and the one you hate. If you do not have a strong reaction, pick an exercise your spouse will appreciate, or give them home field advantage. Don't forget to record your PSA.

In this Bedwork, you will look at the different rituals you currently have, and assess what is working and what changes you would like to make. When asking for changes from your spouse, do so with specificity so your spouse will understand exactly what it is you want to see done differently.

For example, instead of saying, "I want you to kiss me more," say something like, "I want you to kiss me for ten minutes before you touch other parts of my body so I can be thoroughly aroused when you do." (Note: Feel free to use your own words.)

1. **Thinking about Sex.** Put a sticker or some other reminder on your bathroom mirror. When you look at this reminder, make yourself take thirty seconds to think back to a great sexual encounter with your spouse. Remember it with as much detail as possible. Then, take the time to think of this memory (or memories) each time you look at that sticker. If you find you begin to ignore the sticker over time, because you become so accustomed to its presence, move it around your mirror periodically.

2. **Flirting.** Ask your spouse how s/he likes to be flirted with. What time of day is his/her preference? What does s/he want you to say or do? Pay attention to what your spouse likes and then put it into practice. Begin by flirting several times a week and then increase the frequency so you are finding different ways to flirt every day.

3. **Clearing the Slate.** What do you need to do so you can fully engage in intimacy with your spouse? What are the common obstacles that get in the way of sex? How have we overcome those obstacles in the past? What changes (small or large) can we make to remove those obstacles? What will make sex easier, more pleasurable or more frequent? Make a list of what needs to be done, and then figure out how you can help each other with your lists.

4. **Kids' Bedtimes.** Are your children's bedtime routines interfering with time alone with your spouse? If so, what can you do to change the routine? What time should they go to bed so you have at least an hour or two alone with your spouse? If the children are older, and therefore have later bedtimes, what boundaries can you set so you and your spouse still have time alone, even if the children are still awake?

5. **Initiating Rituals.** What do you usually do? What does your spouse usually do? How do you react to them? Are you excited? Annoyed? Defensive? Aroused? Describe what they are and how you react. Do you want to make changes to your initiating rituals? If so, what are they?

6. **The Designated Initiator.** Who is the primary initiator in your relationship? Is this working? Why or why not? Do you enjoy the arrangement you have with your spouse, or do you want to make some changes? If you want to make changes, then write them down as goals (remember to use the PASS technique) for your relationship.

7. **The Don't Say No Experiment.** Try the experiment for two to three weeks. Make sure you tell your spouse you are doing the experiment so you will deactivate his/her fear of rejection and the desperation to get needs met. What changed in your relationship during this time? Did having sex with your spouse become easier, more enjoyable, or more pleasurable? How did your communication develop during this time?

8. **Sex Rituals.** What is "normal" sex in your relationship? How much foreplay do you have? How long does it last? Do both of you get to be recipients of foreplay? Do both of you enjoy orgasm? If so, who goes first? If not, is this something you want to change in your relationship, or are you happy with the pleasure you do experience? Which sex rituals are working for you? Which ones are not? If there are ways your sex life is not meeting your expectations, ask your spouse (again, with specificity) for the changes you would like to see.

9. **Resolution Rituals.** What typically happens after you have sex? Do you stay in the same bed (room, house, etc.) when it is over? Do you stay awake or fall asleep? Do you have conversation? Do you turn on the TV? Once you have answered these questions for yourself, ask your spouse what his/her impressions are. Do you have any requests of your spouse? Does s/he have any requests of you? Together, decide if you like these rituals, or if there are ways you can fine-tune them.

10. **Thank You.** What do you love about the rituals you and your spouse have? Write a thank you note to him/her expressing the things you love about your sex life. Leave it under his/her pillow (or briefcase, or next to his/her toothbrush, etc.) to discover and read.

Element 3: Mystery

"Love enjoys knowing everything about you; desire needs mystery."
Esther Perel – Author and Psychologist

Back in March 2007, writer and producer JJ Abrams spoke at the TED Conference.[1] If you are not familiar with TED, you really should be. It is a conference held each year on topics that relate to technology, entertainment and design. Experts from all around the world are invited to speak about their field of study in eighteen minutes or less. And while it costs about $7,500 to buy a ticket to the conference – and you have to *apply* to purchase them, it's not guaranteed simply because you have the cash – you can watch many of the talks online for free.

In his TED Talk, Abrams spoke on mystery. When he was a young boy, his grandfather was the instrumental person in his life who encouraged his love of mysteries. One of his grandfather's gifts was a box of magic tricks advertised to have $50 worth of magic for only $15. Abrams has carried that box around with him for years, never opening it, as a reminder of his grandfather and the wonder of what the box might actually hold. As long as he keeps it closed, there is mystery.

Abrams contends, "There are times when mystery is more important than knowledge." He continues to explain the reason mystery trumps knowledge is we crave "mystery boxes" in our stories. They are the lifeblood of entertainment. They draw us into the story. They stimulate our imagination. They are the great unknowns. They bond us to the characters. They are the twists and turns we do not expect, but utterly delight us.

If we were to apply Abrams' mystery box concept to the birth of Christ, it would go something like this:

An ordinary teenager is going about life when a bright light suddenly shines in her room. What is going on? **Mystery box!** Then the bright light reveals itself to be an angel of the Lord who tells her she will soon be pregnant. But she is not married. How is she going to get pregnant? **Mystery box!** How is her fiancé going to react? **Mystery box!** Will her community stone her? **Mystery box!** Joseph and Mary delicately navigate the difficulties of a pregnancy out of wedlock, only to find out they have to go on a court-ordered road trip. But Mary is in her final trimester. Where is the baby going to be born? **Mystery box!**

We love mystery boxes when they show up on a movie screen or are found in a story we can quickly read to the end. We intuitively understand they are opportunities the characters are given to become true heroes, to grow into their callings. But what happens when we encounter mystery boxes in our own lives?

Typically, we get very annoyed. They are inconvenient. They deter us from easy and fun things in our lives. They don't fit into our neat and tidy version of a picture-perfect life.

They look a lot like this:

- I just got laid off from my job. What is next? **Mystery box**!
- My teenager has become friends with someone from a different religion. How is this going to affect his faith? **Mystery box**!

- My thirteen-month-old daughter was just diagnosed with a potentially life threatening illness. We don't know what our life will become. **Mystery box**!
- There is a worldwide economic downturn. How are we going to make it financially? **Mystery box**!
- My husband has just been put on antidepressants that are killing his libido. How do we salvage our sex life? **Mystery box**!

In our personal lives, we want to – in fact we *demand* to – rip open the mystery box to see what is inside. The very circumstances that would make our life story a blockbuster hit onscreen are what we want to immediately eradicate. We want all the answers right here, right now. But the irony of the mystery box is that once you rip it open, all the possibilities are gone. Suddenly, the anticipation of $50 worth of magic is replaced by the fact you actually only got a bunch of cheap tricks.

And yet, if you are going to build a healthy sex life with your spouse for a lifetime, and if you are going to experience eroticism and desire in your relationship, then you are going to have to endure a bit of mystery. How on earth do these things have anything to do with mystery?

Think about it. When did you have the most desire and eroticism with your spouse? I would bet the answer lies in the earlier days of your relationship. Those were the days when we would kiss for hours, talk until the wee hours of the morning, could not wait to get a phone call during the day from each other. To quote the band The Police, it was the period in our relationship when "Every little thing she does is magic."

Now, as I mentioned in the Myth-Busting chapter, part of this excitement is born of the rush of hormones we are experiencing. And it is true God had a unique design when He planned how men and women would fall in love. But I believe His plan goes deeper than just our hormonal responses to each other. We are not solely the sum of our biology.

If we think back to those early days, we remember those were also the days when we knew very little about each other. Our hunger to become more knowledgeable of each other drove our passions. The very mystery of this new person sparked eroticism. But as we began to understand each other, to grow deeper in love, and to meld our worlds together, the eroticism faded.

In his book *The Kosher Sutra*, Shmuley Boteach, the "Love Rabbi," describes it as, "It is much like a secret that you long to hear. As soon as its contents are revealed, it has ceased to be a secret and in the process it has ceased to be interesting or erotic."[2]

If I had to wager a guess, I would bet you have a lot of knowledge about your spouse, but not a lot of mystery. I would further guess that you miss the desire you once had in your relationship. Those two circumstances are intrinsically entwined.

So how do we nurture a relationship of intimacy over decades with our spouse and still experience mystery? Before I answer that question, let's explore a bit further why we have such distrust for mystery.

The Devaluation of Mystery

I am not a history teacher by any means, but I have heard the comment that those who do not study the past are destined to repeat it. I understood that statement to be an indictment on ignorance, and I have never wanted to be ignorant. So, to "study the past," I became a student of it, mostly by watching the History Channel and Mel Gibson movies every now and again.

It is fascinating to me how historians look back upon long-ago periods and give them labels. For instance, look at the so-called Dark Ages. It was not until hundreds of years later that scholars began to use those terms, and it quickly took on a derogatory meaning. It became a way to sum up that section of time by focusing on what was deemed to be wrong with it. For a while it was called the "age of faith" because religion reigned supreme in the culture. Later, when this was deemed inappropriate because it is in direct conflict with the subsequent deification of intellect and man, scholars began referring to that period as "barbaric" and "priest-ridden," and spoke of "the centuries of ignorance."

By the same token, these same scholars began calling their own time the "Enlightenment." It was a time in Western philosophy and cultural life in which reason was advocated as the primary source and legitimacy for authority. In fact, during this time, reason was held to be the primary value of society. Reason was prized above authority, intuition, emotion, mysticism, superstition and faith.

Why am I dragging you through this overview of history?

Because there are things we can learn from the past. In fact, our current culture is shaped, in many ways, by our cultural past. Many of our beliefs are passive – we either heard or read it, but did not personally experience it, and yet believe them to be true. So when we hear "Dark Ages," we believe those times to be bad, and when we hear "Enlightenment," we believe those times to be good. What follows from that are logical conclusions we should do like those who were "enlightened" and not be like those who were "ignorant." The pendulum has swung fully from a time where mysticism and faith were revered to a place where reason and understanding is the only litmus test. Anything that cannot be fully known, understood and explained in minute detail is not to be trusted.

The problem with this, like any overreaction, is we have thrown the proverbial baby out with the bathwater. Believe me, I too love to know and understand things. I want to know. I *need* to know. And therefore I tend to not trust things that I do not really understand.

This same philosophy has wormed its way into our belief about relationships. I cannot tell you how many people have told me they "deserve to know" every detail of their lover's past and present in every area of their life. If they don't know every detail, they assume things are being hidden, and if things are being hidden, they must be bad or they wouldn't hide them, and if they hide things, they can't trust them, and if they don't trust them, they cannot truly love them. Round and round the circle goes – each link in the logic chain assuming more and more negative qualities until it becomes a major block in a relationship (if not a causal link to it failing).

Somehow in marriage we have come to the point where we actively and intentionally strive to eliminate all mystery. We lose patience for a spouse who loads the dishwasher differently, drives differently, or approaches parenting differently than we do. We don't even bother to see why they do it a different way. We just know our way is better. We lose all tolerance for ambiguity – everything has to be nice and predictable. Orderly. Able to be quantified and classified. Simple and easy to explain and understand.

The problem with this banal perspective is that it is, well, boring. It eliminates our sense of wonder about each other. I love the wording of that phrase – sense of wonder. The very word bestows us with permission to not know. To wonder is to not be sure – to *not* know. And yet one of the things we revere about children is their unadulterated sense of wonder – their amazing ability to simply look at things in awe without the overwhelming desire to understand it all. They can take things at face value and appreciate them for what they are on the surface. Faith comes easily to them.

We as adults, on the other hand, almost pride ourselves on our cynicism. No one will take advantage of us. We have sayings that permeate our subconscious like, "Fool me once, shame on you. Fool me twice, shame on me," or "If it seems too good to be true, then it is." We require proof. In many ways, we still cling to the pendulum that swung so far.

This is because, in North America, our thinking has been radically impacted by the Age of Enlightenment. We can rationalize and explain virtually everything in our world. Intellectual discourse is high on our list of values. If I can explain things more articulately than you, I win the debate. We put very little value on mystery, on that which cannot be explained. Even our "mystery" shows on TV – *CSI* and *Bones* among others – are tied up neatly with a bow at the end of the episode. Shows that refuse to explain every little nuance – JJ Abrams' show *Lost* comes to mind – drive us insane.

Why do we hate mystery in our own lives?

Mystery Forces Us to Live with Ambiguity

The Franciscan monk Richard Rohr calls this place of ambiguity "liminal space." He says, "It is when you have left the "tried and true" but have not yet been able to replace it with anything else… It is when you are in-between your old comfort zone and any possible new answer. It is no fun."[3]

The Bible is filled with examples of liminal space. We often fail to fully comprehend the impact these seasons made on the people because we skim over the times of ambiguity to get to the heroic finish of the story.

But, ponder with me for a moment. What would you be thinking and feeling if you were stuck in the belly of a great fish for three days? Or wandering in circles in the desert for forty years? Or building an altar upon which you are planning to sacrifice your child? Or marching around the city of Jericho for seven days while being taunted from soldiers on the wall above?

Rohr is right. These times are not fun. However, if we can survive liminal space in our marriages without bailing out too early for cheap and easy answers, we reap incredibly rich rewards. We become adept at dealing with anxiety, living with ambiguity, and even stoking the flames of eroticism and desire.

Dealing with Ambiguity

Lominger International, an organization that trains executives in leadership and management, has compiled a list of sixty-seven competencies essential to running a successful business. Of these competencies, "dealing with ambiguity" is one of the most difficult to learn.

Les Woller, a master associate with Lominger and co-author of the book *The Skill*,[4] says that executives who have a minimal grasp of this competency will tolerate risk and uncertainty. Those who become proficient at this skill set, however, will excel in situations involving risk and insecurity, and will be able to make clear-headed decisions despite the lack of information available. The difference between the two executives is that one begrudgingly works around ambiguity while the other accepts it as a part of business, anticipates it, and enables those around him/her to smoothly navigate during these times of uncertainty. It stands to reason that if executives can integrate this competency into their business, they will rise above the rest because life, very simply put, has lots of ambiguity.

Managing Anxiety

Woller says the main difficulty we face when dealing with ambiguity is that it triggers deep anxiety in most of us. Our primary fear is fear of the unknown. We are fearful of the future because it is uncertain, and we come face to face with the reality that we cannot control it. Our illusion of control comes crumbling down around us. Some of us grow up learning to live with ambiguity and manage anxiety from a young age due to our life circumstances, but some of us don't have this opportunity until later in life.

Think about this in the context of a wife who is watching her husband go through a mid-life crisis. All of a sudden, everything that was *known* is now up for grabs. He isn't the same guy he used to be – in fact, *he* doesn't even know who he is anymore. He loves his wife but isn't "in love" with her. He is not sure the career he picked was the right choice. He realizes he is mortal and quickly running out of time. His hopes and dreams, which were so clear when he was younger, seem more and more out of reach, and this stirs up a deep sense of dissatisfaction with the choices he has made in life.

What is the wife's response? Anxiety.

Internally, she is thinking, "What if he stays like this for the rest of our marriage? What if he never snaps out of it? What if he leaves us? What if he has an affair? Why am I not good enough anymore? What if… What if…"

People who are successful in navigating times of ambiguity have learned to minimize their anxieties and embrace the mystery of their current situation. Therapists have noted the more this woman tries to control the situation, the higher the chance her husband *will* leave. Ironically, the more she insists on stability in the midst of his mid-life crisis, the more likely he will respond by walking out the door. However, if she can learn to lessen her anxiety and lean into the ambiguity of her new life, the odds of her marriage surviving go up exponentially.

Heather was one of my clients who had to learn to do this. When I met her, she and her husband were living separately. Earlier that year, her husband confessed to having an affair and she kicked him out. The plan backfired when he used the space in their relationship to become completely enmeshed with the other woman. Heather was referred to me because she realized the problems in her marriage were a result of the sexless marriage they had for years before he strayed. She thought if she could learn how to be sexual, she would win her husband back. Unfortunately, these things are never so simple. Technique was not going to be the salvation for her marriage.

However, Heather's top priority was a loving and healthy relationship, so she began a slow and arduous process of employing various activities to lessen her anxiety. She also started to date her husband again, despite the fact she knew he was still involved with the other woman. She actively looked for things to appreciate about him, even though there was a plethora of things that were completely unlovable. She learned to be her own person when she was on her own, and to explore things about her own personality that lay dormant for years. She learned to listen to the voice of God and what He was telling her during this tumultuous time. And above all, she practiced being at peace with the fact she was not in control.

Heather's husband broke off his relationship with the other woman seven months later and moved home. There were still many issues to work through in their relationship, and none of them moved along quickly. Many hours were spent in tears, wondering when they were going to make it out of the woods. But over time, things slowly improved.

Heather's husband no longer said, "I love you, I'm just not in love with you." Instead, he said, "I am in love with you and I am thankful you let me come home." The seeds of sexual intimacy were planted and began to grow. They planned a remarriage ceremony. They remembered how to laugh together.

To many people, the process Heather went through seems extremely counterintuitive. In fact, many well-intentioned people in Heather's life were coaching her to kick the scumbag to the curb. And she could have. She was fully within her biblical, moral and legal rights to serve her husband with divorce papers. She was a gorgeous, successful woman who could have had any other guy she wanted. But she chose instead to embrace ambiguity and walk a very rocky path to getting what she truly wanted – the restoration of her marriage.

Was this easy for her? No. Was it fun? Definitely not. But did she have a sense that God had His hand on her marriage? Very much so.

A mid-life crisis is only one way mystery forces itself upon us. It is excessively and annoyingly creative at coming up with new ways to make us pay attention.

But why, when the feelings of ambiguity and anxiety are so uncomfortable, does God allow seasons of mystery?

Mystery Interrupts Habituation

Many couples I meet take a tremendous amount of pride in the fact that they *know* each other. This is a wonderful sentiment when it creates warmth and fondness and a sense of shared history in the relationship.

It can backfire on us, though. When we become so secure in our belief that we know our spouse, we can stop looking for different perspectives on them. We get locked into our point of view, and even worse, we think our opinions of our spouse are the *right* ones. In essence, we get so used to seeing what is in front of us, we no longer look for it any more. Psychologists call this problem habituation. As we become used to the new stimuli, we begin to take it for granted. This can be an incredibly dangerous to the relationship.

On Valentine's Day, a Facebook friend posted this status line: "So, I'm on a date with my honey and we're sitting here with nothing to say. Any ideas for a conversation starter?" This couple finally had a chance to sneak away from their kids for a night out, and had nothing to say. It is both incredibly tragic and extremely common.

The danger of *knowing* each other is that often it means we stop looking for new things. With our spouse, the concept of knowing insidiously devolves into *assuming*. We do not see the devastating consequences of these assumptions until years later. The only group in which the divorce rate is going up right now is empty nesters.[5] Everyone else's divorce rate remains stable or is decreasing. Theirs is skyrocketing. Why? These couples took each other for granted for years, but the cracks in the foundation of their relationship didn't come to light until the kids left home. The irony is after years of knowing each other, we wake up and realize we don't know each other at all!

Mystery interrupts habituation. When confronted with uncertainty and ambiguity in our relationship, we are forced to see our spouse from a fresh perspective. We are forced to learn about them anew. We are given the opportunity to see our assumptions may not be correct.

When we actively seek new perspectives on our spouses, when we are constantly on the lookout for change and growth in them, our intimacy deepens.

Mystery Is an Invitation to Intimacy

When we come to a place of acceptance that mystery has something to teach us, and move from trying to control all our circumstances, we understand the rich invitation to intimacy we are being offered.

There is hope in mystery. It forces us to slow down. It is the divine design for making us pay attention to our surroundings in life. It offers us a gift. When life is ambiguous and our knowledge is limited, we can draw closer to each other.

In our marriages, there is mystery simply because we are on a lifelong journey with our spouses. We acknowledge this in our wedding vows to each other. We promise to love in sickness and health, for richer and poorer, for better or worse. Whether we fully recognize it or not, we are in essence taking the plunge right at the beginning by stating before God and man there are no certainties, no guarantees and no predictability. At that altar, we are waiting for life to unfold and to embrace the unknown.

But if we can learn to appreciate the value of mystery, we not only understand change is inevitable, we also adopt an attitude of anticipation and excitement about this change. We say, "I can't wait to see what is going to happen next in our relationship." We acknowledge there will always be new things to discover. New hopes to hold. Dreams to dream. Uncharted territory to venture into. Seeking mystery matures us, deepens us and teaches us.

Here are two examples of mystery in the sex lives of couples I have coached.

Angela and Tim

Angela developed severe arthritis in her early twenties. This took an extreme toll on her sexual relationship with her husband Tim. There were many days when she just hurt all over. Because they could not predict her good and bad days, they became discouraged and slid into a pattern of sexlessness.

When we met, they were celebrating their ten-year anniversary. Slowly, over a series of many conversations, they realized rather than choosing to have a bad sex life for the rest of their marriage, they would choose to embrace the mystery. Recognizing they could not control her illness and would often not know how her body would respond, they improved their communication skills and increased their creativity so they could have a full repertoire of tactics they could take when she wasn't feeling well. I must say that, despite chronic illness in their relationship – indeed *because* of chronic illness in their relationship – they have one of the most vibrant sex lives I have ever seen.

Maria and John

Maria and John's bout into the realms of mystery looked a little bit different. After more than a decade of being married, Maria finally confessed she wanted to experience orgasm together. She had never had an orgasm with John. Now, in his defense, John had realized this, but Maria always played it off as though it were no big deal. When she finally told him she needed more, it sent the two of them reeling because they were encountering something they had no clue how to fix. When they came to me, they were incredibly frustrated. They had run headlong into mystery, and it made them extremely uncomfortable.

John expressed his discomfort by being extremely anxious Maria would leave him for a man who could bring her to orgasm. Maria, in turn, interpreted John's anxiety as his attempt to control her, and this made her shy further and further away from intimacy with him.

When I encouraged them to see this change as a journey together, they slowly came to understand each other's perspectives. Did their style of lovemaking need to change? Absolutely. But they had more compassion for each other and realized their dilemma did not need to be resolved by a sprint to orgasm. Instead, it was an opportunity to explore a whole new side of their sex life with a new emphasis on what new things they would learn together.

But mystery doesn't just forge intimacy. It also brings back the spark.

Mystery Reignites Eroticism and Desire

In the TV show, *Two and a Half Men*, Charlie and his fiancée reflect on a predicament in which many couples find themselves after years of marriage together. The scene opens as they are sitting in bed. Charlie is watching TV while his fiancée Chelsea is working on her laptop.

Charlie: "Sports Center is over. Time for sex."
Chelsea: "Charlie, please. This report is due tomorrow."
Charlie: "All right. I guess our relationship is getting to that mature, evolved stage they talk about."

Chelsea: "I guess so."

Charlie: "Terrific." Then he mutters under his breath as he moves towards the bathroom, "I hope I die soon."

Chelsea: "What?"

Charlie: "Love you!" Charlie walks into the bathroom and leaves the door open.

Chelsea: "Remember when you used to close the door and try to hit the porcelain so I didn't have to hear you pee?"

Charlie: "Yeah, way back when we used to have sex after Sports Center."

Why is it the more we get to know each other, the more comfortable we become in our relationship, and the more intimacy we cultivate, the more our desire diminishes? You would think as we draw closer and closer, we would have more and more desire. But instead, as we grow comfortable in our relationship, sex ebbs and we no longer take the care to bank our stream off the side of the toilet.

In her book *Mating in Captivity*, Esther Perel describes the paradox of knowledge and mystery: "Love enjoys knowing everything about you; desire needs mystery. Love likes to shrink the distance that exists between me and you, while desire is energized by it. If intimacy grows through repetition and familiarity, eroticism is numbed by repetition. It thrives on the mysterious, the novel, and the unexpected. Love is about having; desire is about wanting... It is less concerned with where it has already been than passionate about where it can still go. But too often, as couples settle into the comforts of love, they cease to fan the flame of desire. They forget that fire needs air."[6]

When you hear this explanation of desire and the erotic, it is easy to see why we have these strong feelings during the infancy of our relationship. Those were the days when all the things that make desire flourish reigned supreme. Everything was new and fresh, waiting to be explored. And then, as we got to know each other, this driving force stalled. We spent so much time together, very little was new. The paradox is the deeper we grow in our closeness with each other, the more elusive eroticism becomes.

It is true there is incredible bonding that happens when a couple builds years of history together. Our knowledge base of each other makes us phenomenal friends and partners. But it doesn't necessarily make us phenomenal lovers.

When it comes to maintaining amazing sex over the years with your spouse, I tend to agree with JJ Abrams – "Mystery is the infinite potential and possibility. It is hope. It is the catalyst for imagination. There are times when it is more important than knowledge."[7] Actively recognizing mystery in your marriage will help keep the spark alive over all those years.

The very elements of mystery – the unknown, the uncertain, the ill defined – are the places where eroticism and desire flourish. Here are some fundamental principles of desire and eroticism.

Desire and Eroticism Need Separateness

Never before has there been so much pressure on relationships as there is in North America today. My husband and I saw how deeply engrained our own cultural biases were when we lived in Kathmandu, Nepal. We quickly came to realize marriages such as our own were termed "love marriages," and they were actually looked down upon! This was quite a shock to us until we learned the rationale behind the disdain.

Many of the older generation had the foresight to realize the young couple, caught in the throes of infatuation and hormones, would not have sufficient wisdom to make a lifelong choice of a spouse. The older generation expected love would grow over the years of participating together in the daily duties of life. In their minds, factors such as financial stability, genetic compatibility, and the support of a wider community were better indicators of a good match.

Now, before we get too critical of the pitfalls of that culture, let's take a look at our own. Today, we put tremendous pressure on our spouses. We expect romance, deep understanding of our wants and needs, spiritual alignment, friendship (indeed the closest of friendship), passion, and agreement in parenting styles. This list goes on and on. We have, in essence, taken "the two will become one" and interpreted it as complete and total enmeshment. Our divorce rates are in part a reflection that our marriages are buckling under the strain of these ludicrously high expectations.

And yet, if you are going to experience the erotic in your relationship, you have to understand that your spouse is indeed a separate person, whose fantasies, sexual tastes and desires might be very different from your own. When you embrace this separateness and allow it room in your relationship, the erotic has space to breathe.

I once had a client tell me a story about her husband. One day, while away on a business trip, he confessed to her that he had a secret sexual fantasy. On the surface, this was completely outside her paradigm, but as she spent some time reflecting on it, she realized it wasn't anything that violated her core values in the marriage. So, instead of feeling threatened and responding with ridicule (such as, "That is so strange and I really don't want to have anything to do with it"), she embraced the concept her husband was a separate person, unique in his tastes, and told him she would be delighted to explore this avenue with him. When she acknowledged and affirmed his individuality within the context of their relationship, they experienced a fresh wave of eroticism.

Why do many people push back from the concept of separateness in marriage? It has a lot to do with fear. Many people think secretly, "If I accept that you are a separate individual, you might ask me to do something outside my own personal comfort zone, you might not want me, or you might define yourself differently than I do."

This mentality leads me to my second point.

Desire and Eroticism Need Fresh Eyes

When Eric and I went to his twenty-year High School reunion, I had the privilege of seeing him through the eyes of people who had not seen him for years. I was able to watch their expressions and hear their comments. Some reflected the man I know. I heard stories of mischief and leadership.

Some described a man foreign to me. One lady talked about how nice and sweet my husband was in high school. Now, I think my husband is the most incredible man alive, but "nice" and "sweet" wouldn't even crack the top ten list of words which spring to mind. For the record, I would list "side-splittingly hilarious," "incessantly perceptive" and "insanely creative," amongst others.

But that is because I have a certain perception of who he is as a person, and her perception was radically different. She gave me new insight into how people perceive him – at least twenty years ago. And that is good information to have too.

Being open to seeing another perspective is important because we often get blinders on about our spouse and neglect to see what is right in front of us. For instance, when your husband's co-worker raves about some amazing thing he did at work, do you catch a new glimpse of how he succeeds? Or do you just think of all the things he failed to do around the house? When a man's gaze lingers a little bit too long on your wife, do you dismiss him as a creep? Or do you have a renewed appreciation for what he is looking at? Do you even notice at all?

I have a friend who has the pleasure (or burden, depending how you look at it) of seeing her husband through the eyes of another almost every time they go out for dinner. Her husband is a very attractive and gregarious guy who manages, *without doing anything inappropriate,* to make the waitresses swoon when he enters the restaurant. Many wives I know would respond to this situation by getting jealous or annoyed. Instead, my friend has deliberately chosen to use these times as reminders of how sexy her husband is to other women. By making this choice, she ensures her perception of him never stales.

Desire and Eroticism Need Delayed Gratification

We are, without a doubt, a culture of instant gratification. It is ingrained even in our children. Numerous studies have been done over the years asking children to choose between getting the object of their desire immediately or waiting a bit and getting even more. In one study done at Stanford, 70 percent of the children simply could not wait.[8] They settled for *less* so they could get it *faster.*

We cart this mentality right into our sex lives. We are besieged with images of couples having sex on first dates (sometimes the second if the couple is extra cautious). When we hop into the sack, it is all about the sprint to orgasm. Wham, bam, thank you ma'am.

And yet, instant gratification numbs eroticism. Eroticism thrives in being put off and delayed. Think back to the first kiss with your lover. Did you spend time thinking about when it was going to happen? How was it going to unfold? Where were you going to be? The delight of anticipation accelerated the desire.

We find the antithesis of this in most modern marriages. Couples zone out in front of the TV all evening, and then will turn to each other and intone the words of UFC referee, Big John McCarthy, "Let's get it on!" It's no wonder so many couples are bored silly with their sex lives.

If you want to have desire and eroticism in your sex life, you are going to have to be deliberate about cultivating it. The anticipation for sex should not begin when Leno goes off. It should begin in the morning or even the day before. You should be flirting, teasing, and touching hours before you ever take your clothes off. Only a small percentage of "sex" should take place when you are naked. The rest takes place when intercourse is not logistically possible, but you are building up to the experience.

Creating Space for Mystery

You might be wondering how the Passion Coach, who uses a solutions-oriented approach to clients, can be espousing the virtues of mystery. To be clear, I am not saying that diligently seeking solutions to life's problems is wrong. I wholeheartedly advocate being solution oriented.

And yet, there are times when we cannot find answers. Times when the prescription medication he is taking to keep him alive has devastating side effects on his libido, and despite all the things you have tried, nothing can take away the ache that he doesn't pursue you like he once did. Times where even though she has never had an orgasm with you, she finally confesses she cannot live like this anymore. Even though you tried and tried, nothing is working, and your fear that she will leave is escalating with each failed attempt.

In these moments, do we stop looking for solutions? No.

Rather, we have to act like a blend of Mulder and Scully from the *X-Files*. While looking for answers, we have to simultaneously learn to embrace the ambiguity of mystery. We choose to learn from the very fact *we do not know the answers*. Contrary to everything our culture teaches us, we realize we can grow from *not* knowing. We choose to see this mystery box as something that will weave richness into our life story, rather than an inconvenience that needs to be immediately eradicated.

If this whole concept of mystery has your head swimming, here are some ways to get started creating space for it in your relationship.

Acknowledge Mystery

When creating space for mystery in our marriage, we begin by acknowledging there is growth in our lives that comes from the journey we take together. We are, in essence, giving God permission to use mystery as a divine tool in our lives. It's not that God needs our permission to use mystery to affect growth in our marriage, but it is a lot easier if we actively surrender.

When we acknowledge the existence of mystery, we grow to understand not everything can be planned and calculated. We realize we have to constantly be in tune with our spouses because they will change – and we will change – over our lifetime together. We accept this change as the natural course of a marriage that stands the test of time. It cannot be fully mapped out, or plotted, or scheduled because we do not have a complete picture of who we are becoming as individuals and as a couple.

Buy It Up

After we acknowledge mystery exists, we need to change our attitude towards it. At this point, we make a conscious choice to see mystery as a *gift* rather than an *annoyance*. When there are changes in our sex life, we choose to see this as an invitation to grow deeper together, learn more about each other, and build a shared history that is uniquely ours. As we change our attitudes, we realize our sex life is not shaped with a cookie cutter – it is the dynamic mixture of our likes, dislikes and adventures together.

My mother had a saying in times like these: "Buy it up. Buy it all up. There are things you can learn right now that are almost impossible to learn at other times in your life, so buy it up." (It always made me think she was buying junk bonds because she knew they would return high yields if she could weather the uncertainty.)

When we buy it up, we choose to shift our attitude from "this sucks" to "this is opportunity." This requires courage. It requires faith that we can deal with the unknowns together and move to deeper intimacy. We are, in essence, moving from autopilot to adaptability. Our brain is learning new patterns of behavior and finding new methods to cope with the unexpected circumstances.

Start Looking Again

Next, we start looking for mystery boxes in our relationship. We renew our interest in our spouses. We let go of our arrogant perspective that we know our spouses inside and out. None of us ever like to be put in a box.

My daughter is in elementary school and when I pick her up, she will often start the conversation about something she learned that day by saying, "Mommy, did you know?" Now, I know a lot about what they learn at that age. I am pretty sure I can read better, write better, and count better than my daughter.

But if I said to her, "Of course I know that!" I would destroy the fun of learning for her. She would become discouraged and stop sharing the new discoveries in her life. But when I respond by saying, "Tell me all about it!" she is able to share a part of herself with me and I am able to enter her world. And as such, I get the experience of getting to know her even better.

In a similar way, we may know the bulk of what our spouse is sharing with us, but the nuances are important. It is the nuances that matter and change. When we are attentive to mystery boxes in our lives, we move out of the danger zone of believing we know our spouse while failing to look at them.

Stoke the Embers of Desire and Eroticism

Finally, we begin to make choices that allow desire and eroticism the space to breathe in our relationships. We give each other permission to be separate individuals. We choose to minimize our anxiety so fear does not block the opportunity we have to explore the hidden aspects of our spouse. We relax more. We accept more. We flirt more. We turn off the TV more. We pay attention more. We choose trust more. We explore more.

Final Thoughts

In her song "The Climb," Miley Cyrus sings:

There's always gonna be another mountain;
I'm always gonna wanna make it move.
Always gonna be an uphill battle;
And sometimes I'm gonna have to lose.
It ain't about how fast I get there,
Ain't about what's waiting on the other side.
It's the climb.[9]

She concludes by saying, "I may not know it / But these are the moments that I am gonna remember most." When we look back over the course of our marriages, it is the times of mystery that weave richness into our lives. The very things that feel uncomfortable and annoying in the moment are opportunities to cultivate the deepest intimacy in our marriages.

As we embrace the mystery in our relationships, we are building the foundation for trust to grow. As we choose exploration rather than fear in our navigation of life's challenges, we grow more confident in our identity as a couple. The beauty of embracing mystery and submitting oneself to the unknown is that in doing so, we build a shared history together. The mystery of our lives is what makes us uniquely us. We will look back and say, "We did that. We accomplished that. We went through that together. We tried that. We laughed at that. We cried at that." And you'll be better for it.

Bedwork: Mystery

PSA: _____

This week, answer at least two questions. If you have a strong emotional reaction to the questions, pick the one you love and the one you hate. If you do not have a strong reaction, pick an exercise your spouse will appreciate, or give them home field advantage. Don't forget to record your PSA.

1. **Permission Statement.** Write out a permission statement (this can be done on your own, or you and your spouse can do this together). In it, give each other permission to change over time, request new things from the relationship, and create new rituals that support those changes. Release each other from the obligation of being the exact same person as when you married. Recognize change is inevitable in life, and accept the journey together as an adventure of rediscovering your spouse over and over again. Give permission to grow through life with each other, and respect the growth you see in the other person.

2. **Challenging Times.** List some of the difficult things that have happened in your life during the course of your marriage. During those times, what brought you and your spouse closer together? What did you learn about your spouse that was new? What did you grow to appreciate about him/her? Did you underestimate or overlook something about your spouse? How did your marriage change and grow under those difficult circumstances? What hope does that offer for the rest of your marriage?

3. **Mystery Boxes.** List some of the mystery boxes in your relationship. What is unknown right now? Do you need to acknowledge the role of mystery boxes in your marriage? Do you need to change your attitude towards mystery? Do you need to start looking for mystery again? If so, write down some specific ways you can do so.

4. **Delayed Gratification.** Practice this principle to turn up the heat of your eroticism for each other. Choose a time when you will <u>*not*</u> have sex for a few days – maybe even a week. Most couples dislike engaging in intercourse when the wife has her period, so this would be an excellent time to choose. Clearly identify with each other when the start and stop dates are for this exercise. During this time, make all forms of orgasm off limits. However, use this time to flirt, kiss, give and receive massages, enjoy long hugs and so forth, all the time knowing it will not culminate in orgasm until the set period of time is over. Pay attention to what this exercise does for the desire you have for each other.

5. **Habituation.** How has habituation crept into your relationship? What can you do this week to pay attention to your spouse? Watch and observe how other people react to your spouse (at a sporting event, a child's activity, church, a work function, etc.). Ask your

spouse's best friend what s/he likes most about your spouse. Actively look for things you have overlooked, forgotten or simply never seen before.

6. **Managing Anxiety.** Scripture is clear we are not to worry. Read these verses: Philippians 4:6-7, I Peter 5:6-7, Psalm 131:1, Proverbs 3:5-8, Luke 12:22-26 and Psalm 34:4. Then write ways you can actively put those principles into practice. Consider what you would be doing with your time if you were not worrying or feeling anxiety. What would you be focusing your thoughts on? What would occupy your time? Choose to do those things instead of worry. Note of encouragement: This is like building muscle. At the beginning, it feels difficult and awkward, but the more you practice, the stronger you become and the easier it is.

7. **Managing Anxiety.** In the contemplative tradition, the Eastern Orthodox Church practices saying a short prayer repeatedly for ten minutes each day. The objective of this practice is to take your mind off whatever is bothering you and place your focus solely on God. Choose a quiet place and time when you decide to do this activity (first thing in the morning before other family members have woken, last thing at night before you fall asleep, etc.), and repeat the prayer. One of the prayers uttered by the Eastern Orthodox Church was, "Lord Jesus Christ, Son of God, have mercy on me, a sinner." You can try this prayer, quote one of the verses in question six or write a prayer of your own. The main point is that your focus is on God.

Element 4: Respect

"If we lose love and respect for each other, this is how we finally die."
Maya Angelou – Author, Poet and Civil Rights Activist

Several years ago, I was working with a woman because she wanted to bring some life back into her marriage. Her children were about to leave for university, and it dawned on her that she was going to be stuck in the house, alone with her husband. This was a terrifying thought to her, because her marriage had been full of drudgery for years. Their sex life in particular had been problematic because it focused mostly on bringing her husband to orgasm, and lacked any creativity. She was bored, frustrated and lonely.

As a response to the state of her marriage, she had chosen to cope by throwing herself into the lives of her children. But with her coping mechanism about to disappear, she realized she needed to work on her marriage if it had any chance of survival. At the time, my course was being offered at her church, and she was quite excited to learn new things about sexuality, which she hoped would inject new life into her marriage as a whole.

During the weeks she attended the sessions, she was filled with hope that things could indeed be better with her husband. For the first time in their twenty-year marriage, she was excited about sex. She believed if they could make some small changes in their sex life, it would have a domino effect of breakthrough in the rest of their relationship. She began to read books on marriage to seek solutions for her problems, sought to bridge the distance between her husband and herself, and asked to try new things in the bedroom.

Unfortunately, her husband did not respond as she hoped. He resented her attempts to make changes in their sex life. At one point, she wrote to me and told me about an exchange they had. "I suggested trying a new position I had read about (nothing radical or uncomfortable). He said, 'What's wrong with you?! Suddenly you're so...' with arms gesturing towards the computer and unable to finish his sentence. We did end up having *regular* sex (same old same old) and afterwards he said, 'See, nothing wrong with that – it works for me!' So I said, 'Well, we're going to have to find something that works for me too.' But he said, 'You take too long.' And that was that."[1]

One of the most heartbreaking parts of my job is when I work with a couple that has failed to put in a foundation of respect for each other. Perhaps they had it at one time, but it has eroded over the years. In other situations, they have never seen the importance of establishing the value of respect in their relationship, and their marriage is consequently crumbling around them.

How do you know if you have a lack of respect in your relationship? This husband summed it up succinctly: "It works for me." Respect is not about you – it is a focus on the other person. Respect says:

- I honor you, even if you are not like me.
- I listen to your input.
- I value your contribution to our relationship.

- I freely allow you to blossom to your full potential without fear.
- I lay down my need to be right and correct.
- I open my mind to the possibility that even though you are very different from me, your perspectives, experiences and choices have value and meaning.
- Regardless of my opinion of your perspective, you are my partner in life and I will revere you as such.

When couples fail to approach each other sexually with a solid grounding in respect, sex quickly becomes a function of marriage rather than an expression of it. It becomes something they do, usually less and less frequently, to get their own needs met or fulfill an obligation they feel they owe the marriage. While this might work in the short term, it is not a sustainable approach. If you want your sex life to thrive, respect has to be one of the essential elements that holds it together.

The Erosion of Respect

Disrespect is insidious and can invade a household under many guises – but all of them are equally damaging. Listed below are a few of the forms that I see most frequently when I speak and coach. For the purpose of understanding them more completely, I will break them down by the major concepts involved. It is interesting to note that often the loss of respect starts in areas *outside* of the bedroom, but no matter where it starts, it always ends *in* the bedroom.

Belittling Men

I Married a Child

Several years ago, my family was having lunch with some friends of ours. This blended family had a very young child as well as a teenage daughter. During the course of the meal, I was talking about our personal struggle with infertility, our deep desire to expand our family, and the possibility of adoption. The teenage girl looked at me and said, "Why would you want another child? You already have two." This immediately pushed my buttons. I explained to her, rather firmly in hindsight, that Eric is my husband, my lover, my friend and my partner in life. He is most certainly *not* my child.

I cannot count the number of times I have heard the idea "he is just one of the kids" from both women and men. When I hear a wife utter this phrase, it is usually accompanied with a look of disgust. When a man makes mention of it, he does so with a spirit of utter surrender, as though this has been the reality spoken in his household for so long, he no longer fights against it.

This attitude is just one of many ways our culture is bending towards a tendency to devalue men. In the movies, we see guys who just cannot get their act together (*40-Year-Old Virgin, Failure to Launch*, etc.). It is more and more common for the media (both entertainment and mainstream) to depict men as necessary for the propagation of the species, but not for much else. The qualities that men contribute are not given much airtime.

For example, studies have shown when men are left alone with their children, they tend to be much more spontaneous, unpredictable, creative and even rough during their playtime than mothers.[2] Furthermore, all these aspects of play have been shown to develop very specific and necessary traits for our children to excel in the world as adults. In our family, these are attributes and abilities my husband brings to parenting that I simply do not come by so easily.

Almost every weekend, Riley begs for what we call a "daddy-daughter date." It is time for just the two of them to be together. They will go get dip cones, or go skating, or go out for a picnic and play on the monkey bars at the playground – any number of things really – all of them child focused and designed to bring Riley as much enjoyment as possible. I never know what they are going to do, and honestly I don't think Eric does until they start. For him, it is all about time together, all the while teaching her how she should be treated by men, and how much her father loves her. These are important messages and important times. From the outside, I often cringe as they roughhouse in the yard, fall off bikes and run through Band-Aids like we own the company. But Riley needs this type of interaction as much as she needs cuddle time with me as we read together.

Now, if I am being transparent, there are times I get frustrated these daddy-daughter dates always seem to happen on the weekend. It's the best time for them, but it is also the best time to clean the house. I wouldn't be completely honest if I said Eric had somehow missed this correlation. He's no dummy. But I intentionally work around that schedule. There is, and will always be, time for chores. But there will not always be time for playing with our daughter. These are precious moments.

So, instead of seeing Eric and Riley's time together as Eric shirking other duties so he can "goof off," I see a man bringing something precious to our family that he is extremely adept at. Others might think he is acting like one of the kids, but the truth is he is being Dad.

Setting Him Up to Fail

Deep down, women are looking for a hero. I was a teenager in the 1980s and I remember watching the movie *Footloose* when it came out. One of the things that still makes me swoon is when I hear Bonnie Tyler's "Holding Out for a Hero." The first verse and chorus sum it up:

Where have all the good men gone
And where are all the gods?
Where's the street-wise Hercules
To fight the rising odds?
Isn't there a white knight upon a fiery steed?
Late at night I toss and I turn and I dream
of what I need

I need a hero
I'm holding out for a hero 'til the end of the night
He's gotta be strong
And he's gotta be fast
And he's gotta be fresh from the fight[3]

As women, we want a Superman. We want a hero. We want him strong and fast and sure of himself. We want him righting wrongs, loosing the chains of injustice and, in a perfect world, we want him moving the furniture when he vacuums the carpets, not just going around it.

Here's the thing: Men truly want to be that hero. They want to swoop in and save the day. They want to make the girls swoon. They want to be admired, praised and respected. But very often, the women in their lives set them up to fail.

In my practice, for example, I find men are often willing to help around the house, but often when they try, their wives nag them because they didn't do the chore perfectly. Frequently, a woman will show up in my coaching practice and complain that her husband is not pitching in enough. When I ask her to describe a situation in which he did actually help, she immediately tells me all the ways he didn't do the chore to her liking. Technically, he did the dishes, but he loaded the dishwasher incorrectly.

Really? What is the *wrong* way to load the dishwasher? You might have a personal style of loading, but if the dishes come out clean (or even mostly clean), is it really worth the fight? What is the worst-case scenario? A few things have to be put back into the dishwasher and run a second time? Is that really worth torpedoing your sexual intimacy within your marriage?

Yes, I just connected loading a dishwasher to sex in marriage. If you ask your husband to do something, but have ridiculous (and even worse – unspoken) expectations, you are intentionally sabotaging your husband. You have set him up to fail. It's the marital version of entrapment. Create enough opportunities for him to fail, and eventually he will simply stop trying. Unless you married a masochist, repeated humiliation at your hands is not going to turn him into the man of your dreams.

When he feels he can't do anything right around the house, or if he knows you just consider him to be one of the kids, or he has just gotten his head bitten off because he didn't do things exactly the way you think they need to be done, what do you think your odds are that he will come to bed at night intent on **giving** you the most mind-blowing orgasm you have ever experienced in your life? Pretty low. He is just going to try to get his needs met so he can feel a little bit better about the day.

Believe me when I tell you that people – men and women – will gravitate towards people and places where they feel successful. Do you know where the number one place is for an affair to begin? The workplace. And it is not because the women in the workplace are ridiculously hot. In fact, most men will say the woman with whom he had an affair was actually less attractive than his wife. It is not about finding someone better looking – it's that men feel they can succeed in the workplace. And when a female co-worker recognizes that success, and demonstrates respect to a man, that is a powerful attractant, especially when he doesn't feel he is getting that at home. Especially if when he leaves work, he morphs from being viewed as Superman during the day to being considered one of the kids at home.

However, when he comes home to a household of people who appreciate him, including a wife who believes he is her hero, and when he comes home to an environment where he is as successful (or more so) than he is at work, he is eager to please. So, give up the right to have things done your way all the time, thank him profusely for what he *did* do, and let him discover his own style of doing it.

Culture of Contempt

Work life, however, is not always the bastion of success and encouragement for men. In society today, some men are finding it harder and harder to achieve the victories they once did in their occupations. It is no secret the recent recession had a more devastating effect on male jobs than it did on those of women. In fact, economists say this "man-cession" was one of the contributing factors to women becoming the majority of the workforce for the first time in history.[4]

But even for men who have been fortunate enough to keep their jobs, they are increasingly expected to excel in areas long considered to be a woman's home field. They are asked to express themselves with a high degree of verbal skills, sit still and focus in lengthy meetings, and tone down their aggression. In this post-industrial society, men can no longer compete on sheer strength or size. Women are finding success in the workforce the likes of which they have never seen. In many areas, the proverbial glass ceiling has been shattered. Women are leapfrogging men for promotions and outperforming them on the newly leveled playing field of classrooms and boardrooms across North America. I am ecstatic to see these new opportunities for women, make no mistake, but with this success comes new challenges and insidious issues.

Within this heady atmosphere of achievement, women are often tempted to undervalue the diversity men bring to the family, and slip into an attitude of contempt. They can easily fall into the trap of believing they are better than their husbands because they might be more adept at a particular task. Discontent with being co-equal, women can slide into the compulsion to prove they are better than their husband in every area – home and work. Pretty soon, they are telling them how to behave and correcting them – just as they do with their kids. This is a dangerous stance to take. Your children are subordinate to you. Your spouse is not.

It is an amazing time we live in where women can truly begin to spread their wings and walk in the fullness of the gifting God has given them. But Luke 12:48 (NIV) helps put things in perspective: "From everyone who has been given much, much will be demanded; and from the one who has been entrusted with much, much more will be asked."

As a woman you have been given much. As a wife you have been entrusted with much. And what is asked of you? "R-E-S-P-E-C-T," to quote Aretha Franklin. Please understand I am fully aware this goes both ways, and I will get to the men next. But for now, this is about you. This is about your marriage and the sex life you have always wanted. If you take an objective look at your situation and find you have become comfortable in the culture of contempt – for men, for masculinity or for your husband – then you need to take action immediately. Remember who you married and why. Your husband can't be your Superman if you are his kryptonite.

Discounting Women

A 1950s Mentality vs. the Millennium Reality

And now it's time to examine the issue of respect from the other side. Just as the attitude of contempt pushes buttons with men, so does the topic of division of household duties with women. It is a huge bone of contention in many marriages. I have had numerous women say to me they withheld sex because their husband didn't help enough around the house. It was, quite frankly, the only way women felt they could strike back as they felt so frustrated and overwhelmed by their sheer workload. Obviously, I don't support this stance, but it underscores the degree of conflict North American couples experience regarding this topic.

For centuries, the roles for men and women were clearly defined. Men went out and hunted, women stayed home with the kids. In the past few decades, though, these roles have become less defined. The number of women in the workplace is growing, but the vast majority of them still carry the bulk of the home chores as well.[5] As a result, they feel angry, bitter and disrespected.[6]

Recently, I met with a team of leaders from a church who wanted me to speak at their Valentine's Day dinner. One leader told me about the feedback she received from other women in the church and, as is frequently the case, the issue of household responsibilities came up. "They don't feel respected by their husbands," she told me. "They feel overwhelmed by everything else they have to do, and sex is just one more thing they have to check off their list."

I don't know any woman who feels she has the work/life balance right. Usually, when the topic comes up, there is a look of guilt that gives way to frustration and then morphs into exhaustion. Men, you need to understand there will be days when your wife really nailed it at work, but she feels like a failure at home. Other days, she really connected with the kids, but blew it at work. You need to appreciate the sense of responsibility she feels is enormous. But the situation is not as straightforward as you might think. Simply giving up her job would most likely not be a solution – emotionally for her or economically for the household.

Feelings of guilt are not limited to women who work outside the home. It applies to women who choose to stay at home as well. The world around them is constantly sending messages that what they do is not sufficient. Their work at home is not given the same value as that of a woman who works in an office, a store or a restaurant. Stay-at-home women are constantly told they should do more, and the implicit directive is they should *be* more. When the world is bludgeoning you with messages of personal inadequacy and disrespect, it is even more imperative you feel respected at home.

Research tells us that despite the fact more and more women are working outside the home, they are still carrying the bulk of responsibility within it.[7] There is a great imbalance of how the household chores are divided up. As I mentioned earlier, sometimes a woman refuses to allow her husband to do the chores because he doesn't do them "correctly." But other times men are just clueless about the amount of work it takes to run a household smoothly. They may not have been raised in a household in which they were expected to participate in these chores, and so they legitimately just don't know. Some men still operate on an antiquated worldview and believe household chores are not their responsibility. Their family of origin might have had very specific roles for men and women, and scrubbing floors didn't show up on the guy's list. Regardless, if this is the situation in your marriage and it is causing problems, it is time for some communication. "It's always been done this way" is not a legitimate reason for continuing with behavior that disrespects your wife.

When Eric and I were going through premarital counseling, it was obvious we came from very different families of origin. My father did all the laundry and organized a thorough clean of the house on Saturday mornings. Dad assigned chores to everyone, and when they were done, we did a fun activity as a family. Mom did all the meals and tidying throughout the week, but the big chores were left for everyone to pitch in and do on the weekends. Eric's household, on the other hand, was quite different. Since his mom did not work outside the home, it was expected she do all the cleaning throughout the day. Men were expected to do the yard work outside (which in Texas was a year-round duty), but participation was not expected inside the house.

Because we had come from such different backgrounds, our pastor recommended we take a list of household chores and divide them up. As was our habit, after our premarital session, Eric and I went to dinner and discussed our homework. That evening, over burgers and fries, we put all the common chores into a "his" or "her" category. For instance, we decided I would take toilets (a task I didn't mind) and Eric would handle meals (something he was far better at than I). Believe me, everything did not fall down stereotypical gender lines, but in fourteen years of marriage, we each still think we got the better end of the deal.

Now, all our efforts to divvy up the work notwithstanding, over our years of marriage there have been times Eric has pitched in with toilets and I have done the cooking. We have learned to give and take when the circumstances became necessary. Certain seasons of life – such as when Riley was a baby, or Eric was studying for his professional exams, or when I was writing this book – called for more flexibility to our original agreement. But our flexibility was enabled by the solid respect we hold for each other, built on years of clear expectations and understanding that everyone pitches in to ensure the smooth running of the household.

If the household chores are beginning to erode the foundation of respect in your household, sit down together with pen and paper and figure it out. If you cannot come to agreement, you might want to consider outsourcing the problem. A housecleaner who comes periodically to ease everyone's burdens is a lot cheaper than couple's therapy or divorce.

Men, if you are having a difficult time wrapping your head around the fact women care so deeply about this subject, look at it this way. Choose to see housework as foreplay. Your wife is wired differently and struggles to compartmentalize the dirty dishes from a sexy rendezvous. It all meshes together for her. So, help lighten her load on the home front. Sometimes just coming home and saying, "Honey, how can I help?" is the very best aphrodisiac.

Everything We've Been Told Is Wrong
We have, without a doubt, a cultural perception that wives are sexually disinterested creatures. We spend hours poking fun in movies and television shows. Men and women alike have bought into this concept that men want sex all the time and women would rather go shopping.

Men, in particular, often pigeonhole their wives as less sexual in general than men. The phrase "Not tonight, I have a headache," is universally perceived as a woman's response to her husband's advances. In fact, there's an old joke that goes, "What's the best way to get a woman to stop having sex with you? Marry her." This cultural stereotype has caused an inordinate amount of despair on both sides of the gender divide.

Shmuley Boteach puts a lot of responsibility for this misperception on the shoulders of men. He asserts women are much more deeply sexual than men. "The Talmud, written two thousand years ago, goes so far as to say that a man of leisure, that is a man whose occupation does not involve strenuous exertion, is obligated to make love to his wife every single night. And that's because his wife wants it every night. The rabbis of the Talmud understood women to be much more sexual than men. And to the extent that today so many married women claim instead to have a headache is because their husbands are having such bad sex with them that they've killed off their libidos."[8]

The very way God created our bodies, Shmuley contends, illustrates the principle that a woman was designed so a man could peel back the layers. It takes time to discover and unlock the depths of a woman's sensuality. A man's penis is fairly simple – hanging outside the body and reacting to stimuli. A woman's body, on the other hand, is truly a wonderland to be explored. Even the design of the labia and vulva working as layers and coverings beckons for her husband to slow down, take his time and browse.

This description parallels what we find in the Song of Songs. This book does not depict a man chasing after a frigid, disinterested woman. The woman is described as someone just as enthusiastic in her sexuality as the man. She rests comfortably in the knowledge her sensuality is a gift she can give the Lover. When women give themselves permission to embrace their sensual birthright, magic happens in their marriages.

Based on conversations in my practice, I believe men also long to discover more about their wives' bodies. Innately, they understand this requires more than just a "quickie." Nothing can be more frustrating to a man that having a desire to explore his wife, but she is unable or unwilling to accept these advances. Very often, when faced with repeated rejection from their wives, men just settle for what they can get. This is a tragic way to live sexually for both of them.

As a Christian culture, we have done a poor job at explaining sensuality to our daughters. Rather than help young women understand this part of God's design for them, it has been much easier to squelch it. Rather than mentor young women to value sensuality as extremely sacred in marriage, it has been easier to pretend it does not exist. And rather than explain to a young girl the wonders of her body, it has been easier to ignore it altogether and let her figure it out on her wedding night.

I know a lot of little girls who were told their private parts were dirty, and have grown up to be women with shameful feelings associated with any act that ventures beyond the most basic of interactions – and even those are usually under the covers with the lights off. It is unrealistic to treat sensuality as shameful for the entirety of a young woman's life, and then expect her to become an enthusiastic lover the moment she says, "I do."

The good news is women who do their shame homework and find freedom in this area become enthusiastic about intimacy with their husbands. I cannot count the number of giggling women who are discovering how they are designed, sharing new ideas and thoughts with their husbands, and enjoying the sexual part of their relationship for the first time in their marriage.

When this happens, however, the onus of responsibility also increases for the man. He has to become a better lover. The one advantage of a disinterested lover is she does not demand a lot from him. A sensual, enthusiastic wife, on the other hand, will have higher expectations. Settling for sex that "works for me" will no longer be sufficient. An unwillingness to slow down and engage your wife in ways that focus on her pleasure is a tangible way to disrespect her. Men, if this is the case, plan on getting some fresh resources, having open dialogue with your wives about what will work for them, and prepare to have a lot of fun.

The Consequences of Disrespect

I have found that many times, when couples fail to respect each other sexually, it is because they come into the relationship with an erroneous belief system, and reinforce that system by interpreting every experience though that lens rather than communicating openly with their spouse. This perpetuates a cycle of increasing animosity and decreasing respect. Funnel the issues I touched on already into this cycle, and you have the makings of a perfect storm.

As men feel less and less competent in their ability to keep up, women are becoming less and less tolerant of their efforts to do so. Women file for 70 percent of divorces,[9] and the prevalent attitude seems to be, "I'm better off without him." But we could not be further from the truth. It is not good for us to be alone. Ecclesiastes 4:9-10 (NIV) tells us, "Two are better than one, because they have a good return for their labor: If either of them falls down, one can help the other up. But pity anyone who falls and has no one to help them up."

As we try to find equilibrium in this new world, it is imperative for women to understand the tremendous value men bring to our relationships and to our families. And men must understand and appreciate the complexities women navigate on a daily basis. Both must continually look for the best in each other, because as I have said before, what you focus on will grow.

Understanding the Patterns of Disrespect

You cannot jump from falling in love directly to bitterness and anger. Believe it or not, there are very specific steps that you must take to move from one to the other. If you want to counteract disrespect in your household, you first have to understand those steps.

Self-Talk Matters

Scientific research suggests we talk to ourselves as much as fifty thousand times a day.[10] We spend an inordinate amount of time listening to our own internal thoughts. It is as though we have iPods that play messages in our heads constantly, sizing up what has happened in our lives and what we think and feel about those events. Furthermore, research also tells us 80 percent of this self-talk is negative. When is comes to our relationships, there are a couple of ways this negative self-talk begins.

One common way for negativity to set into the relationship is through disappointment. Many men and women I meet are extremely disappointed. Life has not turned out the way they anticipated. Their sex lives are not everything they hoped and dreamed. They believe their spouses have let them down. I remember one conversation distinctly, during which my client said, "This is not how I expected my life to turn out." Some couples waited years to have sex, and they were bitterly disappointed when they actually were able to have it. One lady said, when asked whether she was sexually active before marriage, "Well, heck no. If I had, I wouldn't have gotten married!"

Disappointment by itself is not an inherently bad thing. When you recognize it, it can be a catalyst to healthy change in your relationship. However, if you do not address it, it can lead to a spiral of negative thoughts towards your spouse.

Another way for negative self-talk to creep in is when we fail to admire and respect the differences in our genders. As men and women, we are very different creatures. When we fail to understand these differences, and then fail to see the strength of our relationship because of these differences, we get ourselves into trouble. At this point, we can easily slide into an attitude of superiority towards our spouses.

I see men and women do this all the time.

- "He can't multitask."
- "She can't find her way out of a paper bag."
- "He can't tell me how he feels."
- "She won't ever shut up."

Underscoring all these statements is a spouse who, rather than bridging the gender gap to find commonality, is belittling his/her partner for not being as good as him/her. Regardless how negative thoughts begin, they can quickly devolve into "Automatic Negative Thoughts."

ANTs

Dr. Amen, a clinical neuroscientist and psychiatrist, who has spent decades studying the brains of tens of thousands of men and women, coined the phrase "Automatic Negative Thoughts" (ANTs).[11] He breaks down these ANTs into several different categories, some of which are:

- always thinking ("Why does he always leave his socks on the floor?")
- fortune telling ("I know she is going to be cranky when I get home.")
- mind reading ("He said it was ok, but I know he isn't telling me the truth.")
- labeling ("She's such a nag!")

These ANTs have a tendency to worm their way into our subconscious thoughts so we no longer realize how rampant and destructive they are in our relationships. When you fail to be aware of your ANTs, or when you refuse to bring them under control, they can devolve into something powerful enough to bring a deathblow to your marriage.

Contempt

Dr. John Gottman, a giant in the field of relationship research, defines four attributes that will ultimately lead to the demise of a marriage. These "Four Horsemen of the Apocalypse" are: criticism, defensiveness, stonewalling and contempt. The last of this list, contempt, is the best indicator of marital breakdown. Gottman defines it as "Any statement made to a partner from a superior place; to speak down with an air of superiority."[12] He goes on to explain, whether the couple is arguing about parenting, being on time, or a particular base of knowledge, if one partner believes s/he is better than the other, and thereby more correct, the couple is on the track to divorce.

The most common manifestation of contempt is direct insults or name calling. Remember those ANTs? It is a lot easier to call your spouse a jerk if you have practiced it in your head hundreds of times. Contempt is insidious and will grow rapidly if not brought under control.

As you might have suspected by now, respect is the antidote to contempt. When you choose to nurture respect as a value in your relationship, you can overcome and eradicate contempt, ANTs and disappointment. Doing so, however, will take some time and practice.

Nurturing Respect

I once heard a rut is simply a grave with no ends. If you stay in it, you will die. Some of you might be living in a pattern of disrespect with your spouse right now. If you are, take heart. The die has not been cast, and you can break the mold. In fact, it is never too late to remake the mold in the image you want, but it takes effort and intentionality. You did not get here overnight, but there are some specific steps you took to make it this far off-track.

Change Your Self-Talk

You can make it a goal to respect your spouse, but if you do not kick the habit of negative self-talk about your spouse, you will fail. Self-talk will make or break your commitment to respect him/her. This negative undercurrent affects everything we do – how we react to situations, treat our spouses, what mood we are in, and everything in-between. The good news is we have tremendous power to change our lives simply by changing our thoughts.

From the Scriptures, it is obvious that Paul understood the importance of our thought life. In Philippians 4:8 (NIV) he says, "Finally, brothers and sisters, whatever is true, whatever is noble, whatever is right, whatever is pure, whatever is lovely, whatever is admirable – if anything is excellent or praiseworthy – think about such things."

Paul goes on to offer a promise if we take control of our self-talk: "And the God of peace will be with you." Paul understood that when we harness our inner thoughts, we create a new reality. Here are some steps to change your negative thoughts.

Become Self-Aware

Many people have no clue how often they think negative thoughts until they begin to pay attention. These thoughts have played like the soundtrack of their lives for so long, it has become white noise to them. These thoughts have tremendous impact, but people are blissfully unaware because they have tuned out the soundtrack. It is time to turn up the volume so you can recognize what is playing.

Take a couple of days to record your thoughts. Carry around a notepad and pen, and jot down a tally mark every time you say something to yourself that is negative about your spouse. These can be fleeting thoughts like:

- "What does he think I do all day?!"
- "All she does is nag at me!"
- "How come it is so difficult for him to pitch in around here?"
- "She is so selfish!"
- "Is he crazy?! What is he thinking, driving like that?!"
- "What a jerk."

If you notice a pattern emerging (for instance, you internally call your spouse names when s/he is talking to you), then make a note of this as well. You could jot down, "frequent name calling" on your notepad.

Interrupt Your Negative Thoughts

When you are locked into one perspective, it is very difficult to see things differently. However, as a friend of mine says, "A point of view is just a view from a point." Your opinions, thoughts, observations and insights about your spouse are formed through a myriad of factors including how you were raised as a child, the positive or negative experiences you had dating when you were a young adult, the people you keep as counsel in your life, and your level of marriage education.

What your spouse has done or said to you over the years is merely one part of this equation and is, in fact, interpreted through your grid of all those other factors. It is possible you are not giving your spouse the credit s/he deserves. And, to go back to the Pygmalion Effect, when you see your spouse in a negative light, s/he will begin to perform to your levels of expectation. What you focus on grows.

If you are caught in this trap, you need to take a step back and interrupt this vicious cycle. Begin by refusing to think negatively about your spouse. That's right. Stop it. When you begin to spiral into itemizing all the things your spouse has done poorly, say to yourself, "Stop!" If you can say this out loud, it is even more effective. Furthermore, you might want to picture a bright red stop sign.

Then, choose to think about something else. Think about something you love in life – your children, baseball or a recent success at work. You can also refocus your attention on another project – reading a book, playing a game, picking up a musical instrument or going for a run.

This might be difficult at first. If you have practiced, over and over, the art of bad-mouthing your spouse in your head, you have trained your brain to believe this is acceptable behavior. You now need to rewire your brain, and this takes time and practice. Put a rubber band around your wrist and snap it every time you begin to go to that dark place if you have to, but refuse to go there.

Training your thought life is a lot like exercising a muscle. If you have never lifted weights before, the muscle feels extremely weak. But as you continue to work it out, it will get stronger and stronger. And remember, this is not about changing your spouse – this is about changing you.

Cultivate a Culture of Gratitude

As you are beginning to practice interrupting your negative thoughts, begin to look around to discover the good things about your spouse so you can cultivate a culture of gratitude in your marriage. Zig Ziglar, a motivational speaker popular in the 1980s, used to say, "You need an attitude of gratitude!"

To do so, you need to sit down and make a list of all the things your spouse does that you are truly grateful for. No matter how small, notice the positive ways your spouse contributes to your home life, your family, your marriage and your sex life. Focus on how those areas are different from what you contribute in ways beneficial to you and your family.

What are you thankful for? If you cannot come up with anything, start by listing the things that simply don't disappoint you, and grow it from there. As you do the work, you will begin to remember things your own emotions have blinded you to – things you once loved about him/her.

As you begin to recognize and remember, make sure to express this gratefulness to your spouse. So many men and women are desperate to hear a simple "Thank you" from their husbands or wives. Thank them verbally, write notes or send gifts of thanks, or give out hugs of thanks. Thank your spouse as often as you can for whatever you can.

Change Your Perspective

As you begin to recognize your negative self-talk, interrupt this cycle and train your focus on what you are grateful for in your spouse, you might begin to recognize your perspective wasn't fully accurate. I know, that sounds like crazy talk. But as you begin to appreciate your spouse because you have quieted the negative soundtrack in your mind, you are open to see life from his/her perspective.

Choose Mutual Respect

In our relationship, Eric and I have a rule to never dismiss something the other person asks for without careful consideration. If he comes to me with a serious request ("Honey, I want to get the sports package on TV," etc.), it does not matter if I don't understand it or if it doesn't seem like it will have benefit for me. It's not about me. It's about something important to my husband. Likewise, when I approach him about a request I have, I can be assured he will never say no unless he has a well-thought-out reason for doing so. This ground rule encompasses the entirety of our relationship, and extends to our sex life.

When we look at the scriptural foundations for a healthy sexual relationship, the concept of mutual respect is abundantly evident. The principle of reciprocity is built on a foundation of respect for each other's needs, desires, wishes and secret longings.

Here it is again from I Corinthians 7:3-5 (NLT): "The husband should fulfill his wife's sexual needs, and the wife should fulfill her husband's needs. The wife gives authority over her body to her husband, and the husband gives authority over his body to his wife. Do not deprive each other of sexual relations, unless you both agree to refrain from sexual intimacy for a limited time so you can give yourselves more completely to prayer. Afterward, you should come together again so that Satan won't be able to tempt you because of your lack of self-control."

Paul goes on to outline the principle of equality in Galatians 3:28 (NIV) when he says, "So in Christ Jesus you are all children of God through faith, for all of you who were baptized into Christ have clothed yourselves with Christ. There is neither Jew nor Gentile, neither slave nor free, nor is there male and female, for you are all one in Christ Jesus. If you belong to Christ, then you are Abraham's seed, and heirs according to the promise."

When we come into the bedroom with a sense of equality, we understand that while we might be different in our tastes, desires, fantasies and perspectives, we have a foundation of mutual respect for each other. The male and female personhoods encompass the totality of God.[13] God has both male and female characteristics. Respect, therefore, is having a rock-solid confidence this person will partner with you, while constantly challenging you to be a better person because your spouse encapsulates a side of God you do not naturally possess. In this manner, you are two partners, equally responsible before God in the way you treat each other and conduct yourselves in your marriage.

It is important to remember, however, there is no such thing as cookie-cutter people. We each have different strengths, weaknesses, gifts and abilities. Sometimes these attributes fall along stereotypical gender lines, sometimes they don't. My mechanic is a woman who felt God calling her to evangelize to other women by entering a very male-dominated field. In fact, she owns the garage and has quite a few men working for her. While her career choice might be outside "cultural norms," she is having an amazing impact on her community because she had the courage to follow a road less traveled. She found her skills and used them.

The same applies in marriage. In a healthy, functioning marriage, no one person feels the need to lord him/herself over the other. In my marriage I can say without hesitation Eric is far more skilled in certain areas than I, and vice versa. We both acknowledge and celebrate this truth.

You see, respect is rooted in an appreciation for and understanding of each other – even if the other is vastly different. It is an ongoing choice to learn more about our spouses so we have the intellectual as well as emotional understanding of why they operate the way that they do, so we can recognize the value they bring to our lives.

Choose Your Friends Wisely

Jim Rohn, an American entrepreneur, author and motivational speaker, is often quoted as saying, "You're the average of the five people you spend the most time with." If this is true, and your five people disrespect your spouse, then your marriage is in for an extremely bumpy ride. In fact, it is on the fast track to failure.

One of the most important steps you must take to nurture respect in your relationship with your spouse is to become selective in the relationships you have outside your marriage. The most powerful influence in your life is your circle of friends. Your mom was right – it does matter whom you hang out with. If your "friends" have nothing good to say about your spouse, you should stop talking to them. If you need to sever relationships with girlfriends who sit around and complain about their spouses and yours to strengthen your marriage, do so immediately. If your buddies only see your wife as that "nagging harpy" then it is time to move on in your friendships.

Your friends must be the most supportive people you know regarding your spouse. If you find yourself giving in to negative thoughts, they should be the first people you call to encourage you about your marriage in general, and your spouse specifically. If you can't imagine your closest friends doing that, then go find new ones.

Family is a bit tougher. Limiting the number of times you meet with your friend Becky for coffee is a lot easier than worming your way out of Sunday dinner at Mom's house. However, it is still crucial you set clear boundaries with your family that undermining your relationship with your spouse is unacceptable behavior. This might look like sitting down with the family members who are bad-mouthing your spouse, and letting them know you cannot be around them when they act this way. Clearly identify what language or behavior is off limits and give them the opportunity to change. If they steadfastly refuse to change, restrict your time with them.

Recognize Each Other's Strengths

Start paying attention to the things your spouse is good at rather than focusing on when they fail. I like to use the idea of "catching your spouse succeeding." When you are in the habit of catching your husband doing something right, and commenting on it, you are going to see a change in behavior. He is going to gravitate towards the things he is successful at. And your wife will do the same. They are going to do things right every day. Pay attention and surprise them with an "aha!" when you seem them. That might seem simplistic, but the premise holds across your relationship. Find what s/he is good at and celebrate it.

You can also actively look for things your spouse is *better* at than you. When my husband and I had our daughter, we quickly realized he was a supreme swaddler. When I was finished feeding Riley for the night, I passed her to Eric and he put her in the swaddling blanket and tucked her in for the night. Every time I tried, she would be out of her swaddling within two minutes, but he had the knack. After a while, he was so proud of his ability, he was loath to even let me try. It was his guaranteed win.

Final Thoughts

Respect in marriage is paramount. But respect in the bedroom is crucial as well. As two individuals who are different in your preferences and tastes, there will be times when you are trying something simply because it brings pleasure and satisfaction to your spouse. Out of respect for their requests, you incorporate it into your sex life. He wants the lights on during sex? Try it out. She wants to try a new position? Give it a whirl. He wants to squeeze more sex into the schedule? Make it happen. She wants more foreplay? Carve out the time for it.

Ultimately, of course, the goal is the two of you will go back and forth in giving and receiving in your sex life out of respect for each other. When we come into the bedroom with respect for our spouses – respect for their needs, wishes and desires – we give those needs, wishes and desires a place of prominence on our priority lists. As we do so, this respect *unlocks pleasure*. When there is a solid foundation of respect, we have the freedom and security needed to ensure pleasure abounds in our relationship.

Bedwork: Respect

PSA: _____

This week, answer at least two questions. If you have a strong emotional reaction to the questions, pick the one you love and the one you hate. If you do not have a strong reaction, pick an exercise your spouse will appreciate, or give them home field advantage. Don't forget to record your PSA.

1. **Belittling Men.** Have you fallen prey to the "I married a child" belief? Have you set your husband up to fail? Have you perpetuated the culture of contempt for men? If so, reflect on the ways you have been guilty of belittling your husband in these manners. Once you have a clear picture of what you have done, repent of this attitude and create an action plan to redress this in your marriage.

2. **Belittling Men.** If you have fallen into the trap of disrespecting your husband by belittling his contributions to your marriage, sex life and household, then commit to reading a book that will help you understand the inner world of men better. Excellent examples include: *Adam's Return: The Five Promises of Male Initiation,*[14] *Wild at Heart: Discovering the Secret of a Man's Soul,*[15] *The Male Brain: A Breakthrough Understanding of How Boys and Men Think,*[16] and *Secrets of Happily Married Women: How to Get More Out of Your Relationship by Doing Less.*[17]

3. **Discounting Women.** Where have you failed to see the burdens your wife carries? If it escaped your attention, spend the next few days watching what she does and how she does it. What is it like to live in her world? What is it like to be her? Reflect on some ways you can ease her burden and help out. If you need help on what you can do, ask her for specific ideas.

4. **Challenging Cultural Perceptions.** When you read Shmuley Boteach's quote about the libido of women, how did you react? Were you skeptical? Hopeful? Angry? Resentful? How would your sex life change if you believed women were designed to be much more sensual than they seem? What would you change? Based on this information, write down three things you are willing to do in your relationship, and share them with your spouse.

5. **Change Your Self-Talk.** Go through the exercises laid out in this section of the book. Begin by taking two days to write down all the Automatic Negative Thoughts you had about your spouse. Then, practice interrupting these thoughts. Finally, begin to cultivate a culture of gratitude in your marriage.

6. **Choosing Mutual Respect.** Sit down with your spouse and discuss 1) areas in your sex life where you excel at implementing a spirit of mutual respect, and 2) areas in which you could improve at cultivating mutual respect in the bedroom. What can each of you do to respect the wishes and desires of your spouse in the area of sexual intimacy?

7. **Your Top Five.** To go back to Jim Rohn's quote, who are the five people with whom you spend the most time? What qualities do they bring that encourage your marriage to grow and deepen in intimacy? Do those people actively bring a positive perspective when you share about building into your relationship? If not, how are you going to address this situation with them? What do you need to do to surround yourself with positive influences on your relationship?

8. **Cultivating Gratitude.** List out five to ten aspects of your spouse that you respect. What do you respect most about his/her role as husband/wife, father/mother, caretaker, provider, etc., in your household? What do you respect most about his/her abilities in the workplace, with extended family, and in other roles in the community? Once you have made your list, write your spouse a thank you note for the attribute you *most* respect. Give it to him/her directly or put it in a place where s/he will easily "find" it.

9. **Modeling Respect.** In what ways do you model respect for your spouse in front of your children? What actions and words have they witnessed? How are you actively building into their understanding about respect within marriage? How can you get better at modeling to your kids? What do you need to say or do?

10. **Superman.** What are some ways your husband expresses his need to be Superman in your relationship? How do you normally react to this need? Do you need to change your behaviors to demonstrate your respect for him and what he does?

Element 5: Pleasure

"A passion for pleasure is the secret to remaining young."
Oscar Wilde – Author and Playwright

E arly on in my business, I had a young woman come to me who had been married for a year. She had never had an orgasm, and she and her husband couldn't figure out how to get there. While he had been supportive at first, the lack of success had worn on him. He had given up, assuming this was normal. It was at this point she looked at him and said, "You know, honey, if this was your problem, we would have solved it a long time ago."

She is absolutely correct. When erectile dysfunction came to the forefront of our cultural consciousness, we created a $10 billion industry that produced products such as Viagra, Cialis and the like. And you know what? There are a lot of couples that really benefit from those drugs. But women are a bit more complex than men. It is more than just an issue of hydraulics for them. As such, the pharmaceutical industry has been largely unsuccessful in coming up with a female counterpart for Viagra.

In my line of work, I talk all the time of the details of life that drown out our sex lives. I have become a professional problem solver in what it takes to remove the obstacles so your sex life can flourish. One of the biggest impediments to a thriving sex life is when women don't like sex. This lack of interest usually has to do with a lack of pleasure. When women are not experiencing pleasure, they are going to be far less likely to jump over the hurdles life throws at them in order to reach the goal of having sex with their husbands. The incentive, quite frankly, just isn't good enough.

And yet, God created our bodies to be made for pleasure. Scientists are baffled by the biological function of the female orgasm because there is no discernable evolutionary reason for it to exist. A woman does not need to orgasm to get pregnant. She does not need to orgasm to give birth. She doesn't even need to orgasm to be a good parent. The female orgasm is designed simply for pleasure.

This is not that big a stretch when we think about God's creativity on the whole. Our God is not only a God of function and order, but also a God of creativity and pleasure. As such, it makes sense that His design for the most intimate of relationships – that of a man and woman – would reflect His nature and joy in pleasure.

In my practice, I have found sparking a woman's interest and genuine desire for sexual intimacy radically changes the dynamic in a marriage. Generally speaking, men are ready and raring to go, but they have less interested wives. When a couple comes together to unlock the mysteries of her sensuality and sexuality, it becomes a whole new ball game.

The Big Question

The vast majority of women are the Low Desire Spouse (although, as we explored in the Myth-Busting section, this is not always true). Furthermore, we know that statistically speaking, 43 percent of women have some sort of sexual dysfunction.[1] This means they experience chronic low libido, pain during intercourse or inability to orgasm. So, you will probably not be surprised that one of the biggest questions I get asked is, "Why did God make it so difficult for a woman to experience orgasm?"

Here is what is happening in churches all over North America. Many women will come into marriage and spend some time trying to experience orgasm, and when it doesn't work, will give up. Perhaps the young couple wasn't given very good education in the area of sexual intimacy, and so their sexual IQ is low. Perhaps they are expecting the wife to reach orgasm through penetration alone. Perhaps they have received some information but, for whatever reason, it is not working for them. Perhaps she cannot relax enough. Perhaps she can reach the peak of orgasm occasionally, but not on a regular basis.

What usually happens next is the wife begins to think something like, "Sex is my expression of love for my husband. It doesn't matter if I experience pleasure. I will do it for him." It fits with our skewed cultural perspective that you had better make sure his needs are met or he will stray. However, it also falls in line with our theological perspective of sacrificial love.

And, to a great extent, this wife's thinking is true. There will be times in every marriage where both men and women need to take a sacrificial stance of choosing to meet each other's needs purely out of love. This hearkens to Paul's admonitions in I Corinthians 7 – your body does not belong to you alone, but also belongs to your spouse. Sacrificial love can be an extremely healthy thing for your relationship.

However, if this situation goes on indefinitely – maybe kids come along, maybe she is juggling work with home life, or maybe she is highly involved in her church as well as all her other responsibilities. Whatever the reason, if there is no pleasure, it becomes harder and harder to jump that psychological hurdle to come to a place of saying, "I do this out of love" without feeling resentful.

Our brains are hard-wired to do that which brings us pleasure. When God created us, He designed our brains with dopamine and oxytocin and a whole bunch of other endorphins that flood our brain and say, "This is good! I want more of this!" Exercise is a fabulous example. When orchestrating the design of our bodies, God knew in order for us to be at our best, we need to move our bodies. So what did He do? He wired our brains for a rush when we are exercising. It was His design to reinforce healthy activity.

Similar hormones hit our brain when we experience orgasm. They not only give us a rush of pleasure, but they draw us together, bond us to each other, and unify us. It is not just the act of penetration that makes us one. It is the hormonal changes in our bodies after we experience pleasure together that knits us closer together. So, the woman who perpetually says, "This is a sacrifice," misses out on the full design for sex God created. Furthermore, her husband will be drawing closer to her, while she is drifting further away.[2]

Now, back to the original question. Why did God make it so difficult for a woman to experience orgasm? Why did He place the clitoris far out of the way and nearly impossible to reach during intercourse? Why did He wire her brain so she has to consciously stop creating that mental shopping list to focus on her husband? Why did He design her in such a way that, even after she begins to focus, it can take about twenty to forty minutes of warm-up time before she can reach orgasm? Why did God create sex to be like that?

The answer lies in the fact that sexual intimacy is designed to slow us down. To force us to pay attention to each other. To explore. To truly communicate. A man will never find out what really makes his wife's body come alive if they refuse to communicate about the subject. And remember, we aren't just talking about flapping your gums here. Communication takes place in the actions we choose as well.

As I mentioned in the Respect chapter, we have a cultural assumption that women are not as sexual as men. One of the key problems with this notion is couples are too quick to give up looking for solutions when the woman struggles to experience pleasure during sex. Women have tremendous trepidation about embracing the sensual and sexual beings they were created to be, and men have a long way to go in learning how to guide their wives through this process.

The key to unlocking the secrets to the way we were made, as well as developing our unique identity as a couple who experiences pleasure together, is found in the admonition to "browse" in the Song of Songs. It is only when we carve out the time to slow down and explore each other that we will find the fullness of satisfaction with each other.

Basic Sexual IQ

Here are some basic facts about our bodies that help us as we begin the process of seeking pleasure together.

Female Facts

- Vaginal intercourse is an "inefficient method of inducing female orgasm" because around 75 percent of women need some sort of clitoral stimulation to achieve orgasm.[3] This means, for most couples, having face-to-face, simultaneous orgasms is extremely difficult without the extra help of fingers or a bedroom toy.
- In one survey, 48 percent of women admitted to faking an orgasm.[4]
- A woman can take between 20-40 minutes to get warmed up enough to have an orgasm.
- The clitoris has 8,000 nerve endings and serves no function except to bring pleasure.[5]

Male Facts

- The main sex hormone is testosterone and it gradually declines as a man ages.[6]
- The average male orgasm lasts 6 seconds.[7]
- The penis has about 4,000 nerve endings.[8]
- The average time for intercourse is 2-7 minutes.[9]
- Men can fake orgasms as well.[10]

Intercourse Versus Outercourse

Sexual intimacy does not equal penetration. Of course, there is a powerful connection when our bodies are knit together in this manner. But if we are to forge the bonds of pleasure, we cannot get caught in the trap of focusing solely on intercourse. We must also develop our skill in "outercourse."

As mentioned previously, researchers believe only about 25 percent of women can experience orgasm through vaginal penetration. The remaining 75 percent need clitoral stimulation to experience the intensity of orgasm. For some women, they need direct, firm touch on the clitoris itself. Other women are extremely sensitive in this area, and so they need stimulation around the clitoris. Regardless of what type of touch is their preference, they will not achieve orgasm until this area of their body is fully engaged.

It is amazing the amount of misinformation (or complete lack of information) that is out there on this part of the body. I was once speaking to a group of women and a woman in her forties didn't even have a clue what the clitoris was, much less where it was. As a Christian culture, we have strayed far from our heritage where rabbis taught men how to bring their wives to orgasm.[11]

The tip of the clitoris (it extends far into her body) is the little nubby, hidden under a hood, that is located above the urethra. During the arousal stage, the clitoris becomes engorged with blood, and the hood retracts to prepare her body for orgasm. The clitoris can be stimulated manually, orally or with a bedroom toy.

Of course, there are many other regions of a woman's body that bring her pleasure as well, and I highly recommend you spend an inordinate amount of time figuring out where those places are on her. However, the clitoris is the most reliable path to orgasm for most women.

Shifting the focus to outercourse has also been an extremely helpful tool in coaching men and women with issues such as premature ejaculation, inability to hold an erection, pain during intercourse and other similar difficulties. When we shift our attention from intercourse to outercourse, the pressure of performance lessens. We can take the time to figure out what works within the unique context of our sexual relationship.

One couple I coached had never experienced any other form of orgasm except through intercourse. (She was fortunate enough to be in the minority of women who could experience orgasm in this manner.) However, after she went through treatment for breast cancer, vaginal penetration was extremely painful. This couple was suddenly in the position of having to learn about outercourse after decades of marriage. How does manual stimulation work? What areas of your penis do you like touched? How much pressure do I use? It might feel awkward as you begin to learn this new skill set, but it is vitally important as a protection against sliding into a pattern of sexlessness.

Outercourse can be part of foreplay in your relationship, or to use the words of Dr. Ian Kerner, it can become your "coreplay."[12] It is not an inferior form of sexual intimacy – it is merely one of many ways we build pleasure into our relationship. As we increase the intervals of pleasure in our marriage, the hormones released forge deeper and deeper bonds.

Pathways to Pleasure

The good news is there are numerous ways for us to experience pleasure together as we take the time to browse. Let's start with the basics.

Foreplay

Simply put, foreplay is the bridge between her arousal time and his. It might look like something sexual in nature, such as kissing and caressing. On the other hand, it might not look sexual at all. Sometimes the best type of foreplay entails picking up the vacuum cleaner and helping out around the house, or taking a genuine interest in how your spouse's day was. Regardless what works in your relationship, foreplay should begin long before the act of sex begins. Getting the brain engaged, taking the time to think about sex, and getting yourself prepared long before the act takes place is essential.

Hugging

Many couples overlook the importance of hugging. However, "grabbing on to each other" was one of the activities the Beloved and Lover engaged in the Song of Songs. Researchers now tell us that when we hug, our stress hormone (cortisol) comes down and our bonding hormone (oxytocin) rises.[13] Just the act of holding each other causes us to be less stressed and feel closer to each other.

After one of my sessions, a couple shared with me one of the things they were going to do to make their sex life better was to hug for sixty seconds each day. Sixty seconds may not seem like a lot, but believe me, it makes a profound impact on your marriage.

Dr. David Schnarch, in his book *The Passionate Marriage*, encourages couples to "hug until relaxed."[14] While you are standing, put your arms around each other and focus on relaxing. It is a fabulous way to transition from the craziness of the day to the intimacy of the moment. Many couples need this time to slow down after racing around all day. Give yourselves time to physically connect in a nonsexual way as part of your foreplay.

Kissing

Remember how the Beloved and Lover liken kissing to wine? Their kissing was so passionate and intense, that they felt intoxicated by it! It made them feel light-headed and woozy.

Scientists believe when men kiss their wives with those "open mouthed" or "wet" kisses, (you know, the sloppy kind), they transfer testosterone through their saliva to help boost her libido.[15] Testosterone is the main sex hormone and men naturally have more of it than women. The very act of kissing triggers her sex drive because it infuses her with the hormones necessary to desire sex.

Here is your permission to jump into the back seat of a car and remember what it was like to be a teenager. And if you were too virtuous to engage in such activities when you were sixteen, you are due! This is the time when it is healthy for your relationship.

Here are some more fun facts about kissing. There is actually a science that studies kissing called philematology. Scientists study everything from the origins of kissing, to its effect on the brain, to its role in effecting long-term attachment. Here are some of the things they have found:[16]

- There are many nerve endings in the lips and tongue that are stimulated by kissing and make it a pleasurable experience.
- Passionate kissing releases oxytocin and other "feel-good" hormones into the brain.
- Cortisol (the stress hormone) decreases during a session of kissing.

Dr. Helen Fisher has spent years researching and writing about the effects of love on the brain. Dr. Fisher found when subjects looked at pictures of their loved ones as they had their brains scanned with an fMRI machine, the most active areas of the brain were the regions which govern pleasure, motivation and reward.[17] In fact, these are the very areas activated during the use of drugs such as cocaine. It makes sense that when we are deeply in love with one another, it feels like we are on a "high!"

Furthermore, Dr. Fisher believes there are three regions of the brain responsible for mating and reproduction: the sex drive, the passion of being in love, and attachment. According to the fMRI results, the chemicals and hormones released during kissing can activate any or all of these three areas of the brain. So, if you want to increase your sense of passionate love, then kiss! Want to deepen your long-term attachment to your spouse? Kiss! Want to end up in the sack? Kiss!

Sometimes we want to *feel* the intimacy and love and passion before we take *action*. However, if you believe the science, it seems we might have to take action first. So, give yourself permission to act regardless of your feelings, and see where it leads you. You might be surprised when your feelings fall in line.

Browsing

One of the most common exercises sex therapists assign when a couple is experiencing sexual dysfunction is called sensate focus. I also find this exercise to be incredibly helpful for couples that have fallen into the trap of sprinting to orgasm. It forces the couple to slow down and focus on the sensations they are feeling because orgasm is not the goal of the exercise. In essence, sensate focus is structured browsing.

If you want to break the habit of sprinting to orgasm, if you experience anxiety about physical intimacy, or you just want to try something new, there are four stages of the exercise. Each stage is to be done on a different day, and you may decide to stay in one stage for several sessions before moving to the next one.

- **Stage One** – One spouse explores the other person's body without touching the breasts or genitals. The objective is for the exploring spouse to browse the areas of the body (except the restricted zones) that make her/him interested, curious, fascinated or intrigued. The exercise is to be done in quiet, with the exception of the spouse on the receiving end being able to communicate discomfort should the need arise. Sex is not an option during this stage. The purpose is to create an environment where both spouses are fully aware that this exercise is only about touch. Once one partner is done, switch places.
- **Stage Two** – During this stage of exploration, spouses may incorporate contact with the breasts and genitals. It is recommended, however, that this touch is initiated only

after sufficient contact has been made with the rest of the body. Couples practice active communication skills during this stage. For example, the person who is being touched may take his/her hand and guide the other spouse to areas that bring pleasure, indicating the amount of touch and pressure desired. As in the first stage, orgasm is not an option, and once one person is finished, switch places.

- **Stage Three** – At this point, couples can explore each other at the same time, rather than taking turns. Instead of following your own curiosities, now the focus is on what brings your spouse pleasure. Unfortunately, orgasm is still off the table. Don't worry, though, because it is permissible in Stage Four.
- **Stage Four** – Couples continue the mutual touching, focusing on giving and receiving pleasure. At this point, the woman can climb on top of her husband and feel his penis against her. She can rub the head of his penis against her clitoris even if her husband does not have an erection. The couple can stay in this phase of Stage Four for as long as they wish. When they are ready, they can move to penetration, intercourse and orgasm. If either person becomes anxious or nervous, revert to a lower stage and build up to Stage Four again, but at a slower pace.

Ideally, every couple would be educated in the concepts of these stages before they got married so the foundation they build within the first few months of marriage would be deeply rooted in an appreciation for browsing. If we did this, we would most likely avert a ton of sexual dysfunction later in marriage.

Oral Sex

The vast majority of men and women are fully aware of the concept of oral sex. Unless you were living under a rock in the 1990s, you probably had lively discussions about it because it was front and center in American politics. Thank you, President Clinton and Kenneth Starr.

But there still exists ambivalence about the act in Christian circles. This is a bit surprising to me since biblical scholars agree the Song of Songs speaks about the subject. In 2:3 (NIV), the act of a woman performing oral sex on a man is mentioned: "Like an apple tree among the trees of the forest is my beloved among the young men. I delight to sit in his shade, and his fruit is sweet to my taste."

Furthermore, in two places, we see examples of the man performing the act on the woman:

Song of Songs 4:16 (NIV): "Awake, north wind, and come, south wind! Blow on my garden, that its fragrance may spread everywhere. Let my beloved come into his garden and taste its choice fruits."

Song of Songs 8:2 (NIV): "I would lead you and bring you to my mother's house – she who has taught me. I would give you spiced wine to drink, the nectar of my pomegranates."

I advise every couple to incorporate this act into their relationship. Not only do studies indicate it is one of the primary ways women can achieve orgasm consistently, but it also becomes an increasingly helpful skill set to have in your tool belt as you age. Men find oral sex to be of great assistance when they have difficulty getting and maintaining erections later in life. Women who experience thinning of the vaginal lining after menopause often find intercourse to be painful. Developing this skill set early in marriage saves you from having to do so later, when you have run out of other options.

Most Christian couples, however, don't have a clue what to do, and are terrified to go looking for the information. As such, here are some step-by-step basics:

Basics for Her

- **Relax.** Remember oral sex is great foreplay for your husband, even if you are intimidated at first to bring him to ejaculation orally. Oral sex is a skill set you can develop, just like typing. When you first started typing, it felt awkward and strange learning to move your fingers to push the correct keys, but after time and practice, it became second nature. Practice the first few steps of this process, and then add more steps until you are comfortable with finishing all of them.
- **Communicate.** You should communicate clearly before you get started about your intentions so he is not disappointed by unspoken expectations. Saying something like, "Honey, I want to get better at this, but I am going to start slowly, and I may not be able to bring you to orgasm this way at first," sets the stage clearly. Moreover, ask him what he likes about the idea of oral sex so you can incorporate it. Every man is different in what he finds erotic and stimulating, so the best oral sex is always based on what your husband likes.
- **Get ready.** You probably want to have a good lubricant on hand (a water-based, flavored lubricant can make the experience more appealing), so you don't have to be concerned about using only your own saliva during oral sex. This also removes the necessity of having your mouth do all the stimulating of his shaft because you can use your lubricated hand to slide up and down it while your mouth is elsewhere. Many women are terrified of the concept of "deep throating," so remove this fear by being prepared.
- **Remove the barriers.** Most women I meet are nervous about two things: the smells and the taste. We will talk about the latter in just a moment, but for the former, I highly recommend you begin with having a shower or bath together, and incorporate soaping each other down into your foreplay. This ensures hygiene issues will not sideline you and it gets you warmed up (literally and figuratively). The sensation of the water, combined with the slickness of soap, is a great way to enhance the sense of touch. If you enjoy the warmth of the shower and don't mind a bit of splashing, begin oral sex there.
- **Get started.** Begin exploring with your hands and mouth by kissing and stroking the head of the penis, the shaft, the scrotum, the perineum (this area between the anus and testicles is rich with nerve endings) – whatever you are comfortable with and he likes. As you feel comfortable, take the head of the penis into your mouth, lick and suck on it gently. As you get more coordinated, use your hand to stroke the shaft while your lips are paying attention to the top of his penis.
- **"Don't orphan the balls!"** This is one of my favorite quotes from a client who was chatting to his wife about oral sex. Often, women focus too much on the penis to the neglect of the

scrotum and perineum, even though these areas are full of sensitive nerve endings. You can get creative with your touch – vary it from a gentle to firmer massage, to lightly running your nails across him, to a very wet, sloppy kiss.

- **The gag reflex.** As you get used to the sensation of having his penis in your mouth, you can take more in. If you have a sensitive gag reflex, go slowly and take your time. For some women, having a peppermint in their mouths helps calm the gag reflex.

- **Maintain contact.** It is the stroking action on the penis that will bring your husband to ejaculation, and as you become more adept at oral sex, you will be able to recognize the signs that this is about to happen. The most important part of the finish is that you don't break contact, as this is one of the most intimate parts of lovemaking. If you are not comfortable with the concept of swallowing, then keep moving your hand up and down his shaft until it covers (gently) the tip of the penis. This area gets very sensitive after orgasm, so ask your husband how much pressure he likes while he is enjoying his orgasm.

- **Get feedback.** This might seem like the most awkward part of the whole experience, but it deepens your communication skills – and thereby the intimacy that you share together. Ask your husband what he liked and what you can do better next time. I am not suggesting you ask him the moment you two are finished being intimate. Wait a day or two and then ask. You will never become an expert at this (or anything in life) if you don't elicit feedback and, frankly, he is the only one who can give it to you. Understand that talking about sex can be the best thing in your sex life because it shows you care about making it great, are interested in what he thinks, and are enthusiastic. (And those are all great turn-ons for your husband.)

Basics for Him

- **Prepare for the event.** Husbands, make sure your facial hair is well groomed. If you shave, then make sure you have shaved recently. If your wife has a sensitive clitoris, coming in contact with stubble can be incredibly uncomfortable and might even bring the whole session to a screeching halt. Wives, you should also be well groomed. Many couples report that when the wife shaves, trims or waxes her pubic hair, it enhances the sensations and increases the pleasure for both husband and wife.

- **Remove the barriers.** As I mentioned in the basics for her, I highly recommend you begin with having a shower or bath together, and incorporate soaping each other down into your foreplay. This eases any anxiety about hygiene.

- **Take your time.** Men, I cannot stress this enough – do not go straight for the goods! Remember it takes women a while to get warmed up enough to experience orgasm. If you stimulate her clitoris immediately, she will most likely get overstimulated before she gets close to having an orgasm. Instead, spend time exploring the other areas of her body, and enjoy kissing her before you even get close to her pelvic region. Not only will this build intimacy between the two of you, but it will also give her time to become aroused. When you do begin to kiss her vagina, pay attention to it in its entirety, not just the clitoris.

- **Don't get a tongue cramp.** Ok, I don't know if you can actually get a cramp in your tongue. However, it is a muscle (actually a group of muscles), so I guess it is possible. In all seriousness, do a little experiment right now. Stretch your tongue all the way out of your mouth and hold it there for a minute. Feel tired? A lot of men make the mistake of sticking their tongue out as far as possible and then battering the clitoris back and forth with it. They get tired and their wives get annoyed. Instead, think of oral sex as kissing your wife with your lips and use your tongue creatively.
- **Use a variety of touch.** The tongue is an incredibly flexible muscle, so try flattening it out, making it thin, putting light pressure on her and then firm pressure, licking with it slowly or flicking it quickly, drawing figure eights, spelling out words and finding out what her favorite letter is. If you can multitask at this point, use your hands to caress her legs, stomach and inner thighs. You can also take a finger or two and slip them inside her vagina. (Keep a lubricant handy so this is comfortable for her.)
- **Keep the rhythm.** As your wife is getting close to orgasm, make sure you keep the pace and rhythm of what you are doing consistent. Nothing is worse for a woman than being on the verge of orgasm and then feeling the touch change to something that isn't as pleasant. If your wife is responding to what you are doing, then for goodness' sake, don't stop!
- **Get feedback.** Every woman is different in what type of sexual touch she prefers, and so to understand how your wife ticks and what makes her tingle, you have to ask her. Some women need the hood of the clitoris to be pulled back so you can get direct stimulation on her clitoris. Some women need the hood of the clitoris to keep it covered because direct stimulation can be painful. Some women need a very firm touch, while others need a soft one. If your wife has not yet discovered what type of touch she enjoys, encourage her to be honest and learn together.

G-Spot

The G-spot is named after the German gynecologist Ernst Gräfenberg who first noted it in the 1950s. The term "spot" is a bit misleading, because it is actually a region of tissue highly sensitive to stimulation and can induce orgasm. It is located about one to three inches inside the vagina on the anterior wall. (If you are lying down on your back, it is towards your navel, not your spine.)

Because it is located close to the urethra, when it is touched, many women interpret the feeling as the need to use the bathroom. (If this makes you uncomfortable, empty your bladder before embarking on any G-spot finding expeditions!) As you continue to stimulate the G-spot, this sensation fades and gives way to another sensation. Some women find the new sensation mildly pleasant, others arousing, and still others find intense and orgasmic pleasure.

There is intense debate in the academic world as to whether the G-spot orgasm is actually a clitoral orgasm[18] or an orgasm unique unto its own.[19] Regardless of *how* a woman achieves orgasm through the G-spot region, or *what* type of orgasm it gets labeled as, it's a pleasurable orgasm. Research (and my professional experience) shows while the clitoral orgasm seems to be centralized around the pelvic region, the G-spot orgasm reverberates through the whole body.

One woman told me, "I knew you could have a good orgasm. I even knew you could have a great orgasm. But I didn't know you could have an *Exorcist* orgasm." I responded, "Well, when your head is spinning around, you know that you have found the G-spot."

Some women who achieve this orgasm will also have female ejaculation. (They will often come up to me with a shy smile and whisper, "I squirt!") This ejaculate comes out of the urethra and so women are often afraid they have urinated in the bed. However, this fluid is completely different than urine. It is clear (vs. yellow), has a sweet smell (vs. pungent), and won't stain your bed sheets. Having said that, there can be quite a bit of it, so I always recommend you are prepared with some towels on your bed, just to make the cleanup easier.

If I have you curious, and you want to embark on a hunt for your G-spot, here are some thoughts on finding it. It is a process – it takes time, experience, and a high degree of comfort with your body and your spouse to experience orgasm through this form of stimulation. Most women report they are very relaxed and highly aroused when they experience this type of orgasm for the first time.

If your husband inserts two fingers in your vagina, and strokes the G-spot in a firm "come hither" motion, this can be extremely successful. Many women have also found that using a vibrator is most helpful, especially as they are just learning to find it, because the toy will put firm pressure on the area. Finally, let me encourage you – even if it takes time to find, don't give up! If you allow yourself, you will enjoy the journey as well as the destination.

Anal Sex

Anal sex is, without a doubt, the most frequently broached topic in my experience with individuals and groups. Get a group of Christians together, and someone will ask about it. The form in which the question presents itself varies from, "Is my husband secretly gay if he is asking for anal sex?" to "Is it permissible biblically?" to "How do you do it?" I suppose it should not be surprising that the question comes up so frequently for it is a topic that most Christians avoid like the plague.

I officially stay neutral on this subject. I have seen anal sex be incredibly detrimental to a relationship, and I have also seen it lead to incredible breakthroughs in intimacy for couples. I believe the subject is something that must be addressed in the privacy of each couple's bedroom, and they must decide together whether it is something they want to explore.

Let's begin with addressing what Scripture says about it. Very simply, there is no prohibition in Scripture against anal sex between a man and a woman. Since this is not an area which has been prohibited by Scripture, couples are responsible (as with absolutely everything written in this book) to live out I Corinthians 7:3-5 when grappling with this issue. Beyond having simple intellectual knowledge of this verse, it is incumbent on all couples to really know it. One of my dear friends calls this process "getting it into your bones." When a couple has internalized the concept of giving to each other and never demanding from each other something hurtful, there is freedom for trust to flourish. Trust is an essential element that allows for freedom in a couple's sexual relationship.

Moving beyond the scriptural parameters that govern this area of sexuality, one of the most basic questions I get is, "Why would you want to?" The simple answer is because it feels good. The anus is rich in nerve endings, so both men and women can enjoy stimulation in this area.

Women report stimulation in this area (Note: This does not necessarily mean full penile penetration) brings them to orgasm more quickly. There is much speculation as to why this is the case. Some experts believe it is easier to stimulate the G-spot anally than vaginally. Other experts believe stimulation in the anus activates the pelvic nerve, which is also activated by the vagina and the cervix, and thereby carries the same pleasurable message to the brain.[20]

Men also report that, because the anus is tighter than the vagina, they like the sensation anal penetration creates. They are also aroused by the pleasure their wives experience through this form of sexual intimacy. When men are stimulated anally and their prostate gland (often referred to as the "male G-spot") is massaged, this can be intensely pleasurable as well.

Finally, there is a level of attraction to anal sex because it is still largely taboo. Just the fact it is considered kinky in some circles can heighten the arousal experience for both spouses.

For the couple that wants to explore this in their marriage, there are a few essential ground rules:

- **Go slowly.** This is incredibly important to remember the entire time you are engaging in anal exploration. Going slowly ensures you have the ability to communicate effectively with each other. If you feel pain, then ask your spouse to stop.
- **Use lots of lubricant.** Unlike the vagina, which lubricates on its own, the anus has no natural lubrication. Water-based lubricant is the easiest to clean afterwards, but some couples prefer a silicone-based lubricant because it lasts longer. Regardless what type you use, more is better.
- **Use a condom.** Regardless if you are using fingers, a bedroom toy, or your husband's penis, wrap that rascal. It eliminates the risk of transferring unwanted bacteria and semen into the area. Unlike the vaginal system (in which what goes up must come down), the anus is connected to the intestines. It is safer and cleaner to use a condom.
- **Relax.** The natural tendency is to clench your muscles (in this case, the anal sphincter) when you are nervous. This will lead to a painful encounter. Most couples find the most successful way to relax is when they are highly aroused. Again, take it slowly.
- **Start with fingers.** Whether or not you have any intention of moving on to penile penetration, it is important to begin with your fingers. They are small and you can get a good sense of whether or not you enjoy the sensation of penetration. If you do enjoy it, your spouse can move from one finger to two.
- **Move on to penile penetration.** If, and only if, both spouses are fully on board and still enjoying the experience, take it to the next level.

As with every area of sexual intimacy in your marriage, communication is key. Letting your spouse know what you think and feel about various sexual acts is important. While we must always grow and deepen our intimacy with each other, this does not mean we have to participate in all the options for this to happen.

Enhancing Pleasure

As you explore together the various avenues to pleasure, you might want to know there are many products and exercises that can make this journey easier.

Lubricants

Years ago, one of my clients told me I saved her marriage. "You recommended a good lubricant to me," she said rather matter-of-factly. I was a bit slow on the uptake and wasn't sure how something this simple could have such a dramatic effect on her relationship, but she continued on: "I was allergic to [insert name of the most popular over-the-counter brand], but it was the only stuff I knew to buy. So, when I would use it, I would have to have sex quickly and then immediately hop into the shower because it would begin to burn. It was killing our sex life! But when I got a good lubricant from you, it didn't burn. Now I actually enjoy having sex with my husband again!"

If women do not have sufficient lubrication, sex is going to be uncomfortable at best and excessively painful at worst. There are all sorts of reasons why a woman might not have enough lubrication. She might:

- not be aroused enough
- be on a medication that hinders lubrication (allergy and cold relief medications, antidepressants, and even the birth control pill are notorious for having this side effect)
- be headed into menopause, and the drop in estrogen levels is causing changes in the way the body produces lubrication
- be nervous, stressed or exhausted
- have recently given birth or is still breastfeeding
- be a smoker.

There is nothing worse than wanting to be intimate with your husband, but being betrayed by your body when it refuses to lubricate properly. It creates a vicious cycle because next time you are considering having sex, you might hesitate because you are worried. Not only are you dealing with something physiological, but now it is psychological too.

A great lubricant will take the pressure off. You will no longer have to worry about getting wet enough so sex doesn't hurt. It allows you to relax and focus on enjoying yourself and him. And this makes for a much more satisfying sex life for both of you.

Thankfully, we live in a time when good lubricants are readily available. You can have one on your bedside table drawer, another in your travel bag, and another in the shower. A lady once told me lubricants are like lipstick – no woman should only have one!

Here's a rundown of the different types of lubricants:

Type	Pros	Cons
Water-based	Easy and safe to use almost anywhere. They do not stain, are simple to wash off and are safe for use with condoms or diaphragms.	Cannot use in water (as it will wash off) and are not long-lasting. Some brands can be sticky.
Silicone-based	Great for water. They are long-lasting, non-sticky and usually have a silky texture.	Harder to wash off (as they are designed to last in water).
Petroleum-based	An option for anal sex.	Cannot be used with condoms, diaphragms or cervical caps. Can be irritating vaginally. They are difficult to wash off and can stain the sheets.
Oil-based	Made from vegetable or nut oils.	Can feel greasy and stain the sheets. They are not recommended for use with condoms.

It might seem obvious I prefer water- and silicone-based lubricants. However, you have lots of options, so enjoy finding one (or more) that work for you.

Kegel Exercises

Kegel exercises are a safe, cheap, and easy way to enhance the pleasure in your sexual relationship. Both men and women can do these exercises daily.

For Her

The pelvic floor is like a basket of muscle. It holds in the bladder, uterus and other sexual reproductive organs. As women get older, have children and gain weight, this muscle can begin to sag and lose overall tightness. When this happens, women can also can experience decreased sexual sensation.

To combat this deterioration, doctors recommend women do kegel exercises. There is quite a list of benefits that comes from doing these exercises on a regular basis. They can:

- strengthen the pubococcygeus muscle
- make childbirth easier
- increase the odds your perineum will more likely be intact (fewer tears and episiotomies) throughout childbirth
- enhance sexual enjoyment for both men and women (including better orgasms!)
- prevent prolapses (slipping out of place) of pelvic organs
- prevent leaking urine when you sneeze, cough or jump on a trampoline.

The best way to illustrate a kegel exercise is this: Sit on the toilet, and as you begin to pee, stop the flow of urine. This muscle you are using is your pubococcygeus muscle, more commonly referred to as your PC muscle. Make sure you are actually working your PC muscle and not cheating by using your thighs or buttocks muscles. If you want to make sure you are only using your PC muscle, spread your legs on either side of the toilet as you begin to pee. This will ensure you isolate and use only the PC muscle. Once you have figured out what your PC muscle feels like on the toilet, you can do kegels anywhere.

The goal is to squeeze your PC muscle as tight as possible and hold it for ten seconds. However, when you are starting, clench it for as long as you can and work up to ten seconds. Doctors recommend you work up to twenty reps, three times a day.

It is also surprisingly easy to find time in your daily routine to do these exercises. Since no one can actually see you doing a kegel, you can do them just about anywhere. Sitting at a red light? Do some kegels. Standing in line at a grocery store? Do some kegels. Watching your favorite show on TV? Do some kegels. Although it takes some awareness and mental discipline, it is really quite easy to do.

For Him

There is a joke that goes "Who is the most popular man at a nudist colony? The man who can carry two cups of coffee and a dozen donuts." (No, I am not endorsing or recommending nudist colonies, coffee or donuts for that matter. It's just a joke.)

We often overlook the fact that there are a whole host of benefits for men when they do kegel exercises as well. Regular exercise can:

- help you achieve stronger erections
- help with premature ejaculation
- increase the intensity of your orgasms
- increase the strength of your erections
- help increase overall control in the pelvic region
- increase your odds of having multiple orgasms.

Just like with women, these exercises do not take a lot of time, and can be done without anyone noticing. You can do them in your car on your commute to work, sitting at your desk at the office, or while watching TV.

In order to find the PC muscle for the first time, go to the bathroom. As you begin to pee, stop the flow of urine. This muscle that you use to halt the urination is your pubococcygeus or PC muscle. Once you have identified your PC muscle, you can begin doing kegel exercises.

Squeeze your PC muscle as tight as possible and hold it for five seconds, and then release for five seconds. (When you are starting, clench it for as long as you can and work up to five seconds.) Doctors recommend you work up to ten reps, three times a day.

You might want to note, however, just like building your biceps takes time, so does building your PC muscle. Work on it daily and you will definitely see an improvement in the next couple of months.

Bedroom Toys

Over the years, I have frequently been asked why bedroom toys are such a good idea. Some people consider them to be dirty and kinky, a replacement for a spouse, or simply unnecessary. But over the years, I have seen them be instrumental in revitalizing the sex lives of countless couples for several reasons.

They Open the Lines of Communication

Communication is the most important element to having great sex. That is why, in the diagram of essential elements, it is in the center. All the other elements hinge on having clear, open and effective communication. And yet, it is one of the scariest things to do, or even try, for most couples.

Toys help alleviate this fear and lessen the stress by giving a focal point for both parties to start with. Think about it – it is virtually impossible to throw one of these items on the bed and not have some level of conversation about it – even if you are just laughing. (And remember, laughter in the bedroom can be a good thing too.)

At one of my parties, I met a woman who had been married for thirty years and seemed to be deeply in love with her husband. Their sex life, however, had been put on the back burner for quite some time. She did not come out and say they lived in a sexless marriage, but implied quite heavily this was the case. I chatted with her about her specific circumstances and recommended a small starter toy.

Three months later, I saw her at another party. As I began my discussion about how bedroom toys can open the lines of communication, she raised her hand and asked if she could share her story. Evidently, when she left that first party with her toy, she called her husband and told him she had bought a couples' toy and needed him to get out the batteries for it. When she got home, every single battery in the house was laid out on the bed, he was in the bed looking chipper as can be, and quipped, "I didn't know what kind you wanted."

When she finished her story, she said to the other ladies that moment was the turning point in their relationship. It started conversation and reignited the spark. Thirty years into marriage, this couple had found the key to talking about their sex life.

They Reduce the Ego Factor

One of the reasons talking about sex is difficult is because we are afraid of hurting each other's feelings. I have had women tell me if their husbands are doing something with his body that is just not working, it can be very difficult to say stop because they are afraid he is going to feel inadequate. I have also met men who are secretly afraid if they say no to anything their wives are trying, then she will stop experimenting altogether – after all, many of us feel that getting something is better than nothing, right?

But when you are figuring out what works and what doesn't with a bedroom toy, it takes a lot of the pressure off. For example, saying, "I don't like how the toy feels there" is much less intimidating to say (or hear) than, "I don't like it when you do that." This way you are both learning together and no one is to blame if either of you don't like it. And if you do like it, you have opened up a whole new world of enjoyment for you both.

They Help with Sexual Dysfunction

Research tells us that 43 percent of women and 31 percent of men have some sort of sexual dysfunction in the bedroom.[21] These dysfunctions can run the gambit from low libido to erectile difficulties to complete inability to orgasm. A woman who has never been able to orgasm or has "lost" her orgasm due to menopause might be able to experience this pleasure with the help of a vibrator. A man who is having a hard time keeping an erection might benefit from a c-ring (a penis ring). And men and women who struggle with low libido discover sex can be easier and faster with the use of bedroom toys.

They Add Variety and Fun

If we are going to have relationships that last a lifetime, we have to become experts in two areas – recognizing when we are in a rut, and knowing how to get out of it.

Bedroom toys are a great way to spice things up by trying something we haven't tried before. One client of mine had always thought the face-to-face simultaneous orgasm was an invention of Hollywood and could never be achieved in real life. But when she and her husband used a couple's toy for the first time, they realized it did not just happen in the movies.

Considering all these things, it is easy to see why I am an advocate of bedroom toys. I do not mean to imply that toys can fix all the issues a couple has, nor would I push anyone to try them if they are not comfortable with the idea. But if you are having any of these issues, or are just looking to try something new, then I think bedroom toys are a great place to start.

Finding Bedroom Toys

My primary concern with bedroom toys is finding the proper place to purchase them. Most stores in which they are sold have two issues (perhaps more, depending on the store) – they carry porn, and the toys are sold with graphic images on them. Many Christians do not want to have to walk past shelves of porn to get to the toys, or have a scantily clad woman on the packaging of a vibrator.

At one of my conferences, a man raised his hand and said, "If you want to do home improvement, you go to Home Depot. I want to do some marriage improvement. Where do I go for this stuff?"

That is an excellent question. On my website, www.erynfaye.com, under the Resources tab, I have listed links to companies that offer discreet and tasteful products. I do, however, encourage you to do your own research to find a company that suits you best.

Regardless of what the two of you decide are the most enjoyable pathways to pleasure, actively working to enhance pleasure should be a priority in your marriage. Understanding how pleasure works also means having education on what can hinder it.

Interferences to Pleasure

The Greek philosopher Heraclitus said, "The only thing constant is change." This truism is exceedingly obvious in our bodies as we go through life. As we age and face new health concerns, we run into issues that can curtail the amount of pleasure we experience in our sex lives with our spouses.

Medications

Modern medicine, without a doubt, saves lives. Doctors are devoted to ensuring you live for as long, and as comfortably, as possible. When they prescribe a medicine, it is with the express purpose of treating the particular health issue you have. Doctors are amazing allies.

Still, they are often less concerned about the sexual side effects of the drugs they are prescribing. Given the options of saving your life from dangerous epileptic episodes or increasing your libido, they will choose the former. That is their job.

However, you, as the patient, have the responsibility and right to discuss all side effects candidly with your doctor. Their objective is primarily to keep you alive and well – your objective as a patient is to advocate for balance in all areas of your life. Sometimes these two objectives are on opposite ends of the spectrum and difficult to reconcile. Other times, however, you do not have to forego one for the other.

I recently had a conversation with a friend who was relapsing into depression after years off medication. She was fully aware that, for her own health as well as that of her family, she needed to go back on medication, but was loathe to go back on the drug her doctor had previously prescribed. She already struggled with low libido, and this other drug made things considerably worse. I recommended she ask her doctor about Wellbutrin, a drug with considerable success treating depression without obliterating libido.

A few months later, this woman came back to me and thanked me for my suggestion. When I asked how things were going, she responded, "Not only am I not depressed anymore, but Wellbutrin curbs my appetite, gives me energy and boosts my libido. It should be in the drinking water!"

(Note: I am not a medical doctor, nor is this woman. As always, if you are considering pharmaceutical avenues, you should have a full conversation with your doctor and talk about all your concerns. The effects this one drug had on this woman may not be the same for all patients.)

Unfortunately, stories do not always turn out this well. But you can guarantee they will not go well if you don't summon the courage to have a frank conversation with your doctor about libido. Whether it is a prescription for the birth control pill or heart medication, ask about the sexual side effects and what you can do to manage, mitigate or eliminate them.

Pain

One of the most problematic areas of sexual intimacy is the physical pain that many women feel in the pelvic region of their bodies. This might include vulvodynia, pudendal nerve pain, endometriosis, vestibulodynia or a whole host of other conditions. Doctors are rarely given specialized training in this complex field, and so when women go for medical help, they can sometimes leave the doctor's office feeling even more confused and isolated.

If you are unable to find someone who can clearly explain your condition and treat the problem, the physical pain will not only drown out any sense of pleasure, but it can also impact the interpersonal dynamics of your marriage. Diagnosing, understanding and treating pain quickly and effectively are imperative for the overall wellbeing of your relationship. If you are experiencing pain, here are some tips:

- Get quality information. One of the best books on the subject is *Healing Painful Sex: A Woman's Guide to Confronting, Diagnosing, and Treating Sexual Pain* by Deborah Coady and Nancy Fish. This book reassures you that you are not alone, helps you figure out what is wrong, gives you tips on finding a doctor who can effectively help you, and provides practical information on taking care of your body.
- Have a candid conversation. Some of my clients are fearful of letting their husbands know the full extent of their pain. You might be concerned that full disclosure will disappoint your husband and lead to a complete lack of physical intimacy, someone might have convinced you that the pain is just "in your head" so you feel foolish talking about it, or you might think that things will never change so you should just "suck it up." However, to use the Texan colloquialism, this isn't your problem, this is *y'alls* problem. It might be your body, but it impacts both of you. The two of you will work through this season much better if you are honest and supportive of each other.
- Build a support team of experts. Obviously, you need to have a doctor who is overseeing your care, but it is also highly likely you will need a physical therapist who is an expert in pelvic floor care. You might also want to add a therapist, counselor or coach who can help you navigate the interpersonal ramifications of sexual pain. Having a team working on your behalf will lift your spirits in the discouraging times and move you towards complete healing faster.

Aging

It is inevitable that as the years pass our bodies will change. What works in the bedroom tonight may not work as well in five or ten years' time. The very best defense against a stale love life, or one constantly failing to meet your hopes and dreams, is education and communication.

Menopause

When I first started my business, I went around to all my female friends and asked them about the state of their sex lives as market research. During one of these conversations, I asked one lady about menopause. I soft-peddled my question and said, "I hear that lubrication is a bit erratic during menopause." She looked at me and laughed. "Erratic? It's *nonexistent*!"

Over the years, I have met many women who are going, or have gone through, menopause and are asking for help with their sex life. They might be dealing with hormonal fluctuations which can be annoying at best and frightening at worst (one lady described menopause as "an alien has landed in my body"), vaginal dryness, thinning of the vaginal lining (which makes sex incredibly uncomfortable if you are not prepared), changes to your orgasm (many women said they "lost" their orgasm during menopause), or a host of other symptoms. And yet, before women actually go through "The Change," very few have any idea what to expect.

Here is a rundown on the basics of menopause. During a lifetime, a woman has a limited number of eggs in her ovaries. Each month, the primary sex hormone in her body (estrogen) regulates the release of these eggs so she can get pregnant (or get a visit from Aunt Flo if she does not). Contrary to commonly held beliefs, menopause is not an event, but rather a series of phases.

As she comes to the end of her eggs, the estrogen in her body begins to decrease. This phase is called perimenopause because she will still have her periods, but they will not come consistently each month. This is because her ovaries are not releasing an egg each month. This phase can start as early as a woman's late thirties, but more commonly begins sometime during her forties. During this phase, she might notice that she has "fuzzy" brain (where she cannot think as clearly as she once could), hot flashes and night sweats, insomnia, irregular periods, emotional ups and downs, depression, vaginal dryness, decreased libido and other similarly disruptive symptoms.

As this phase can last for a few years and has health implications (increased risk of osteoporosis, higher cholesterol counts, etc.), it is important to recognize the symptoms and talk to your doctor about them.

The second phase is menopause, and this phase is technically defined as having gone a full year without a period. At this point, the symptoms of perimenopause tend to decrease because the levels of estrogen (although significantly less than prior to perimenopause) have leveled off and are more consistent.

The good news is women eventually transition into post-menopause. Gail Sheehy, author of *Menopause: The Silent Passage,*[22] writes that women in this phase experience a "post-menopausal zest" in which they have a heightened sense of focus, clarity and even energy. They have a deeper and more accepting sense of self which enables them to live their later years with less self-criticism.

At the end of the day, the best way to prepare for menopause is by educating yourself about what is to come and what your options are in dealing with it. But for those of you who are waiting to get to the "zest" stage, here are some recommendations:

- Get a good doctor who will listen seriously to the things you are feeling in your body.
- Discuss the latest research on the pros/cons of hormone replacement therapy (HRT).
- Do your research. Gail Sheehy's book is an excellent place to start.
- Increase your intake of calcium, antioxidants and B vitamins.
- Decrease your intake of fatty foods (Of course. You go through hell, why not take away your pizza and burgers too?!)

As you get educated about what actually happens in menopause, make sure you keep those lines of communication open with your spouse so the two of you can process the changes together.

The same holds true for andropause.

Andropause

Andropause is the gradual loss of testosterone over a man's lifetime. Unlike menopause, where there is an obvious demarcation point (missing periods), the testosterone levels in men begin to slowly taper off in their mid-fifties and sixties. While men can still produce sperm (and consequently reproduce) during this season, they will begin to experience a host of new symptoms. These symptoms can include changes in mood, loss of physical agility, lower sex drive, weight gain and depression. Furthermore, since testosterone in males is essential for sexual behavior, men might find difficulty sustaining erections.

It is important couples realize that men enter this season in life. If the wife is not aware of these changes, it is quite possible that she will interpret her husband's change in behavior as something to do with her. Furthermore, if her husband is unaware of andropause, it is easy to feel isolated very quickly. The loss of testosterone is not something you normally sit around and discuss with your hockey buddies.

Here are some recommendations for men who are beginning to feel the effects of andropause:

- Go for a checkup with your doctor and have your testosterone levels tested.
- If your levels are low, discuss treatment options with your doctor in light of your own medical history. It is possible you could begin a course of testosterone replacement therapy (TRP) taken by oral capsules, injections or skin patches.
- Do your research into natural alternatives to testosterone replacement therapy (the maca root, Asian ginseng, ginkgo and L-arginine have all had success boosting libido and blood flow in men).

Final Thoughts

The body is an amazing creation. It was designed in ways we are still discovering, and yet these mysteries are known to our Creator. He took careful consideration as He knit us together, knowing full well we would share pleasure with each other. I heard it once said that Satan's biggest agenda was to get us into bed with each other before marriage, and keep us out of bed after we are wed. Do not fall into that trap. Take the time to discover the pleasure you can bring each other – pleasure that was planned for eons ago.

Bedwork: Pleasure

PSA: _____

This week, answer at least two questions. If you have a strong emotional reaction to the questions, pick the one you love and the one you hate. If you do not have a strong reaction, pick an exercise your spouse will appreciate, or give them home field advantage. Don't forget to record your PSA.

1. **Foreplay.** Pick one time this week with your spouse and explore foreplay. Here are the rules: You can explore as much as you want (sensual massage, kissing, holding, etc.), but hold off on any activity which leads to orgasm for at least twenty to thirty minutes. This is your time to explore each other, and find new ways to pleasure each other without "sprinting to orgasm."

2. **Kissing.** Experiment with different types of kisses this week. (If you have a spouse who takes any form of kissing as a signal you want to immediately hop into bed, then lovingly explain the objective of this exercise is to practice building pleasure and foreplay.) Vary the type of kiss as well its placement. Try pecks on the cheek, a kiss on the head, a warm kiss on the palm of your husband's hand, a closed-mouth kiss after a deep gaze into your wife's eyes, a lingering wet kiss. Try kissing with your eyes open. Kiss with your eyes closed. Have fun and enjoy!

3. **Kissing.** Feeling like you are about to fight? Try kissing instead. I know you won't feel like it, but do this experiment. See what happens to your disagreement. Worst-case scenario, you end up fighting after the kiss, but you were well on your way to doing that anyways. Maybe kissing will remind you why you are together, boost your levels of oxytocin, and help you come to a more productive resolution to your dispute.

4. **Old Messages.** If you have difficulty experiencing pleasurable touch in marriage because of messages given to you during childhood:
   - Write out messages communicated to you verbally or nonverbally.
   - How did you interpret those messages as a child? (What did you tell yourself about pleasure?)
   - Do you have distinct memories around this subject? What are they? What emotions do you remember having? What role do they still play in your marriage?
   - What do you want to believe now about pleasurable touch in your marriage? What does Scripture say? What feelings do you want the subject to invoke in you now? Write out those current beliefs, read them aloud, and use them as new messages to tell yourself.
   - Prayer. At this point, I offer a sample prayer for you to say, but you can change it to better suit your own wording if you wish.

Father God, I realize for my entire life, I have been operating under the assumption that pleasurable touch is _____. I realize now these beliefs have undermined what you designed sexual intimacy to be in my marriage. Through examination of your Word, I now realize intimacy with my spouse should be _____. Please remind me of your truth every day so I can have freedom in this area of my marriage.

5. **Browsing.** Try the sensate focus exercise as a couple. Did you find any breakthroughs in your relationship? What happened when you forced yourselves to take orgasm out of the equation? What did you discover about your spouse that was new? What was your favorite part of the exercise? What was your spouse's favorite part?

6. **Interferences to Pleasure.** What has been standing in your way of achieving pleasure with your spouse? What can you do to problem solve this situation? Do you need to read a book on the subject? Visit your doctor? Do some research on natural remedies? (Always consult with your doctor about anything you are taking to ensure it does not interact poorly with current medication.)

7. **Enhancing Pleasure.** What can you do this week to enhance the level of pleasure in your marriage? Do you want to introduce a new accoutrement into your sex life? Do you need to begin doing kegels each day? How did your body respond to this new exercise or accoutrement? Is this something that will enhance the pleasure you enjoy together?

8. **Pathways to Pleasure.** Is there a pathway you would like to try for the first time? Or perhaps there is one you have tried before, but did not take the time to develop the skill set? Have a conversation with your spouse to assess how s/he is feeling about the idea of introducing something new into your sex life.

9. **New Information.** What did you learn for the first time about pleasure? Was there a fact or bit of information you had never heard before? Share this information with your spouse and chat about how it can impact the pleasure in your relationship.

Element 6: Trust

"Trust in the LORD with all your heart and lean not on your own understanding;
in all your ways acknowledge Him, and He will make your paths straight."
Proverbs 3:5-6 (NIV)

I stopped praying when my dad died. I was done. I had spent more than a decade praying that first my mom, and then my dad, would get better and survive their cancers. They didn't. Prayer seemed like a colossal waste of time. Why pray to a God who – if He listened at all – was probably too preoccupied with the starving children in Africa to listen to me?

This went on for years. For reasons I don't fully understand, I continued to move in Christian circles. So, to look like the cool Christians, I would open my mouth and utter words during prayer times. I was a pastor's kid, so I am sure no one had a clue I was faking it. I knew the language. I knew what to say. But I didn't have any conviction that God was on the other end of the phone. In my private life, away from the eyes of other, holier Christians, I never prayed. My heart had closed.

This went on until one day when I got really desperate. I was running late to a very important appointment, and needed to find a parking spot immediately. If I remember correctly, there was a big work contract that hung on the line, and it was imperative I made the right impression.

"God! I need a parking spot right now!" I barked. At that very moment, a car slid out of a space in the front row of the office complex, and I took the spot. Focused on dashing into the building to make my appointment, I didn't give the incident much thought.

A few weeks later, I was at the mall looking for a parking spot – again. This time, I wasn't in a rush, but was feeling a bit cheeky. I remembered the prayer incident and thought, "I wonder if that was a fluke?" So, I prayed for a parking spot. Again, within moments, a space opened at the front of the parking lot.

Pretty soon, I let Eric know about my new experiments. He was fully aware of my silent treatment of God, and found it utterly fascinating I found parking spots anytime I asked. He laughed and said, "You have a parking angel. We'll call him 'St. Henry' because we have a Ford."

St. Henry and I bonded for a full year – my only prayers were for parking spots – before I opened the door a bit more to God. A group of ladies was beginning the book *The Power of a Praying Wife,*[1] by Stormie Omartian, and my interest was piqued. First, I really loved my husband. He was, and still is, the most amazing guy. So, praying for him seemed like a good thing to do. Second, there was absolutely nothing wrong in our marriage at the time, so the risk was extremely low. St. Henry had begun to bolster my confidence in prayer, and this seemed to be the next logical baby step.

I fell in love with the process of praying for my husband. The group of women was great and the book was life changing. I still recommend women read it and implement Omartian's suggestions. Eric was thrilled I was praying for him, and the intimacy in our marriage deepened.

And slowly, over the following months and years, I began to heal. I began to open my heart to God with my prayers again. If He could be the God of parking spots, if He could reach down and care for something so seemingly trivial and mundane in my life, then perhaps I could trust Him with larger areas of my life.

To this day, I don't know if it was "God's will" for my parents to die so young. There are all sorts of theological stances on why bad things happen to good people. However, I do know this without a shadow of a doubt. I would not be the person I am today – I would not have the same levels of compassion, the rock-solid understanding of life in the midst of ambiguity, the gift of being marked by pain, the deep conviction that change takes place as a series of small, consistent choices, or had the opportunity to meet St. Henry – had I not walked through the fiery road of extended illness, death and grief. Wisdom is mined in the dark places of life. Trust and faith help you survive the mining process.

Trust in your relationship begins with the belief that God cares about your relationship, He gives a damn whether you succeed or fail as a couple, He loves you enough to take time away from His focus on the other atrocities in the world to nurture the two of you, and He cares enough about your marriage to be concerned about your sex life.

Trust Your God

If you are a believer, then you can – indeed you must – hold on to the faith that God is an active member of your marriage. He is instrumental in working in you so your marriage can deepen in intimacy over the years. And He will be at work on your spouse as well. Your spouse may not believe in God, or you might feel his/her faith is not as strong as yours. But this does not erase His influence.

I have met many people who were holding on to one hope for the restoration of their marriage – that God cared and wanted their relationship to remain intact. In these situations, each spouse felt very alone in their pain and struggled to see a way forward. When one woman shared her story of redemption, she reflected on the pain during this period in her marriage: "It's such a lonely place – to be locked in a prison of pain where the only other person who knows about your misery seems to you to be the one who caused it. And though they might dare to want to be your strength, they feel locked in their own pain, and are almost certain you're to blame. For us, it was like an uncrossable chasm."[2]

However, during these rocky times, there is another party in your relationship, and He is a powerful ally. Don't get me wrong. It is not that God is taking sides with you against your spouse. In fact, often He is going to work on you first. If you are asking for help, He is going to respond by putting you to work on your own issues.

I remember listening to a couple share during a weekend marriage retreat about a fight they had. As they lay fuming in the darkness, the husband told God, "God, you have to admit that this fight is 90 percent her fault." God responded, "Yes, but your 10 percent caused her 90 percent." Even if you are only responsible for 10 percent of the argument, it is probably that 10 percent that is causing your spouse's 90 percent. And God will address the 10 percent first.

If you have done any reading on the Christian perspective of marriage, you have no doubt run across the illustration of the triangle. The triangle is the strongest and most stable shape in geometry because each side braces the two opposite sides and prevents movement. Many structures are reinforced with triangles to give the construction the necessary stability.

I have to admit, in the early years of my marriage, I found the triangle illustration a bit cheesy because I liked my husband a whole lot more than God at the time. But, as I have studied relationships and sexual intimacy (not to mention the fact I have come to like God again), I have learned to appreciate the value of the illustration. Here it is:

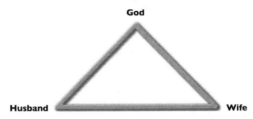

Ideally, the husband deepens his relationship with God and so does the wife. As they develop their relationship together, God is the third party providing strength and stability in the relationship.

I have found that often with Christians we slip into believing it is incumbent on us alone to develop our relationship with God. However, this neglects the power of God to work in our lives. God is very actively working to draw us into relationship with Him. The whole story of the Gospel concerns an omniscient God who came down to reach humankind through the most humble of circumstances. The words of John 1:14 (NIV) are powerful in this regard, "The Word became flesh and made His dwelling among us." Here is the most powerful force of the universe, reaching out to us because He so deeply desires relationship with us.

Not only did He come, but He *died*. John explains later in 3:16 (NIV), "For God so loved the world, that He gave His one and only son." This is a God who so longed for relationship with us, He was willing to pay an enormous price. He created us for relationship, hard-wired the need for connection into our DNA, and when we chose to reject Him, implemented a drastic strategy to win us back. This is a God who cares deeply.

So, if you have a spouse who is not responding to Christ, you can trust that Christ can get to him/her. This understanding takes an enormous pressure of responsibility off your shoulders. During times when your spouse is not willing or cannot seek Him, He is still seeking him/her. This also means you do not have to strong-arm your spouse into following God. God is responsible for His relationship with your husband or wife. That is their business.

In the meantime, your business is to pursue the calling on your heart and deepen your relationship with God. Obviously, we would love for the relationship to work like this:

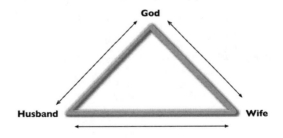

However, in times when it is not going this way, rest assured God is a lot bigger and more powerful than you, and loves your spouse a whole lot more than you do. In the meantime, your spouse's relationship with God should have little to no impact on how you should act in your sex life. (Obviously, if your spouse asks you to do something that violates Scripture, this is the exception.) Your spouse's choice not to follow God does not let you off the hook from doing everything in your power to be the best husband or wife you can be.

In fact, Paul tells us in I Corinthians 7:14 (NIV), "For the unbelieving husband has been sanctified through his wife, and the unbelieving wife has been sanctified through her believing husband." In essence, you should allow your love and devotion to your spouse to permeate your relationship. Remember what I said in the Faith chapter about Christians should have the best sex? Allow it to be your witness to your spouse.

Trusting that God cares about your relationship gives you the freedom to trust Him in the hard times. It is also the first step to trusting yourself.

Trust Yourself

Interestingly enough, the more secure and confident you become with yourself – the better you know and accept yourself, and the more you recognize that your happiness does not rise and fall with your spouse – the easier it becomes to trust.

Most of us grew up believing that love = enmeshment. We were raised in families of origin in which love only grows when it is tightly controlled and organized. Everyone has their roles within the family system, and it is difficult to find love if you are not dutifully fulfilling your role. Often, individuality and separateness are not values to be held dearly because they are threats to the family system.

Emotional Fusion

When this dysfunction worms its way into relationships, psychiatrists call it emotional fusion. Emotional fusion is losing your sense of self within the wider context of your spouse and family. There is little room for individual perspectives, thoughts, emotions, ideas or separateness.

Emotional fusion in a marriage might look like:

- low self-esteem
- being dependent on your spouse's opinion for your validation of self
- being heavily influenced by your spouse's moods
- trying to fix all your spouse's problems for him/her
- the inability to separate your emotions from those of your spouse
- putting honesty on the back burner for fear of rejection.

It might also show itself by:

- refusing to leave your spouse's side at a party
- jealousy over the people your spouse works with
- balking when your spouse wants time with the girls/guys

- being in a great mood until your spouse comes home grumpy, and then being in a bad mood yourself
- not expressing what you truly think and feel about your relationship for fear your partner will get angry, sad or depressed.

Emotional fusion creeps into the bedroom as well. If you are unable to express your true needs and desires, you are going to settle for a sex life far less than what you dream. If your sense of self is wrapped up in what your spouse sees in you, you are not going to have a good enough idea of what you want out of your sex life because you haven't given it sufficient thought. And if you cannot see your spouse as an individual with his/her own desires, needs and wants, you are going to be completely unable to be a good lover because you cannot get outside yourself enough to meet those desires, needs and wants.

Differentiation

In a healthy relationship, couples are differentiated. They are able to hold two opposites – separateness and togetherness – in tandem. As I mentioned earlier, we often take the admonition "The two will become one"[3] and interpret this as total enmeshment. This is not oneness – this is emotional fusion. Becoming one in a healthy manner is much more complex. It means recognizing and honoring you and your spouse's unique designs, while still basking in your time together.

In this place, you can love and accept your spouse as different, and bring different perspectives to your marriage without this threatening your unique perspectives. Furthermore, you embrace your togetherness as a couple. Your identity, your personhood, your value, and most importantly your status as a child of God, does not rise or fall on the attitudes, perspective or emotions of your spouse.

Do not confuse this with extreme individualism. Murray Bowen, the psychiatrist who developed the theory of differentiation, said, "I consider rugged individualism to be an exaggerated pretend posture of a person struggling against emotional fusion. The differentiated person is always aware of others and the relationship system around him."[4] If you are dogmatically asserting your individual needs, thoughts and opinions on those around you, you are not doing so out of a calm sense of assuredness. This is a red flag you are pushing against the enmeshment you feel in your relationship. As Hamlet said, "The lady doth protest too much, methinks."

This happens all the time in the midst of mid-life crises. Many couples I meet in this predicament are there as a reaction to years of emotional fusion with their spouse and other close relationships. Feeling a desperate need to break free, they often interpret freedom as getting out. The "love" they were feeling was completely smothering them. The sad fact is when one spouse begins down this road, the other tends to grab on tighter, which just exacerbates the smothering.

When you clearly know who you are as an individual in your marriage, when you know who you are created to be as a child of God, when you truly recognize your value, you can trust yourself. You are not at the mercy of the emotional well being of those around you. You have the freedom to communicate your deepest desires because you know what they are, and you have enough sense of self to express them. You do not live in fear of making poor choices because your choices emanate from a place of confidence. But when you do make poor choices – because no one is perfect – you know you are fully capable of putting them right and moving on with your life.

And when the intolerance for separateness and boundaries is gone, it gives your relationship space to breathe and trust to flourish.

Trust Your Spouse

It is no secret that a healthy relationship is built on a bedrock of trust. How we develop trust, however, is subject to debate. We have a phrase in our culture that says, "Trust is not given – it is earned." On my Facebook page, I quoted this and then asked for feedback on whether people agreed with the statement. I immediately started to get responses.

Some people were adamant it was a true statement. Trust is definitely earned. Others claimed it is indeed given. And still others opened the door to the concept that trust is both given and earned. One lady put it this way: "You have my trust until you screw me over, and then you have to earn it back."

Trust in your spouse is essential to building a great sex life. In order for sex to be good and intimacy to develop, you have to be willing to become vulnerable to your lover – let him/her know where and how you like to be touched, what you like to talk about in bed, and even what your secret fantasies are. When we trust, we can be honest, and we can be transparent. Trust allows our communication to deepen when we share this intimate part of ourselves.

On the other hand, lack of trust is the root of much sexual dysfunction.[5] Researchers believe lack of trust is one of the primary psychological issues for men experiencing erectile dysfunction. The inability to feel safe enough to relax keeps women from experiencing orgasm. The violation of trust in survivors of childhood sexual assault makes it exceedingly difficult for them to build relationships entailing trust. Trust is clearly a key to the quality of our sex lives.

Trust is given, but it is also earned. If we enter our relationship constantly on the lookout for our spouse to "screw" us, chances are pretty high we are going to find it. When we withhold trust, intimacy cannot flourish. It is stymied by the expectation of failure. So, we must enter into the marriage covenant giving our spouse the gift of trust.

However, trust either deepens or sours over time mainly due to the manner in which we treat each other. It is incumbent on us to actively develop trust over the years through our words and actions. Interestingly, trust is a self-perpetuating cycle. The more trust we have, the easier it is to trust. Here are some ways to develop it.

Establishing Clear Expectations

In the Faith chapter, I outlined the various sexual behaviors that are boundaried-out in Scripture. Once you get into a marriage relationship, there are very few. Yes, you cannot get a prostitute, have a liaison with your neighbor's wife or use animals to bring you sexual pleasure. Third parties are pretty much out. But beyond that, the field is fairly wide open. There is a lot of space and freedom for the two of you to explore.

That being said, it is important to set parameters so you don't take little steps that can lead towards violating those scriptural prohibitions. As you build trust with each other, I recommend you sit down as a couple, and talk about (at the very least) or write down (an even better plan) the expectations and boundaries you have in your marriage. This might look like:

- The maximum amount of time you will go without having sex (barring catastrophic illness or extended travel). If you begin to creep up to this amount of time, you can lovingly remind each other it is time to reconnect sexually.
- The ground rules for introducing creativity into your sexual relationship. What constitutes a "suggestion" and when does it cross the line into "pressure"?
- Restrictions on Internet and TV usage so one or both of you cannot slide into unhealthy relationships or viewing.
- A clear understanding of what Scriptures around the topic of sex mean to you as a couple, combined with the agreement that you will not violate them.
- Limits on the amount of time, as well as the time and place you meet with members of the opposite sex.
- A practice of setting aside time for the two of you to be alone including date nights, weekends away and so forth.
- Practices that you will engage in, or refrain from, while out of town, away from each other (traveling companions, alcohol consumption, etc.).

These are just a few examples of having conversation so you are both very clear on the expectations and boundaries in your marriage. Touch base with each other throughout the years to make sure you are both still on the same page and redefine your list if necessary. As you put those ground rules into practice in your relationship, trust will grow.

Consistency In Word and Deed

One of the simplest ways to build trust in your marriage is to say what you mean, and mean what you say. When you make a promise to your spouse, keep it. If you have a problem with keeping your promises, then use a new tactic – under promise and over deliver. But stop disappointing your spouse.

One of the most consistent wounds I see spouses inflict on each other is when one (usually the Low Desire Spouse) makes an implication or promise of sex at some later time. The High Desire Spouse gets excited in anticipation of the event, but when it rolls around, the Low Desire Spouse is no longer interested. A pattern of this sort of behavior is devastating to the person who continually gets their hopes up, only to have them dashed repeatedly.

If it is impossible for you to predict what mood you are going to be in later, and whether you will want sex, then don't make any promises. It is much fairer to your spouse, not to mention authentic of you, to remain silent about your thoughts. Later, if you are indeed interested, then initiate at that time. But don't set your spouse up for disappointment. It erodes their trust in you.

Of course, this principle is not restricted to the bedroom. If you are constantly disappointing your spouse by promising something you do not deliver in any area of your relationship, this has a good chance of spilling over into the bedroom as well.

Guarding Our Words

What we say to each other during sex – or even about sex – is extremely sensitive. It is incredibly easy to hurt each other by opening our mouths without thinking. Often spouses will use the excuse "I'm just being honest," but this type of "honesty" was not balanced with kindness or a good sense of timing.

I once had a lady tell me that, even though she was the Low Desire Spouse, she decided to surprise her husband one night and dress up for him. She went to the lingerie store and picked up something sexy and red – the color of passion. When she put on the outfit for her husband, he looked at her and told her she looked like a tomato.

She was absolutely mortified. Not only had he failed to see the effort she put into creating an intimate moment with him, but he had tapped into something that made her feel very shameful – her body image. This one-two punch was impossible for her to recover from. Right then and there, she resolved never to surprise him in the bedroom again, and lingerie was no longer an option for their sex life. There was no way she was going to open herself up for potential future ridicule and pain.

What we say to each other during our most private of moments, how we respond to what our lover brings to us, is incredibly precious and needs to be treated as such. Use your intimate times together to build each other up. If you have a serious concern with your spouse, approach the subject lovingly and with good timing. Bringing it up in the heat of the moment is rarely the best idea.

Transparency

Hiding things in our lives from each other is extremely detrimental to trust. When couples ask me, "What do I have to tell her/him? Everything?" I recommend they ask themselves a simple question anytime they are concerned they might be hiding something. "If I were to ask my spouse about this activity and say, 'What do you think about this?' then what would my spouse say? How would s/he react?"

If you cannot ask your spouse this question about something in your life (whether this be your shopping and spending habits, online relationships, the colleague at work who you habitually take to lunch, or the sexually explicit websites you visit), then you can rest assured it has a high potential to undermine the trust in your relationship. Trust is built through transparency.

Want to know how much I spent? Feel free to look at the receipts. Want to ensure my conversations with a friend on Facebook aren't crossing the line? Here's my password. Want to know if my texting is with buddies only? Here is my phone – take a look.

But what about privacy? Privacy is great. It is fabulous when you want to get some time in the bathroom alone. It is wonderful when you need time out with the girls or the guys. It is healthy when you are having a conversation with a friend who is going through a difficult time. It is not so hot when it is used as an excuse to cover up activities that are going to undermine your relationship. When there is an easy, open air of transparency in the relationship, trust has room to flourish.

Faithfulness

Monogamy is a foundational element to the vast majority of modern marriages. When we say, "Until death do us part," we commit to being faithful to that one person for life. Sometimes we idealize monogamy in Christian circles. The way we teach about marriage gives the impression that, as long as we communicate and love each other well, monogamy will not be a challenge. Wrong.

No matter how much you love your spouse, how happy you are together, how well you communicate, or how often you have sex, there will still be other people who catch your eye. You might run into them at work, in the airport, or at the grocery store. But at some point in your marriage, you will make contact with someone who sparks your interest in a way that exceeds appropriate bounds. In that moment, every married person – if they are honest with themselves – realizes monogamy is not easy. It's a *choice*. It can be an extremely gratifying choice, but make no mistake. It is a choice.

Dave Carder, a counselor who specializes in working with couples recovering from affairs, believes every person has a "dangerous partner profile."[6] You might be attracted to someone who:

- listens when your spouse does not
- is very different from your spouse
- has a particular look
- admires and encourages you
- enjoys the same hobbies and interests as you
- reminds you of your "darker," "riskier" side
- reminds you of who you want to be in life
- makes you feel safe.

The more you understand what your dangerous partner profile entails, the better you can protect yourself and your marriage by creating clear boundaries around such people. Letting your spouse know what that dangerous partner profile looks like provides another layer of protection. In fact, listening to your spouse's perspective is always a wise course of action when it comes to people who might threaten your marriage.

There also will be times in your marriage when you are completely unaware that someone else is attracted to you. Your spouse can give you crucial backup by watching out for you and alerting you when this happens. Often we can recognize it when people around us are attracted to our spouses faster than our spouses.

Eric and I use the code phrase "That person has hit my radar" when this happens. While we have only had to use it on a few occasions, there have been times when one of us has had concerns about a third party paying copious amounts of attention to the other. In these times, it is our pattern just to make each other aware. It might go something like this: "Hey, babe. I think this person is looking to you to meet her needs when really her husband should be doing that." It's not an issue of jealousy, but watching each other's backs so we can guard our marriage.

Emotional

Being vigilant about guarding your marriage begins with keeping an eye out for emotional attachments that can form through work relationships, social circles or online activity. These relationships usually begin as a seemingly innocent friendship that can cross the line into an emotionally laden one.

Emotional affairs are no longer restricted to face-to-face contact. In fact, they are skyrocketing due to our increasing involvement with social networks. For example, according to a survey done by the American Academy of Matrimonial Lawyers, 81 percent of their members have seen an increase in the number of divorces that involve social media.[7] Facebook was the top offender, being linked to 66 percent of divorces. Unwittingly, men and women are getting caught in entanglements as they hunt down lost loves and old friends. When your marriage isn't going so well, it is easy to idealize the feelings you had with an old flame, especially when you only "see" them for a few moments during the day. They don't live in the daily frustrations of your life – they get to be your escape.

While it is common for these emotional affairs to escalate into physical ones, they don't always. Even if they remain emotional, though, they still have a devastating effect because one spouse is taking time, attention and energy away from the marriage.

Another area that tempts the faithfulness of couples is the sinister world of pornography.

Visual

The number of men and women who are finding stimulation through online pornography is increasing exponentially. The statistics around the growth in the pornography industry are staggering. Here are a few:[8]

- According to www.xxxchurch.com, a website devoted to helping men and women recover from the world of porn addiction, 47 percent of Christian marriages are polluted by pornography. Most often, the man is involved (72 percent) but it could be the wife instead (28 percent).
- A Christianity Today Leadership survey done in 2001 determined 51 percent of pastors said cyber-porn was a possible temptation and 37 percent said it was a current struggle.
- A 1996 Promise Keepers' survey revealed over 50 percent of the men in attendance were involved with pornography within one week of attending the event.
- The Barna Group reported 29 percent of born-again adults in the U.S. feel it is morally acceptable to view movies with explicit sexual behavior.
- The American Academy of Matrimonial Lawyers estimates 56 percent of divorces involved one person having an obsessive interest in porn sites.

Here are the problems with porn. Not only does it contravene the boundaried-out items given to us in Scripture, but it is also devastating on a marriage in several ways. First, it feels like cheating to the spouse who is not participating in the pornographic activity. When I was answering questions from the viewers at *Marriage Uncensored with Dave and Christie*, the number of women who wrote in for support was excruciatingly sad. These women genuinely felt their husbands had cheated on them, even though there was no physical contact with flesh-and-blood women. Their husbands' indulgences completely undermined their self-confidence in their sexual relationships.

One woman wrote: "I have a lot of deep emotions going on inside me, and one that I am struggling with right now in regards to pornography is wondering how do I maintain in my mind and feelings that God made me beautiful just the way that I am when my husband lusts after these women in vulgar positions doing gross things (out of the context of marriage). How do I not always wonder if when we're making love, or just touching each other, wonder if he's picturing those women he's seen on the computer, and not cherishing me?"[9]

Furthermore, researchers are finding more and more incidences of men who view pornography becoming unable to bond sexually with their wives. Sex therapist Dr. Ian Kerner calls this "Sexual Attention Deficit Disorder" (SADD).[10] In this disorder, men become so accustomed to achieving orgasm through masturbation while being stimulated by pornographic images, they can no longer become aroused with their own wives. The dopamine and oxytocin rush they feel becomes intrinsically linked to porn, and it becomes extremely difficult to find this intimacy outside this insidious online world.

Finally, when men and women get their sex education from pornography, they fail to understand that porn isn't real sex. Men don't last that long. Women don't get aroused that quickly. And most of them do not like to have semen spewed all over their faces. Furthermore, the positions porn stars manipulate themselves into are all for the camera angles, not for pleasure.

It is a fake world. But when you have young men and women who believe it *is* real, they come into the marriage bed with grossly inaccurate perceptions of what real intimacy looks like. This leads to unrealistic expectations and disappointment, and erodes the overall trust in their relationship.

Physical

When someone uses the term "affair," the physical type is often what springs to mind. When a third party enters a marriage relationship, it is like Pandora's box – if you open it you will release all the sorrows in the world. There is quite simply no way to estimate how much an affair hurts until you have personally walked this road. You cannot fathom the amount of pain, insecurity, turmoil and agony both the cheater and the spouse who has been betrayed experience in the aftermath of infidelity.

Is it possible to heal after an affair? Yes. But it takes time, lots of talking and forgiveness to make your way out of the woods.

Healing Broken Trust

Time Heals

When our spouse has hurt us, it takes time to heal. The amount of time it takes depends on the degree to which our trust was violated. If it is a passing hurtful comment, it might be relatively easy to forgive and move on. If it was an affair, it could take years.

I have had people call me and say, "My spouse cheated a year ago and can't figure out why I am not over it yet. Am I crazy for still struggling with this issue?" When it comes to an affair, a year is an extremely short period of time.

Healing from infidelity is an extremely bumpy road. Shirley Glass, dubbed "the godmother of infidelity research," noted in her book *NOT Just Friends: Protect Your Relationship from Infidelity and Heal the Trauma of Betrayal*,[11] spouses who have been cheated on can demonstrate symptoms of post traumatic stress disorder (PTSD). The betrayal is so traumatic, that the healing process comes as a series of two steps forward, one step back.

I have worked with people who were doing extremely well on their road to recovery until something benign happens, like meeting a person with the same name as the "other woman." All of a sudden, the betrayed wife is catapulted back to the memories of the affair, and it's as fresh as the day she found out.

If you are in this place as a couple, be patient with yourselves and each other. Recovery from infidelity is possible, but it takes a long time.

Talk about It

One of the key factors to restoring trust is the freedom to talk about the issue with your spouse. Some couples need to talk extensively. Others can discuss the incident once or twice, and it is sufficient to move into healing. The key is acknowledging the needs of each spouse in this situation.

This is particularly important when a couple is recovering from an affair because it is the avenue to peel back the layers of the trauma and loss. In this situation, the betrayed spouse needs to ask as much as s/he needs to ask. For some people, the idea of finding out the details of their spouses' indiscretions is too much to bear. This is ok. If you don't want to know because knowing would make things worse for you, then your healing process can excel without this information.

However, if the niggling worries about the details are interrupting your healing process, and knowing the details will help you move on with your life, then ask. This is a painful process for both spouses, and should be directed by the betrayed spouse and respected by the betrayer. If you are in this situation, having a professional third party to facilitate this process is something you should seriously consider. A counselor or therapist, who is skilled in helping marriages through the aftermath of an affair, can keep the conversation from getting derailed by the pain in the midst of this process.

Eventually, if you truly want to trust your spouse again, you are going to have to forgive.

Forgiveness

Some years ago, my husband went through a certification process on a relapse prevention program. He was a fundraiser for a nonprofit that worked with addicts breaking their addictions and getting back on their feet. The course wasn't strictly necessary for his position, but he felt it was important to know what the counselors dealt with on a regular basis so he could more effectively tell their stories to potential funders.

The course was intensive and the participants were required to do homework each night. One evening when he came home, he told me they had gone through the section on forgiveness that is an essential section for any addict who wants to truly leave their compulsions behind and move on. I was intrigued with the conversation until he turned to me and said, "I think we should go through the exercise and talk about your dad."

Oh, no.

In the later years of his life, my father had made some – to put it mildly – *poor decisions* that had huge ramifications for his kids. I tried to forgive him. I thought I had done a decent job of it.

But here's the thing about forgiveness – it is a large, ambiguous, and difficult-to-pin-down concept. Sure, we have all heard the quote that refusing to forgive someone is like drinking poison and expecting them to die. But how do you know when you have actually done it? What do you say and do? Can you ever move to the place of having fondness for the person?

Out of sheer love for my husband, I decided to listen to the perspective he had gained at the course. Michael Dye, the author of the course,[12] had an interesting spin on forgiveness. It wasn't just a question of what the person did and how you can let go. It was an in-depth look at what meaning you had ascribed to the event and the person.

Through my tears, Eric helped me fill out the chart. Here is an example:

Person	Offense	Judgment	Vow	Effect On Me	Person's Debt
Dad	Married four months after Mom died.	He is selfish and weak, unable to live without a woman.	I will never need a man.	Trust issues in my relationship with Eric, which have taken years to address properly.	He owed me the right to grieve at my own pace without a stepmother. A year would have been nice.

There were actually a list of offenses, but I won't bore you with all the sordid details. Eric sat next to me on the couch and wouldn't let me leave until I had put everything on paper. It took hours. Listing the offenses was the easy part. What took a while was writing them all down. Once I started, the memories of all the hurts started flowing, and I was able to remember everything he had done that hurt me. Then, figuring out the debts he owed me took much longer.

What's the Debt?

But it is the debt part of this exercise that is profound. Typically, we are taught to forgive the offense and the offender, but we do not pay heed to the ramifications of the offense in our current lives. However, unless you actually know what you are forgiving a person for – what debt you are releasing them from – it is impossible to truly forgive them. If you try to address the offense, but never dig deeper to the debt, you will be spinning your wheels.

The best way of clarifying the debt is by asking yourself: If it were a perfect world and s/he hadn't done that to me, what would I have? What did s/he steal from me? What did I lose because of what s/he did? What would be different in my life now?

Keep in mind, the debt might not be logical at all. It is your emotional response to the hurt you have experienced. For example, you could be forgiving your mother for being an absentee parent during your childhood. She might "owe" you all the years of coming home to an empty house.

Your younger brother might "owe" you the attention he stole because he was the favored child. Your boss might "owe" you the new car you planned to buy with the promotion you worked incredibly hard for, but she gave to someone else. Your hopes, dreams and expectations are what were stolen when you were hurt.

Acknowledging the debt and choosing to forgive is the path to freedom in your present life. To move on, we must fully resolve the past. Jack Canfield calls it the "need to complete the past to embrace the future."[13] Lack of forgiveness is an anchor that holds us back from moving forward.

The Effects of Forgiveness

I encounter the issue of forgiveness most frequently with women and men who have issues in their sex lives. I have clients who were underappreciated and ignored, cheated on, and even abused by their current or former spouses. I meet a significant number of people who have been unable to move past the offenses and the accompanying debts they incurred. A lot of these people are still married but can't figure out why their sex lives are languishing. Let me tell you, if you think you can have a thriving sex life while holding on to some offense you have against your spouse, you are out to lunch. Sex is one of the most intimate ways we express ourselves with our partners, and this expression will be severely curtailed by unforgiveness. It festers and grows until it becomes all-encompassing, spilling over into other areas of our relationship.

Many of us underestimate the effects forgiveness will bring. One of my clients, Tiffany, told me she had been raped when she was fourteen years old. She couldn't figure out why, years later, she was struggling with inhibitions in her sex life and pain during intercourse. She had been to the gynecologist, who ran extensive tests and concluded that her problem was not physical but psychological. When Tiffany chose to begin the journey of forgiving her rapist (which for the record was neither easy nor quick), her sex life began to be enjoyable and the physical problems began to disappear. Had Tiffany not made the choice to forgive, who knows how many more years she would have lived without the full enjoyment of this intimate part of her relationship with her husband.

Forgiveness Is Unilateral

Tiffany's story brings up an important point. Forgiveness is a unilateral act. You do not need an apology, an acknowledgement or even a public allocution from your spouse or other offenders to forgive. Would that be satisfying? Absolutely. But is it necessary? Not at all. My father had been dead for years when Eric and I went through the exercise. It was for me and me alone. And it brought me enormous freedom that I did not even know I was missing until I saw the effects of choosing to forgive.

Once the participants have completed their lists in the exercise, Michael Dye has them verbally articulate a forgiveness statement. When I meet with clients who make this choice, I typically have them write their own statements because it is much more powerful when you express this declaration in your own words. The statement should be in present tense, include an acknowledgement of choosing freedom, and a release of the offender, the offense, and the debt owed to you. If you need a starting place, start with this:

Today, I choose to forgive ____(name)____. I choose to release him/her from the debt s/he owes me, which is _____. I realize that by holding on to this debt, I have restricted my own freedom to live a full life. I choose instead to release him/her from this debt so I can be free. ____(Name)___, I forgive you and I release you from the debt you owe me.

For some people, repeating this statement a few times is sufficient. Others need to verbalize it several times a day for days, weeks or even months. Reading your statement is making an active choice to forgive time and time again until the anchor holding you in the past is finally severed. Over time, when that old debt floats to mind, it will feel odd and uncomfortable because you have consciously chosen so many times to release the offender.

For me personally, after forgiving my father I was able, for the first time since he died, to remember the good things he did for me. It was as if all the anger had been a cloud preventing me from seeing him for what he truly was – a man, not a monster. He was like all of us – capable of making some very good, as well as some very bad decisions. While I will never forget the hurtful things he did, I can now remember the man who taught me to face my fears in life, was undaunted by any question I had about sex during my teen years, and took out personal loans so I could attend law school overseas. This man helped mold me into the person I am today. And had I not forgiven, I would have forgotten about him.

Final Thoughts

As we forgive more, as we trust more, and as we fall deeper in love with our spouses, we realize how vulnerable we become. This can be terrifying. This person has insight that no one else can claim, which also means s/he can hurt us more than anyone else. Some people cannot tolerate this level of vulnerability, and respond by numbing or distancing themselves to feel safer.

For those who dare to risk, however, the rewards are immeasurable. For on the other side of the door of this deep vulnerability lies a vast sea of intimacy. And it is also where we discover creativity.

Bedwork: Trust

PSA: _____

This week, answer at least two questions. If you have a strong emotional reaction to the questions, pick the one you love and the one you hate. If you do not have a strong reaction, pick an exercise your spouse will appreciate, or give them home field advantage. Don't forget to record your PSA.

1. **Trusting God.** Have you ever stopped to consider how much God cares about your relationship? Have you ever realized that He, and not you, is ultimately responsible for His relationship with your spouse? Are there areas in your relationship you need to relinquish control to God?

2. **Emotional Fusion and Differentiation.** How would you rate your relationship? Do you have a clear sense of individuality within the context of your marriage? Or do the two of you feel enmeshed? What are some ways you can diffuse the emotional fusion in your marriage and move towards differentiation? If you want to read a book on the subject, *Passionate Marriage* by David Schnarch[14] is an excellent resource.

3. **Establishing Clear Boundaries.** (Note: This is an exercise you do together.) Sit down individually and consider the question: What boundaries to you consider crucial to the safety and well being of your marriage? What do you need to establish so trust can flourish? Write down all the expectations and boundaries you can think of, and then share this list with your spouse. How is your spouse's list different? Decide which items make your combined list. Print out a copy for each spouse to keep.

4. **Dangerous Partner Profile.** What type of person are you attracted to? List the qualities of that type of person. Does that person give you something you are missing in your marriage? What are some ways you can introduce those missing qualities into your marriage? Now that you recognize your profile, what can you do to safeguard each other's lives when you see someone who hits your radar?

5. **Consistency with Words and Deeds.** Have you been guilty of making promises to your spouse and failing to follow through? Where, when and what were those things? Do you need to apologize? What can you do to make your promises selectively, and then do what you say?

6. **Guarding Our Words.** Have you said things that have hurt your spouse, particularly when you were being intimate? Do you need to ask your spouse if you have hurt them?

Do you need to apologize for anything you said? Do you need to forgive your spouse for something s/he said?

7. **Transparency.** Are there things you are hiding from your spouse? Things that if you were to say, "What do you think about this, honey?" your spouse would be concerned or hurt? How can you cultivate an atmosphere of transparency in your marriage so your trust in each other grows, fortified by your honesty with each other?

8. **Forgiveness.** Is there someone in your life who you have not yet forgiven? (This might be your spouse or someone else.) Fill in this chart:

Person	Offense	Judgment	Vow	Effect On Me	Person's Debt
Who was it?	What did they do?	What did you decide about this person because of what they did?	What did you tell yourself would never happen again as a result?	How has that inner vow affected you throughout your life?	What are you holding on to that the offending person still "owes" you?

After you have completed this chart, write your own forgiveness statement. Here is the example I give to coaching clients. Take the example, but add your own words so that it will fit your individual circumstances. You might even want to include Bible verses that speak of forgiveness.

Today, I choose to forgive ___(name)___. I choose to release him/her from the debt s/he owes me, which is _____. I realize that by holding on to this debt, I have restricted my own freedom to live a full life. I choose instead to release him/her from this debt so I can be free. ___(Name)___, I forgive you and I release you from the debt you owe me.

Element 7: Creativity

"To live a creative life, we must lose our fear of being wrong."
Joseph Chilton Pearce – Author

Our daughter is not crazy about spicy foods. It is probably my fault, at least in part, because when I was pregnant with her, I avoided anything and everything that could intensify my heartburn. In our family, however, we value multiculturalism. Eric and I have traveled extensively overseas, and believe there is a lot to be learned from exploring and experiencing other cultures. As a result, we vary our menu with foods from other countries.

Sometimes, much to the chagrin of our daughter, those foods are spicy. When she complains about the food, our typical response is something along the lines of, "If you want to travel around the world with us, you have to learn to eat new kinds of food." Since she is desperate to go to overseas, this response is usually sufficient to get her to pick up her fork with a big glass of water handy. While she doesn't necessarily love everything we make her try, she has a fairly extensive pallet for a child her age. Sushi currently sits at the top of her favorite foods list, a food I personally did not get to experience until adulthood.

How did you find out you liked your steak cooked medium-rare? Or that tiramisu is your favorite dessert? Or that you prefer to mix your mashed potatoes with gravy? At some point in your life, you tried it, and realized you liked it. Perhaps you learned your preferences around your family table growing up. Perhaps a person you really wanted to impress offered something new to try, and you took them up on the offer. I am responsible for the fact that Eric now drinks coffee. When we first started dating, I invited him into my world of addiction to caffeine and he has been lurking in darkened coffee shops with me ever since.

You will never know whether you enjoy something new unless you try it.

If you are aiming to have a sexual relationship with the same person for decades, then creativity, variety and spontaneity need to be tools in your tool belt. This doesn't mean you won't have your tried and true favorites. There is absolutely nothing wrong with having a favorite position, time of day, or type of lighting during your sexual encounters. My husband's favorite flavor of ice cream is vanilla. No lie. But the reason he knows this is his favorite is that he tried a bunch of other flavors. That is the difference between having a *favorite* and an *only*. Couples that have years of sex filled with *onlys* risk succumbing to the most subtle but deadly threats – boredom. Sex ceases to be fun. It becomes routine. And the marriage is at risk.

When we begin to recognize the importance of creativity, it points us right back to God.

The Great Creator

When I meet with clients, no matter their background, experiences or present state of relationship, I believe, as children of God, they were created in His image. We were created to reflect the majesty of God here on earth. As such, I believe people are naturally creative, imaginative and resourceful.

I love the children's movie *Tinker Bell*. Scene after scene is devoted to the diligence and care the fairies take to usher in the beauty of each new season. Any young girl can tell you there are garden fairies, water fairies, light fairies and, of course, tinker fairies. I find this movie captivating because, with childlike innocence, it breaks down the incredible detail and beauty in nature.

Of course, as adults, we do not believe Tinker Bell and her fairy friends are responsible for the dew on the grass in the morning, the changing of the leaves, or the first dusting of snow in winter. But this movie is a vivid reminder of the incredible detail God took when creating the earth.

We serve a God who embodies the essence of creativity. The details of creation are just one glimpse of His vast artistic abilities. He is also the God who created the stirrings and vision in the hearts of Monet, Michelangelo, and da Vinci. Whether they had a personal relationship with Him or not, they were created to reflect the creative expression – the limitless imagination and profound insightfulness of God. Their works of art and accomplishments were mere tastes of what we are designed to dream, imagine and invent.

This natural tendency to be imaginative, creative and resourceful should extend to our sexual expression with our spouses. When we shut down this aspect of God in our most intimate moments with each other, we deny one of His most fundamental and obvious gifts.

The Power of Veto

I meet a lot of people who, out of fear, shut down any creativity in their sexual relationship. Often, when I inquire about the reasons for this inaction, I am given a reason such as, "It just doesn't feel right." Usually, I am given this response by one spouse to justify his/her refusal to try anything different than what the couple has done for their entire marriage. Furthermore, this excuse is often used to cover up insecurities such as lack of biblical understanding, shame or guilt about sex, fear of vulnerability, perfectionism, mistrust in the relationship, lack of anatomical knowledge, and so forth.

However, the refusal to venture into any areas of creativity deadens sexual intimacy. Just as the Low Desire Spouse holds the power of veto on the amount of sex in a couple's relationship, so does the person who says no to creativity. The husband or wife who refuses to accept an invitation from his/her spouse into something new shuts down and aborts the process of deepening intimacy.

One of my clients came to me because her husband was uncertain he still wanted to be married after decades together. His love language was physical touch, and yet their sex life together had been marked with long stretches of inactivity. Over the years, the rejection this man felt piled up until he was no longer certain he was with the right woman. During one of their many conversations about fixing their marriage, he said something profound to her, and I believe his wisdom should be heeded by all of us in how we approach creativity in the bedroom. He said, "Just be open to my ideas. I care less if you say no than if you dismiss them without serious thought. Take some time, think about them, and then let me know. But please don't just say no."

As I mentioned in the chapter on Respect, Eric and I have an agreement that we will not refuse a genuine request from each other. When it comes to applying this rule to the creative aspect of our sexual relationship, we feel safe with this ground rule in our relationship for a number of reasons:

- We have a very clear sense of boundaries. We know the other person will never ask us to do something that violates our biblical understanding of Godly sexual interaction.
- We use I Corinthians 7:3-5 as the foundation for our sexual interactions and therefore consider each other first. If either of us was to slide into a "my way or the highway" stance, it would be a violation of these verses.
- We both do our shame homework so we recognize when our resistance is due to getting our shame buttons pushed. We know what shame feels like, know how to address it, and pursue healing quickly so it does not bog down our intimacy with each other.
- We have grown in our trust for each other over the years. Trust is the essential element that pairs with creativity. As we deepen our trust, we are more responsive to our spouses' desire to be creative.

Slowing Down

Sometimes I meet with clients who are not resistant to creativity because it triggers their shame or insecurities, but rather who are simply exhausted. For these people, the idea of adding "be creative" to their list is overwhelming. I understand this sentiment. I have said it before, and will say it again. The vast majority of us live a breakneck speed in life. We rush from one activity to another with barely a moment to pause and reflect.

My husband, God bless him, has the unique ability to home in on the precious moments in the midst of chaos. Recently, we were driving together and I was nattering away about something trivial when he suddenly interrupted me. "Look! The trees are lining the street and we can see all the way into the city!" The view – once I stopped long enough to experience it – was truly breathtaking.

At that moment, I paused and reflected on the lives our forefathers lived. Had they been driving down that street with the beautiful fall trees, they most likely would have been walking or in a horse-drawn buggy. Instead of taking ten minutes to get to the grocery store, it would have taken at least thirty. There would have been no radio or distractions. They would have had time to think and reflect.

Our modern pace of life drains us of the ability to be creative. If we are constantly running on empty, finding space for creativity is daunting. The only solution to getting our tanks filled back up is to set aside time to check in with the ultimate source of creativity.

Morning Pages

Over the years, I have realized that my place of meeting the Great Creator is done on my "morning pages." I developed this practice when going through the book *The Artist's Way*,[1] and it has revolutionized my thinking on quiet times with God. For years, I struggled with the concept of reading a verse and then sitting silently. I did it because I believed it was an important discipline in my Christian walk, but it was very difficult for me. And while I still believe that meditating on the Word of God is an important exercise, and one I still pursue, it is not the way I construct my daily quiet times anymore.

Instead, each morning, I wake up and write three pages. I do not edit what I write – I just dump all my thoughts onto the page. They are my words, unfiltered, to God. Usually, the first page or two is full of clutter. It contains my fears about the day, my concerns for my family, my anxiety about the sheer volume of work I have to wade through in the next ten hours. I write about relationship hiccups, problems I am trying to solve, frustrations I battle.

And then, the fog clears. As I write, my hand is active, my mind is focused, and my heart is open to hear God. I clear the thoughts in my head by putting them down on paper, and in the process I make the space for God to speak. Usually by my third page, I am reminded to call a friend who is hurting, nudged to memorize a verse that is significant for this season in my life, given gentle reproaches about my parenting style, reminded of ways to love my husband, and discover an abundance of creativity. Most of my articles, chapters and talks have been written, or at the very least started, in my morning pages.

I believe this exercise of slowing down is crucial if we are to hear the promptings of God in our journey of sexual intimacy. Often, when we ask the Great Creator for help in our personal lives, we do not recognize it when He speaks. In part, this is due to the fact that we do not silence the chatter from our lives so we can get quiet enough to hear Him.

When we believe our God desires creative expression in every area of our lives, and when we trust Him enough to be real in our relationships, we begin to soften to the concept of creativity in the bedroom.

Getting Started

Once we come to the place where we recognize that creativity is essential for the long-term health of our relationships, the question becomes, "What can I do to be creative?" As you ask yourself this question, remember marriage is a marathon, not a sprint, and so you must set realistic goals. I usually encourage couples to try one new thing each month. The husband can choose one month, and then the wife can choose the next. Set aside the time you need to set yourselves up for success. Do your research ahead of time (so you know what you are going to try), make sure the kids are taken care of (this is a great time to send them to Grandma's house), and get ready (buy, acquire, make, set up anything you need for your new thing).

As you take the plunge into something new, always try your new thing twice. (The exception to this rule is if you experience pain.) The first time can be strained under ludicrous expectations and the task of navigating the technical details. This is normal. Embrace the concept of practice sex (if you have forgotten it, go back to the Myth-Busting chapter), and learn together. Most importantly, be willing to make mistakes. Practice is the goal, rather than perfection.

If you fall in love with the new position, time of day or accoutrement, then congratulate yourselves. You can add this item to your expanding list of intimate expressions with each other. If, however, you hate this new experience, give yourselves a break. Not everything is for everyone. You are in the process of developing a deep intimacy that reflects the personality of your relationship. Now you have more knowledge of what does not work for the two of you.

On this note, however, it is worth adding a reminder that we change (emotionally, intellectually and physically) over time. Something you enjoyed together in your thirties might not work so well in your fifties. Conversely, something that you disliked in your thirties might bring a high degree of pleasure and enjoyment in your fifties. Keep an open mind during your adventure together.

Avenues of Creativity

The avenues to creativity in the bedroom are vast and ever expanding. As you read through the rest of this chapter, keep in mind this is just a sample of what is available, and you can continue to do research on your own.

Positions

Whenever I speak to couples about the concept of creativity, the first thing they talk about is different sexual positions. Perhaps we have been culturally indoctrinated to believe that a new position in the bedroom is the height of creativity, or perhaps it is just the most basic and fundamental way couples branch out to spice up their sex life. Regardless, there is no doubt that there is a lot of material on positions. In fact, the oldest sex manual in the world is the Chinese *Handbooks of Sex* written five thousand years ago by Emperor Huang-Ti.[2]

Over the centuries, men and women have been trying all sorts of positions and giving them interesting names. Here are a few:

Viennese Oyster. The Amazon. The Hammock. Reverse Spoon. The Snow Plow. The Butterfly Effect. The Rickshaw. The Happy Landing. Yin-Yang. The Three O'clock Appointment. The Slinky. The Splitter. The Lazy Dog.

And yet, despite the wide variety of options we have imagined, conceived and invented, couples still report their favorites to be:

- Man on top (Missionary Position)
- Woman on top (Cowgirl)
- Rear-entry position (Doggie-Style)

Now, there are obvious advantages to these positions. In the Doggie-Style position, a husband is able to view his wife from behind, which can be very visually stimulating. Women also enjoy this position because it allows for deep penetration and G-spot stimulation. In the Cowgirl position, a wife can often control the thrusting, as well as receive adequate stimulation to the clitoris, so she can have an orgasm. Furthermore, in this position, a husband is able to see his wife's body stretching out above him. Finally, the Missionary Position is popular for its intimacy as the couple is face to face with a high degree of body contact. Although only about 25 percent of women report they can orgasm through this position, they still rank it as a favorite.[3]

Experimenting with new positions wards off boredom, allows you to see each other in different ways (literally and figuratively), and gives you the opportunity to experience new avenues to pleasure. You can also feel new sensations during intercourse, extend the amount of time you are enjoying intercourse, find different ways to orgasm (by finding your G-spot, for example) and explore new perspectives (sight and touch).

When you are ready to move on to new positions, there are numerous books and websites devoted to enlightening people on their options. When I research these books, I look for those with two elements. First, I want sufficient detail so trying a new position doesn't turn into a completely frustrating endeavor. Second, I want to find books that do not have live couples photographed for the purposes of demonstration. There are plenty of books on the market that have tastefully drawn diagrams, or have excellent explanations without any pictures. (For some suggestions, go to the Resources tab on www.erynfaye.com.)

Timing

The time of day or night you engage in sex is a great way to inject creativity into your relationship. Most couples fall into a pattern in which they have sex at the same time, every time. A simple way to try something new is to change that up.

Here are some ideas:

- Wake up half an hour early and have morning sex. An orgasm is a great way to start your day on a good note. Note: You might need to go to bed a bit earlier the night before to make this happen, so plan ahead.
- Meet your spouse for lunch while the kids are in school and take him/her to a hotel instead. One of my clients did this for her husband's birthday one year. She decided that men having affairs got to have the excitement of stealing away to a hotel for sex in the middle of the day, and why should her husband miss out on that fun because he was faithful?
- If you want to meet your spouse for "lunch" but have small children at home, see if a friend will babysit for a few hours so you can sneak away. Then, return the favor at a later date.
- Many couples will take a "nap" on the weekends and sneak off to have sex in the middle of the afternoon. Note: Please lock your bedroom door as not to traumatize any inquisitive children.
- Put the kids to bed at night and then have sex within the next half hour. Waiting until you both retire to bed usually means you will both be too tired. So have sex and then watch your favorite TV show. If you have older children who retire after you, lock the door and be quiet. For some couples, the thrill of having to be secretive can be its own form of aphrodisiac.
- Try the middle of the night. One client would get up in the middle of the night to feed her infant, and then wake her husband up on her way back to bed for a quickie.

Setting and Location

In the popular movie, *When Harry Met Sally*, Sally comments that she and her boyfriend had decided not to have kids so they would never be held back from having passionate sex on the kitchen floor – but then they never had sex there anyways. Most of the time couples stick to the bed when having sex. Sometimes this is solely for comfort. Older clients have noted that their backs can't handle the kitchen table anymore. But other times the bed is just a rut that couples fall into.

Why is vacation sex the best? You have no choice but to change the setting and the location of where you are having sex. The bed in this new place is not intrinsically associated with getting up in the middle of the night with the kids – it is new and fresh. We don't look around and see all the chores to be done. And this injects life. It makes us feel more relaxed.

Change in location also increases the possibility of getting caught. Believe it or not, this is an aphrodisiac to many couples. The idea that they are doing something forbidden brings a spark back into what was previously absent. One couple told me one of their favorite experiences was in their walk-in closet while they were packing their house to move. It was spontaneous, it was different, and they had to be quiet so other members of the household didn't catch them. All this created an air of excitement that had been previously lacking in their marriage.

When was the last time you had a passionate kiss in an elevator? On your couch? On the floor in front of the fireplace? Outdoors? In your closet? The dressing room of your local mall? The back seat of your car? Perhaps it is time to write a list with your spouse of places you always imagined.

Length of Time

Once when teaching my course, I was speaking to a group of pastors and their spouses. As I began to talk about the concept of *making love* versus having a *quickie*, one woman called out, "Sometimes you just need a nice, light snack!" The room dissolved into laughter and even the most shy in the room were giggling in approval.

As I mentioned earlier, one of the common complaints I hear is the woman wants to "make love" and feels her husband just wants to have "a quickie." The former evokes images of a couple looking into each other's eyes and kissing deeply, while the latter conjures up the picture of getting pinned against the wall and being taken right there and then. Both can be deeply passionate, just different forms of expressing the passion.

Sometimes sex will be a deep, soul-connecting intimacy with our spouse. Other times it will just be a way to experience pleasure together quickly. Sometimes it will be a two-hour encounter. Sometimes it won't last ten minutes. Sometimes it will be long and luxurious. Other times it will be fast and frantic. Sometimes both spouses will walk away having experienced orgasm. Other times the focus is on one person alone.

Difficulty arises, however, when couples fall into a rut of believing that it has to be one or the other – all the time. I have seen husbands refuse to acknowledge the need to make love, and met wives who insist each and every sexual encounter *must* be making love. A dogmatic adherence to one or the other undermines true intimacy. A steady diet of quickies denies the concepts of exploration, creativity and deep communication because, amongst other reasons, there is simply no time to venture into those areas. On the other hand, if couples only have sex when they have time to make love, they might never get to it out of sheer busyness.

Both types of sex build intimacy if they are done in balance. Sometimes you need a snack – sometimes you need a gourmet meal.

Bedroom Accoutrements

When I chat with couples, I define bedroom accoutrements as anything they bring, besides their own bodies, to enhance the experience of sex with their spouses. With this definition, you could obviously create a very long list. In fact, I may neglect to mention your favorite. Consider the following as a starter list. As you develop your list, pick activities that incorporate all the senses. Frequently, we focus on one or two, but overlook the others.

Sight

- **Lighting.** According to one study, 76 percent of men want the lights on versus 36 percent of women when they are having sex.[4] Because men are highly stimulated visually, they want to see their wives during sex. As such, the lighting you choose can increase the variety and creativity of your expression together. If you are a woman who feels awkward or uncomfortable about your body, try different forms of lighting. You do not have to be stuck with only two options – lights on or off. Instead, install a dimmer switch, use candles, or pick a softer light bulb for your bedside table lamp.

- **Mirrors.** This is a creative way to heighten your sense of sight in the bedroom. You will be able to see each other from angles you have never seen before. Even if you have body image issues (which we will discuss later in the Attraction chapter), I promise you that is not what your spouse is focused on.

- **Lingerie.** Many men love the look of their wives in lingerie. It might not stay on for long, but they enjoy it while it lasts. When I met with Christine Morton, the lingerie designer behind the brand Christine,[5] she emphasized that you must try on the lingerie to decide if it is for you. There is no way to tell how something will look without going into the fitting room and trying it on. Many designers strive to create a line that fits women of all shapes and sizes, so you can find something perfect for you.

- **Blindfolds.** Just as enhancing each other's visual stimulation can be erotic, so can removing that sense of sight with an item such as a blindfold. This is often an exercise I will assign to couples so they can practice trust. One spouse wears the blindfold while the other browses his/her body. Because the person with the blindfold cannot see what is coming next, it forces him/her to pay full attention to the sensations, and builds his/her sense of trust when s/he cannot be in control of the experience. Often couples like to allow one spouse to be blindfolded first, and then switch so that both parties can enjoy the pleasure of being explored.

Taste

- **Food.** When was the last time you brought chocolate pudding to bed? Or strawberries? Or grapes? Or whipping cream? Adding food to the mix is a fantastic way of incorporating your sense of taste. Try eating a strawberry and then kissing your wife. Or licking that pudding off your husband. Note: Do not put any item containing sugar in the vagina as this can lead to irritation and infection. Outside that little guideline, get creative.

- **Aphrodisiacs.** These are foods that increase the libido of the person consuming them. Oysters, coffee, chocolate, chilies, avocados, black beans, strawberries, and more have all been proclaimed foods that will satisfy your appetite for more than just food. If this is something that interests you, there are aphrodisiac cookbooks on the market to help you prepare these delights.[6] This puts a whole new twist on the idea of a five-course meal!
- **Edibles.** Retailers design these items specifically for the sexual experience. Often they come in a gel or lotion. They can be used for "kissable" massages or can be applied to the genital area. Sometimes the flavor is accompanied with a tingling sensation that helps speed up the arousal process. Again, do not put anything sugar based inside the vagina.

Touch

- **Water.** When you add water to your experience, the sensations of sex change. Bodies feel slicker. They are easier to slide over. You feel things differently than you do on dry land. This is also a great option for women who are chronically cold. Jumping into a warm shower and enjoying sex there ensures he can see you (because you are no longer bundled under layers of bedding), but you will be able to stay warm.
- **Bedroom toys.** I have covered this topic at greater length in the Pleasure chapter. These items are great options for couples who want to increase their odds of face-to-face simultaneous orgasms, explore new types of orgasm (such as the G-spot), prolong the period of a husband's erection, help a wife orgasm faster (or at all), or just to add variety.
- **Lubricants.** Having a good lubricant takes the pressure off your sexual relationship. If a husband is ready to have sex, and his wife's body is not yet ready for intercourse, she can be confident sex will not be painful. Just knowing this will often help her relax enough to enjoy the experience.
  - **Textures.** The sense of touch can be enhanced by something as simple as changing the sheets and trying a new kind of fabric. Silk, satin, and flannel have different feels and add new sensations.

Sound

- **Music.** Having a playlist of songs that remind you of your lover is always a great idea because it is easy to keep them in mind throughout the day. Whenever I hear a Bob Marley song, I think of Eric because Marley's music was a favorite at the restaurant we frequented during our honeymoon. Furthermore, putting on the playlist as background music when you are together is a great way to get into the mood. It also has the added bonus of drowning out any noise the two of you are making if there are other people in the house.
- **Ocean or nature sounds.** This is an idea that comes up for my clients frequently. Couples have told me that having a playlist of ocean sounds, water crashing on a beach, or birds singing, will remind them of a vacation they had together. They are transported to a romantic, intimate time when they hear the music. Even if these sounds don't work for you, there might be some similar sound that reminds you of sexy times you had together.

Smell

- **Aphrodisiacs.** It might surprise you to learn that a powerful aspect of our arousal process is our sense of smell. One study showed that the smell of pumpkin pie, doughnuts, black licorice and lavender increased blood flow to the penis (some by as much as 40 percent.)[7] The most commonly reported aphrodisiac for women, however, is the smell of their husband's shirt. Men love the smell of their wife's perfume. Paying attention to what your spouse loves to smell is important as you open up the avenues to intimacy.
- **Pheromones.** Pheromones are the scents that animals emit in order to sexually attract a mate. While it is debatable whether humans give off pheromones as defined in the animal kingdom (the field of research is in its infancy), there is some evidence that we too emit chemicals of attraction in our sweat and skin cells. Some perfumes and bath products claim to have pheromones in a bottle. Whether or not it is a marketing ploy, it might be a fun avenue for the two of you to explore and see if it increases your enjoyment of each other.

Final Thoughts

For couples who have never integrated creativity into the bedroom, or for those who are still novices in this area, my advice is to go slowly. You are building a sexual relationship that will last for a lifetime, so do not feel any pressure to rush. Instead, start with something that sounds interesting but is not intimidating.

After you have had your practice sex with this new experience, talk about it as a couple. Here are some conversation starters:

- What did you like about this new experience?
- Did you experience new pleasure, greater intimacy with me, or have more fun?
- Was there anything you didn't like?
- If so, what was it and why did you not like it?
- How could we make this better for next time?
- Is it going on our "favorites" list or the "been there, done that" list?

Ask open-ended questions and then listen carefully to each other's perspectives. Sometimes, the communication about the experience is just as important – in fact, sometimes more important – than the experience itself.

Bedwork: Creativity

This week, answer at least two questions. If you have a strong emotional reaction to the questions, pick the one you love and the one you hate. If you do not have a strong reaction, pick an exercise your spouse will appreciate, or give them home field advantage. Don't forget to record your PSA.

1. **Resistance.** If you are resistant to the concept of creativity, spend time this week to journal about it. As you write, ask yourself:
   - Why am I resistant to this concept?
   - What is in my past, the way I was raised, the messages I was taught which hinder me from creative expression with my spouse?
   - What makes me afraid when I think of the subject of creativity? What is the source of my fear?
   - Are those messages, fears and concerns that I have rooted in biblical truth?
   - If I am dealing with shame (rather than genuine conviction), to whom can I tell my story and receive an empathetic and compassionate response?
   - What baby steps can I take to slowly incorporate creativity into my relationship?

2. **Slowing Down.** Carve out twenty to thirty minutes in your day to intentionally get quiet and write three pages. This exercise works best when you do it first thing in the morning (get up a bit earlier if you have to), but if this is impractical for you, then choose another time. Before you begin to write, ask God for the insight you need in your life and marriage, and trust Him to show up.

3. **Clarification of Boundaries.** Either separately or together, write out your list of things you do not want to try in the bedroom. Next to each item, write why you will not try it. For example, you might write, "I won't have a threesome because I believe it violates the biblical basis of a healthy marriage." Once the two of you know clearly what you will not try, and the reasons why, there is a greater sense of safety in the bedroom to ask for new avenues of creativity.

4. **Communication.** Go on a date with your spouse to talk about the creativity in your love life. Remember to ask open-ended questions and then listen to the answers without interruption. Here are some sample questions:
   - What was the most appealing part of this chapter for you? Why?
   - Is there anything you have thought of trying that we haven't yet explored?
   - What excites you the most about the idea of incorporating more creativity into our sex life? Why? What scares you the most? Why?

- Did this chapter remind you of things we used to do but have neglected over the years?
- Is there anything we used to do that we should try again?

5. **Creative Experience.** Pick a new position, time of day, or place to have sex and try it. If you love it, add it to your list of favorites together. If you don't, then put it on the "been there, done that" list. Regardless of which list it lands on, congratulate yourself on being creative in your love life this week, and talk about the experience using the conversation starters in the conclusion of this chapter.

6. **Creative Experience.** Try bringing something as a new accoutrement into the bedroom. Have you always wanted to try satin sheets? Can you soften the lighting in your room so you aren't stuck with on and off as your only options? Would your spouse enjoy his/her favorite food served in bed? Is there a piece of lingerie you have been eyeing that you might be able to buy as a surprise? Experiment with this new experience and then talk about it afterwards, using the conversation starters in the Conclusion.

7. **Calendar.** Sit down as a couple and schedule your time to try something new each month. When will you have a date night, and use that night as a time to incorporate something new into your sex life? Plan out your dates, and decide which spouse will be in charge of picking the "something new" each month. Sometimes you might want to switch back and forth each month (he chooses this month, she chooses next, etc.), but have your personal schedules dictate what works best for you as a couple.

Element 8: Passion

"Nothing great in the world has ever been accomplished without passion."
Georg Wilhelm Friedrich Hegel – Philosopher

In the movie *The Bridges of Madison County*, Meryl Streep plays Francesca Johnson, a lonely woman who has a weekend-long affair with a photojournalist while her family is out of town. Throughout the entirety of the film, the director projects the stereotypical depiction of a passionless marriage pitted against the naively romanticized intensity of an affair. The message is clear. According to Hollywood, passion cannot survive within marriage. It is reserved for longing glances, secretive caresses and torrid affairs.

And yet, a desire for passion beats within the heart of every marriage I have ever encountered. This desire runs so deep that it frequently spills over into coaching sessions, speaking engagements and personal conversations with men and women.

When Doug and Marlene came to see me, Doug was in agony. This fully capable businessman, who no doubt could settle lucrative deals in his sleep, sat on my couch in tears. "I want her to feel passion for me again." Marlene looked at him sympathetically, but emotionally had checked out of the marriage months before. Years of misunderstanding and turmoil had drained the life out of her, and it was only her faith that kept her hanging on. The passion was gone.

In one study on divorce, 80 percent of couples said they still loved each other, but none of them had any passion for each other anymore.[1] Losing the passion is a huge fear for couples today. They fear if the passion is gone, they will never get it back, and they will be trapped in passionless marriages. It causes them terrible anxiety.

What's So Special about Passion?

Over the years, I have had the privilege of talking to thousands of men and women about passion, sensuality and sexuality. In all of these conversations, the best way I have heard the word defined was by a woman in California. She said to me, "Passion is what allows me to breathe, and yet it is passion that takes my breath away."

In that simple, yet profound statement, she summed up the two sides of passion. On one hand, it is the essence of life because it makes us feel alive and connected. It underpins our hopes and dreams. It is the *why* to our *what* and *how*. It is the inner compass we were given so we won't lose our way on the journey of life. It points to the unique direction we are supposed to go.

The poet Henry David Thoreau describes it: "I went into the woods because I wanted to live deliberately. I wanted to live deep and suck out all the marrow of life, to put to rout all that was not life; and not, when I came to die, discover that I had not lived." The modern-day bard, Jon Bon Jovi, described it as waking up to "French kiss the morning."[2] Passion drove David to dance nearly naked before the Lord in front of all of Israel.[3] It was passion at work within Bilbo Baggins when he felt the Tookish part of him waking up as the dwarves were singing in his home.[4] The boys of *Dead Poets Society* answered the call of passion as they stood on their desks reciting "Oh Captain! My Captain!"[5]

Passion allows us to breathe.

But passion can also be a lightning bolt that hits us out of the blue. It is that moment when you are blown away by a performance or burst into tears while listening to a song on the radio. It is that "ah-ha" moment where everything is just snaps into focus and is crystal clear. A look across the room that just makes your knees weak. Almásy and Katherine[6] embracing in a side corridor of the dance hall. Edward and Bella[7] lying next to each other in the middle of a vast, lush field.

Passion takes our breath away.

Unfortunately, we often allow it to drop to the bottom of our priority list. It gets drowned out by the details of life. We sacrifice it on the altar of the convenient, the immediate, the proper, the conventional and the expected.

One of my professional challenges is teaching couples how to make the transition from the roles they play during the day (mother, father, sister, brother, daughter, son, friend, employee, employer, neighbor) to the roles of sexy, passionate men and women at night. We pour our energies into the people and tasks around us all day long. A boss needs something done, and we try to get it done efficiently and with excellence. A friend calls up sobbing because her teenager is doing drugs, and we listen and empathize. A co-worker is on the verge of having an affair because his home life is boring, predictable and lonely, and we invest time over lunch trying to convince him why this isn't such a good idea.

When we return home, our children need us to help with homework, or kiss their boo-boos, or drive them to their games or dance classes. Later, we feed, bathe and tuck them into bed. And then, tired and worn out, we stumble into the bedroom at night, and look at our spouses, who may or may not even like us at the moment. Passion is the furthest thing from our minds.

And so now it is simpler to make sure little Susie gets to school on time than to realize that something you dreamed of in your own childhood has been neglected for years. It is safer to plop down in front of the tube and see other people's passions play out onscreen than giving life to your own passions. It is easier to become roommates with your spouse, rather than putting in the effort to reignite the spark that drew you together in the first place.

Passion does not have to disappear. But it is completely ludicrous to expect that we can squelch our passions in life – living only to fulfill all our duties – and still have passion in the bedroom. You cannot live in a state of perpetual physical and emotional burnout and expect to experience waves of passion with your spouse. Passion is not a light you can turn on and off as you please.

Rather, it is like a pot of water on the stove. If the water is cold, it is going to take a lot of time, energy and effort to get it to boiling. However, if it is simmering, getting it to boiling is easy. So, if you want hot, steamy passion at night, you have to be looking for and cultivating it during the day.

If it is nurtured, it will stay alive. The author Erwin McManus puts it this way: "The better world you keep waiting for needs you to accept your life's calling and responsibility, and then to create it."[8] Passion gives you clues about your calling, but you must take action to see it happen.

What's Your Cause?™

My husband is a professional fundraiser. His bread and butter comes from getting people to open their wallets and give money to his organization. As such, he absolutely loathes sitting down on an airplane and hearing the question, "So, what do you do?" He has often confided to me that the only response he could give that would be worse was if he were a pastor. People pick up their books or computers with extreme haste once they find out what Eric does.

He now takes a different approach to these awkward conversations. When people begin to inquire about him, he responds by saying, "I change the world. What do you deeply and passionately care about?" Eric is not asking to be flippant – rather, he believes we are all called to care about something. Since we are created in the image of God, we reflect parts of God's heart for the world. We are designed to believe in, care about and champion a cause that is important to God.

When Eric asks this question, he is tapping into our essence as humans. Why are we here? What were we designed for? What does God want for us in this life? How should we then act?

In fact, those are such important questions that he wove them into the ethos of his organization and entitled the campaign, "What's Your Cause?" Instead of approaching fundraising as an expert on hunger and poverty, paternalistically telling people what they *should* care about, Eric now invites them into conversation about what God is urging them to care about.

I meet people all the time who have no answer to Eric's questions. If we want to label this place in life, we call it mid-life crisis. Men and women come to me all the time with no sense of purpose in life. For so many years, they have plugged away at life and fulfilled all their obligations, dutifully checking off their to-do lists – finish school, get a job, get married, have kids. Then they wake up one morning and realize they have no passion. "Why am I here? What is my purpose? What am I doing with my life?" As they begin to answer these questions, the tragedy is these men and women often come to the conclusion that their paths no longer include their spouses.

In order to have a relationship that spans a lifetime, we have to stoke the flames of passion together, and that begins by paying attention to who we were created to be as individuals, as well as a couple. When couples have a deep-seated sense of purpose and passion about their individual callings, and this purpose extends to their calling as a couple, they are able to tend to the fire of passion so it does not go out.

To do this, we must begin with some fundamental questions.

What Do You Want? Who Are You?

I must confess I am a bit of a science fiction and fantasy nut. I grew up nursed on stories from The Chronicles of Narnia, The Lord of the Rings, the Star Wars trilogy, and John White's The Archives of Anthropos series. My mother and I would have lengthy conversations about these stories, and I am still a sucker for the rich imagination of worlds beyond our own.

As such, one of my favorite TV series was *Babylon 5*. Written by J. Michael Straczynski, the story paints a picture of life hundreds of years in the future. Mankind has discovered that many other species exist, and the Babylon 5 project is a huge space station where all races can come together to trade, negotiate and pave the way for peace.

As ambassadors from the various colonies negotiate, it becomes clear there are members of powerful ancient races who hover in the background, choosing whether or not to interfere with the younger races. To simplify the complex storyline, there are two types of ancients. The good guys are the Vorlons, and the bad guys are the Shadows.

When the Shadows interact with other races, they do so with the question, "What do you want?" Fundamentally, they are calling upon the person's desires for success, acquisition and power. These characters always remind me of the serpent in the Garden of Eden – luring weak beings to give in to their foolish impulses.

On the other hand, the Vorlons ask, "Who are you?" In this, they call forth the unique design and identity of the person. It is only once you know who you are that you will discern your purpose and thereby direction in life.

Many people make the mistake of thinking that passion is the answer to the Shadows' question when, in fact, discovering passion lies in the heart of the Vorlons' question. Passion is the compass that points to your purpose in life. It tells you how you were created. It lets you know who you were meant to be. It is your clue to why you are on this earth. If you feel passion, stop and pay attention, because it is a clue to how God designed you.

Awakening Sexual Passion

The development of the passionate side of you emanates from within, as you understand who you are created to be, but spreads to your relationship. As you begin to move from translating your understanding of passion as an individual to the two of you as a couple, do not get the term *passion* confused with the hormones you experienced during the infatuation phase of your relationship. While you might encounter moments of euphoric high throughout your years together, most often the passion you feel for each other will be different than the initial buzz.

That is not to say, however, that you won't derive clues from those early days of your relationship. That chemical cocktail flooding your brain was not the only thing stoking your passions for each other in the early days. You reinforced your body's hormones by spending a lot of time with each other, touching each other frequently, being kind and considerate to each other, and sharing your hopes and dreams. Many couples are amazed that when they begin to reenact their actions from the early days, how quickly they once again feel passion for each other.

As you begin the process of nurturing passion in the bedroom, begin by asking:

- When do I feel passion for my spouse? Where am I? What am I doing? What am I saying? How am I acting? What am I wearing?
- What does my spouse do which brings out the passion in me? What does she say? What does he do? What is she wearing? How is he acting? (If you struggle to answer that question, what do you think s/he could do?)
- Think back to a time when you had passion. What were the circumstances of that time? What was different? Did you have more energy? Were the kids gone? Were you

on vacation? Had you just watched a romantic comedy? Was it a certain time of day or specific position? Had one of you just returned from a trip?

As you answer these questions, you will get insight into the unique blend of passion in your marriage. Furthermore, once you know what works, you can clear time and space so the circumstances under which you feel the most passion will arise more frequently.

Passion Comes In Different Forms

At one of my Passion Salons, one woman told the group that her favorite way to initiate sex is to tackle her husband and throw him to the ground. "Of course," she noted, "I have to make sure that all the kids' toys are out of the way first."

This type of passion is what I like to call "demonstrative passion." It says, "I want you right here, right now." There is no mistaking this woman's intentions when she jumps her husband. Demonstrative passion might look like pinning your wife to the wall and kissing her fervently. It might be dragging your husband out of the party early and not going straight home.

And yet, passion can present itself as a "quiet passion" as well. This passion runs deep, but does not look the same on the surface as demonstrative passion. There is a love scene in the movie *Out of Africa* that demonstrates this quiet passion very well. Robert Redford and Meryl Streep are beginning to have sex and he says to her, "Don't move." She responds, "But I want to move." The emotion is just as intense as the couple that is falling to the ground, but looks much different.

The wonder of a lifetime with one person is you can explore different types of passion and find your rhythm as a couple. It is true that passion will ebb and flow during various seasons of your relationship. If it has been too long since you felt the fire of passion, look back to a time when it existed. It existed then for a reason. The circumstances allowed passion the space to breathe. What were those circumstances? How can you duplicate them today?

Look for Whispers of Passion

For some people, passion does not come as a wave of intense emotion, but as a small voice even subtler than quiet passion. Sometimes people act like Elijah,[9] expecting an earthquake or powerful wind, but instead the answer comes as a gentle whisper. Dr. Pat Love, co-author of *Hot Monogamy*[10] suggests that people with chronic low desire may never feel earth-shattering passion. "If you wait for a tidal wave of passion to wash over you, you might wait a long, long time." Instead, she urges people, "When you feel the slightest pulse of desire, follow through on it."

If you believe you might be one of these people, then slow down, remove the clutter and actively look for fleeting thoughts. For you, "passion" might mean you realize your husband looks good today, or smells nice, or has a sweet smile. It might be a movie you watched that made you feel amorous. You might appreciate how good your wife looks in that shirt, or you have a passing thought of her alone – while the kids are at school. When you have these whispers of thoughts, take action. Use them as a catalyst to tell your spouse what you are thinking, reach out physically, or even initiate sex.

Warning: Passion Can Be Unstable

In Exodus, we are told the story of a young Moses. Even though he was raised in Pharaoh's household, Scripture is clear he was aware of his heritage, and felt a kinship with the Hebrew people.

As recounted in Acts 7:24 (NIV), one day, he went to watch his people and, "He saw one of them being mistreated by an Egyptian, so he went to his defense and avenged him by killing the Egyptian." What on earth possessed a man, who had every comfort and luxury in the world to kill another man? Passion.

Even though Moses had no clue what the calling on his life was when he watched the Egyptian administer the beating, he had a deep sense of passion about the protection of the Hebrew people. His reaction foreshadowed the mantle he would divinely receive a full forty years later. Part of what he was designed to be was triggered when he witnessed the injustice, and he lost control and killed someone.

If we were to sell passion in the stores, it would have an explosive symbol on it. Passion is a powerful compound that can be combustible.

In Dr. Gottman's research,[11] he discovered that couples with the most passion in their sex lives are the most "volatile" outside the bedroom too. They have a high degree of conflict, and yet they balance this with a high degree of physical affection. Surprisingly, these couples have a great chance of success in their relationship, as long as their acts of affection outweigh those of conflict and they don't fall prey to the Four Horsemen of the Apocalypse.

When you have passion in your life, it spills over into the bedroom. You cannot be dead to passion in one area and expect to have it in abundance in others. It doesn't work like that. If you are a passionate person, it will emanate from you and manifest itself in every area. This might not look neat and tidy all the time.

At one of sessions I was teaching, a pastor spoke lovingly about his wife. He was fully aware she was vocal, gutsy, fearless and passionate in everything she did and said. In some church cultures, this can be quite a liability for the pastor and his wife. It can cause problems, offend people and be a bit messy. And yet, this man said, "I love my wife the way she is. I would never try to change her." He intuitively understood that to damper her passion would affect all areas of her life.

Rather than trying to squelch passion, we should teach people how to properly manage it. For instance, if you are a couple that Dr. Gottman would term as "volatile," you need to understand that research indicates you need to have five acts of affection for every act of conflict. If you are a couple who fights frequently (or even if you rarely fight), you need to have a list of fair fighting rules so your conflict does not stray into contempt, criticism, defensiveness or stonewalling. If you are outspoken about the callings God has given you, you might need to become adept at political savvy skills as well. As we grow to understand our passion and nurture it, we can become more mature in managing it.

Nurturing Passion

To stay alive, passion must be nurtured. If it has been so long since you paid heed to the inner compass of your passion, you might need some help rediscovering it. Here are some tips as you go on this journey.

Remember Your Childhood

Here is the encouraging part of discovering passion – it has always been with you. You may have buried it deep down years ago because it was inconvenient to your life's plan, or maybe your parents didn't like the activities you were passionate about. Regardless of what caused you to stash it away, it is still there.

In his book *The Windows of the Soul*,[12] Ken Gire states that the person God created you to be is echoed in the hallways of your youth. What did you love to do as a child? What did you play with? What were your favorite toys and activities? What consumed hours of your free time? What did you read? What brought you joy? These are all clues to the person God designed you to be.

I have a dear friend who grew up playing with LEGO®. While all the other little girls were dressing their dolls, Jennifer was constructing structures. When she was old enough to discover LEGO® Mindstorms® (robotic LEGO®), she thought she had died and gone to heaven. She grew up to be a successful engineer, meticulously analyzing the construct of computers to build a better world around her. Her childhood pleasures led to a solid understanding and development of her talents, capabilities and giftings.

The calling on your life is not alien to you. In fact, it should bring you great joy. The psalmist jubilantly expresses, "I praise you because I am fearfully and wonderfully made."[13] This is not a guy who is ticked off with how he has been designed. Instead, he embraces it because it emanates from his very soul.

Slow Down

One of the greatest battles we fight as modern human beings is the war waged on our time. When we refuse to carve out time to slow down, be quiet and listen to our God, we lose touch with a piece of our souls. The modern pace at which we live is not healthy. We are chronically exhausted, hyperstimulated and overmedicated in our attempts to keep up. This is not how we were designed to live. This is not the place from which we can make the greatest impact on our world.

Discovering your passion entails slowing down. You must choose to carve out time in your day to be alone and quiet. You must "Be still and know that I am God."[14] As you make time to connect with the Creator of the universe, you will peel back the layers that cover your true calling in life.

Furthermore, as you go about your day, do so at a pace in which you can see and truly recognize the details. I am already teaching my eight-year-old how to look for passion in her life. I use the term "spark" because it is a word that resonates with her. When she comes home from school, I will often ask her, "Riley, did you discover any sparks today?" As she learns to go about her day on the lookout for sparks, she is discovering more and more who she is designed to be. As I ask her questions, I also gain insight on this marvelous creation entrusted to me. As adults – and as spouses – we need to cultivate this practice as well.

What is really going on in your world? What gives you a spark? What energizes you? How are people responding to you? Are you making an impact? What brings you joy?

Simplify

In order to slow down enough to answer these questions, you might need to simplify your life. Let's face it: There are a lot of things in life that compete for our attention. For most of us, if we were to accept every invitation we were extended, we would be occupied about one hundred hours a day. (Yes, this is impossible.) However, when we know what we are about and what we are called to, we can deepen our focus by eliminating the clutter and drilling down to what is most important to us.

In his book *Small Footprint, Big Handprint*,[15] Tri Robinson teaches people how to simplify their life (footprint) so they can maximize the impact of their life on the world around them (handprint). As you get a clearer picture of your passions, you gain a better perspective on how God can use you. But often this entails some sacrifice. We like our stuff – even if the sheer amount of it is killing us – and it can be hard to let go.

When my clients take inventories of their lives to see what they can simplify, I ask them these three questions:

- What do I need to delegate or outsource?
- What do I need to give up?
- What do I need to ask for help with?

As you work through this exercise, you pave the way to focus on activities that truly reflect your values and passions.

Eric and I discovered this accidentally when we moved from British Columbia to Ontario. We now refer to the move as The Great Purge of 2010. We had been given a moving allowance that was, in our minds, quite generous, but when we got quotes from various moving companies, we realized we were three thousand pounds' worth of household items over our budget. We had a choice: pay more or shed weight. We chose the latter.

Some of those three thousand pounds were several TVs that we owned. They were old-school TVs and thus enormously heavy. To be honest, we had no intention of eliminating TV from our lives, but we just couldn't justify paying someone to haul those bulky things across the country. To this day, Eric will tell you he expected to get a flat screen of epic proportions the minute we moved into our new place.

However, once we reached Toronto, we found that we didn't miss TV as much as we thought. In fact, we had a whole lot more time with each other and our family than ever before. We went on lengthy walks together. We lingered over dinner longer. We invited people over to our home more often. We found other forms of entertainment.

When we cleared away the excess clutter, we were able to focus on the activities which furthered our purpose and calling in life.

Pay Attention to Your Spouse

Just like you, your spouse has passions. The more you understand, encourage and support these passions, the closer you two will be as a couple. There is something about a couple that has a clear sense of purpose together. It directs their choices, activities, parenting and finances. They also have a sense of peace that follows them because they are not battling with identifying their purpose – they already know it.

I met one such couple at a dinner party. As many of the people at the party did not know each other, the hostess asked each guest to share his/her personal story. It made for an extremely entertaining evening since all of us had made very different journeys in life to arrive at that same table.

One couple stood out for me. They had been married for nearly forty years and life had taken them all over Canada. They had very different pursuits and careers – he was a pastor and she was in the medical field – but it amazed me how they had been able to knit these differences together to create a marriage that had supported, and indeed enhanced, each other.

Sometimes, however, finding out what a spouse is passionate about can feel threatening. At one of my conferences, this topic sparked a lively debate between a husband and his wife. Evidently, he has a passion for motorcycle riding, and this pastime terrifies her. They have young children and she fears something harmful might happen to him.

There are times when your passion for a particular activity might need to be curbed for a season due to practical considerations. One of my clients' husbands wanted to become a bush pilot. Since the mortality rate for people in this profession is higher than she was comfortable with, she asked him to get his license once the kids were older. In the meantime, he found other ways to pursue the underlining source of his passion – adventure and travel.

Final Thoughts

You cannot expect to schedule passion into your day and have it arrive obediently if you have not created the circumstances for it to thrive. However, as you clear time and space, simplifying your life and homing in on what is truly important to each of you, you give sexual passion room to flourish. Passion, just like fire, needs air to breathe. You cannot stifle it and expect it to grow.

As couples begin to practice the skill set of creating space for sexual passion, I often recommend that they schedule time away from home. Take a vacation together without the kids. It can be a short time away – a weekend, for example – or a full week. Here is the primary ground rule: Do not pack tons of activities into your time together. Yes, schedule a hike, or a trip to an art gallery, or go to a concert or a sporting event – whatever you like to do as a couple. But do not fall into the trap of over-scheduling your time. Your objective during this trip is to reconnect as a couple, rediscover the joys of being together, and give passion a chance to emerge.

When you feel the whispers or the intensity of passion, take note. This is important. This is part of how the two of you connect this way. Once you know what works, you can create the circumstances necessary to rediscover it if it slides off your radar again.

Bedwork: Passion

PSA: _____

This week, answer at least two questions. If you have a strong emotional reaction to the questions, pick the one you love and the one you hate. If you do not have a strong reaction, pick an exercise your spouse will appreciate, or give them home field advantage. Don't forget to record your PSA.

1. **Childhood Passions.** Spend an hour at the park with a journal. Watch the kids on the playground and remember what you were like as a child. What did you dream about? What made you most happy? What did you want to be when you grew up? What captured your imagination? What did you find interesting? What did you play with? What do these things tell you about how God created you?

2. **Discovering Passion.** Watch your favorite movie. What do you love about it? Why? What draws you to its characters? Why do you like or hate them? How does this movie inspire you to live? Does it reflect anything you would like to emulate?

3. **Discovering Passion.** Listen to music that deeply moves you. Reflect on the meaning of the words or the rise and fall of the notes. What is it that evokes emotion within you? Why do you cry or laugh when you hear it? Not sure which song to choose? Here are some suggestions:
   - "I Hope You Dance" by Lee Ann Womack
   - Vivaldi's "Four Seasons"
   - "Love You Like a Love Song" by Selena Gomez
   - "God of This City" by Chris Tomlin
   - "Standing outside the Fire" by Garth Brooks
   - "Bed of Roses" by Bon Jovi
   - "The Sacrifice" by Michael Nyman (theme song to the movie *The Piano*)
   - "Just a Kiss" by Lady Antebellum
   - "Holy, Holy, Holy" by Reginald Heber
   - "Gonna Fly Now" (theme song to the movie *Rocky*).

4. **Passion with Your Spouse.** Remember your first date with your spouse. What did you enjoy the most? What did you laugh about together? Where did you go? Have you ever gone back to that place? What did you talk about? Why did you decide to go on a second date?

5. **What Question Are You Answering?** Have you gotten caught up in the question "What do you want?" If so, give some thought to the question "Who are you?" and journal about what you discover.

6. **Discovering Passion.** Park near the airport in a place where the planes are visible. Watch them taking off or landing and think about places you want to visit, things you want to see, and people you want to meet. (Hint: This makes a great date too!)

7. **Old Messages.** Think about the messages your parents gave you about passion. Was it important in your household? Were you told that you were being silly? Or did they open doors to help you explore your passions? How have you incorporated these messages into the way you think now? What are the messages you send to your children? What messages do you want to send?

8. **Calling As a Couple.** Sit down together and brainstorm what you feel called to as a couple. Why do you think God brought you together? What are the two of you passionate about as a couple? What is your cause? How can you simplify your lives and choose your activities wisely so you can make room for this passion to grow?

9. **Passion in Your Spouse.** Take a moment to think about your spouse's passions. What have you done to nurture it? Have you actively campaigned against it? Do you even know what his/her passions are? What type of person would your spouse be if s/he were fully living out his/her passions?

10. **Whispers of Passion.** What are some of the small whispers of passion you feel for your spouse? When have you felt them? What were the circumstances of the time? What can you do to actively pay attention to them when they happen in the future?

Element 9: Attraction

"All we've ever wanted is to look good naked / Hope that someone can take it.
God save me rejection from my reflection / I want perfection."
Robbie Williams – Singer-Songwriter

The room had gone completely silent. The fun banter of chitchat had abruptly died. Rachel's comment had stopped everyone cold. "I hate looking at myself in the mirror. I can't stand to see my reflection."

As she continued her story, her eyes filled with tears and her hands plucked nervously with her clothing. "I don't know how to be okay with myself. Does any woman really feel comfortable and grow to accept who she is?"

The group of women was quiet. The room was full of women of all shapes, sizes and ages. No one had an answer. Every one of them struggled with what Rachel was talking about. After all, if Rachel, who is a stunningly beautiful, thin and fashionable woman, has these hang-ups, what hope did the rest of us have?

According to researchers, appearance is a universal shame trigger.[1] Few other issues will make us feel so small and insignificant so quickly. And, contrary to popular opinion, it does not restrict itself to women. Men have these hang-ups too. They silently size themselves up in comparison to other men. They are secretly afraid their penises are too small, they have too much hair and their bellies are too big.

There is no doubt we live in a society that puts extremely demanding expectations on how we dress, groom ourselves, maintain our appearance and our weight. And under this constant pressure, most of us buckle and give in to feelings of insecurity, inadequacy and self-hatred. This is a problem.

However, there is another side of this issue that we don't like to talk about either. If resisting the ludicrous pressure to look a certain way takes courage, opening yourself up to discover what your partner finds attractive takes even more.

One of the Internet memes going around on Facebook was "Random Things About Me." Friends would write up lists about themselves and then tag other people – they would send their list to friends and request that they too make a list. It was an amazing way to find out quirky facts about associates, friends and family that you had never known before. The reason these sorts of applications are so popular is because deep within the heart of humanity is the desire to be known.

We bring this desire right into our relationships. We desperately want to be heard, understood and recognized for our contributions to the world. We want a relationship where we can completely relax and be ourselves – our true selves. Within this environment, we long to drop the façades we put on for work, school or church, and just be *us*.

The cry echoed in every fledgling relationship is "I want to be loved for me!" The disappointment when this fails to materialize is devastating. The actress Rita Hayworth once said, "They go to bed with Gilda [her most famous part], and they wake up with me." We long to be accepted as the imperfect beings that we truly are. Achieving this state with your spouse is the most intimate thing in the world. Sometimes, however, this comfort level crosses over from intimacy to unattractiveness.

Men and women will privately say things to me they wouldn't dream of saying to their spouses. "I miss the days when she took care of herself. Now, she is always in sweats and a ponytail." Or how about this one: "He wants to be intimate with me, but comes to bed with a scruffy face and thinks that farting under the covers is a turn-on." These men and women deeply love their spouses, but the sheer amount of comfort that has crept into their relationship is threatening to undermine their attraction to each other.

When this happens, those unattractive qualities stand like the proverbial eight hundred-pound gorilla in the bedrooms of these couples, silently and awkwardly hovering in the background. These are big issues that can fester under the surface if they are not addressed successfully.

Attraction Killers

Each couple knits together the personalities, perspectives, thoughts and desires of two unique individuals. As such, there is no *right* or *wrong* way to enhance – or even kill – the attraction in your marriage. Rather, you must define what is important for you, and then begin to address the issue.

The following list of attraction killers are some of the issues men and women have raised with me as areas of frustration. My guess is that you have very little idea what might be an attraction killer for your spouse because you are terrified to bring it up. In fact, what you personally find unattractive might not even be on this list, but it is a starting point for conversation.

Negative Body Image

I am fascinated by the British series *How to Look Good Naked*. During each show the host, Gok Wan, will home in on the deepest insecurities of a female guest, and discover which body part she despises most about herself. He will then have her strip down to her "knickers" (or *underwear* for you non-British folk out there), and introduce her to a lineup of average-looking women who are also in their undies. Gok explains to the guest that these women are lined up from smallest to largest of the hated body part. The woman then has to place herself where she thinks she fits in the lineup. So, for example, if she is really concerned about her thighs, he arranges the women from smallest to largest thighs, and then has the guest decide where she believes she measures up.

I have never seen a show where the guest didn't go right near the end where the largest body part was. Sometimes, while she does this, she is in tears completely undone by her own self-loathing. However, Gok will then move her to the place where she actually belongs – often nearer the smaller end. The brilliant point the show makes is that when it comes to body image, how we perceive ourselves is not necessarily reality.

We are besieged every day by images of "beauty" as defined by marketers. We somehow forget it is their job to make us feel insecure about ourselves so we will go out and buy their product. This advertising is difficult to escape. Experts estimate we are hit by up to five thousand ads a day.[2] As a result, men and women are increasingly unsatisfied with how they look. They fall into the trap of believing it is actually possible to be the ideal that is presented in the airbrushed images we see around us.

A few years ago, Dove began their Dove for Real Beauty Campaign. As part of this campaign, they released a video in which a model went from being completely natural to gracing a billboard.[3] During the video, we see the evolution of the model as industry people put on her makeup, do her hair, and then proceed to the photo shoot. The shocking part, however, was when her photo was loaded onto the computer and the graphic alterations began. Her neck was lengthened, her eyes enlarged, the shape of her skull altered, and the line of her neck slimmed down. The aim of the video, of course, was to expose the fact that many young women are desperately trying to look like the models on magazine covers and billboards, and yet they fail to understand that even the models don't look like that!

We get so caught up in what beauty is supposed to look like, that when our lovers tells us how good we look, we grimace and respond with an ungracious comment such as "You need to get your eyes checked." Internally, we are running through a checklist – formed through our consumption of media images – of all the reasons why they are wrong. In one of the *How to Look Good Naked* episodes, the woman's fiancé thought she was gorgeous, but she could not see this in herself. In fact, she had put a hold on their wedding because she was so repulsed by her body.

Here's the problem with negative body image. It kills your sex life. It poisons the intimacy the two of you can have together by making sex centered wholly and completely on you. Instead of being a safe place for the two of you to explore, it becomes all about *your* thoughts, *your* opinions, *your* perspectives and *your* demands. If it is allowed to run unchecked, your insecurities will morph into the rudder that directs your sexual relationship.

I have met many people who are held back from having a thriving sex life because of their negative body image. One lady told me this was the reason why she insisted on having the lights off during sex. She couldn't stand to see herself, and didn't want him to see her either. Can you imagine decades of sex hidden under the covers with as little visual stimulation as possible? It's tragic! When people harbor negative internal messages about their bodies, it is very difficult to have the freedom that a successful sex life entails.

Weight
Very often, negative body image is often enmeshed with the issue of weight.

Cultural Influences
I was appalled when I saw that the actress Jennifer Love Hewitt had to defend the fact she is a size two.[4] Just so we are all on the same page, a size two has a twenty-five-inch waist. It is tiny. And yet she was being derided in the media as "fat." Remember when size six was considered the perfect size? Now the perfect size is zero. A friend of mine in the movie industry once told me that when a size six actress walks on set, she gets called a "heavy roller."

There is a growing disparity between what we see on magazine covers and what we see in the grocery store, the mall or at work. Twenty years ago, the average model weighed 8 percent less than the average woman, now she weighs 23 percent less.[5] In fact, most models today qualify as anorexic on the body mass index. The drive to be thin is at the root of the fact that there are millions of girls and women who have eating disorders such as bulimia and anorexia.

There is no doubt that the expectations set for us by the media and advertising are ludicrous and dangerous. Teaching children to have self-esteem in spite of the assault of images is one of the greatest challenges facing educators and parents today. We must teach our kids that, no matter what they look like and no matter how much they weigh, they are "fearfully and wonderfully made."[6] The value of their character, their essence, their personhood does not depend on their weight.

And yet, there is no refuting the fact that, as North Americans, we are grossly overweight. Not only do we rank high on the list of "World's Fattest Countries,"[7] but experts agree the problem is only getting worse. Moreover, the problem has trickled down to our children, which does not bode well for the future unless there is major intervention.

As we look to address the overall problem, it is important to recognize that while battling ludicrous expectations is on one end of the spectrum, on the other end there exists a prevalence of thought that it is a person's right to be as big as they please. The attitude says, "I can put whatever I want in my body, in whatever quantity I please, because it's *my* body!" This reaction runs the gambit from people who genuinely believe it is their God-given right despite the health consequences, to the people who echo this cry as a way to cover their deep shame and embarrassment over their weight.

One such person exemplified this stance on Facebook, saying: "You know who your friends are when they accept you when you [are] FAT, skinny, short or tall. Not just when its makes them feel good. Got a call from a dear friend and was told to measure two miles so I could run off my excess weight. I thought about it after a while, yes I was very mad, but then I thought that this friend did me a very big favor. I was shown through the actions of one person that it is up to me to [be] happy with me rather than take the views of someone who is superficial and shallow. Thank you my 'friend' for allowing me to see how [I] look through your eyes."[8] When I read this, my heart went out to both the author as well as his friend. His friend very well could have been acting out of deep concern for this man, encouraging him to begin a lifestyle that would keep him alive a bit longer for his wife and kids. I don't know how diplomatically the friend brought up the issue – the sentiment could have been delivered well or poorly. But the author became enraged and refused to hear the heart of the message.

It is dangerous to live in either end of the spectrum. On one end, people are wholeheartedly buying into the propaganda that our bodies are meant to be starved in order to be valued by others. On the other end, people pollute their bodies with unhealthy lifestyles, and accuse anyone who addresses this matter as shallow and superficial. Living in either extreme puts us at risk.

The answer, experts believe, lies in the middle. Maintaining a healthy lifestyle means becoming active and eating well without striving to achieve ridiculous standards. Furthermore, we should always choose compassion and care for *all* people, no matter how they look, because they are created in the image of God, while still encouraging everyone to treat their bodies as "temples,"[9] and thereby taking care of them properly.

When Weight Is Your Place of Safety

It is imperative to recognize that weight gain cannot simply be attributed to a lazy, undisciplined, or slothful nature of the person who is overweight. We often put overweight people in this category unfairly. We are only beginning to scratch the surface of why it is so difficult to break our addictions to sugar, processed foods and other impediments to weight loss. Sometimes, however, there is something deeper going on in this person's life. One lady who took my course opened my eyes to this fact.

During my interview with Shannon about the ravages of infertility, she explained that she and her husband had slid into a sexless marriage. Each and every sexual encounter served to remind her that she could not have what she so deeply longed for – children. Thankfully, over the years, this couple had filled their home with adopted children, but the act of sex still triggered her feelings of inadequacy and failure. As she was putting on her jacket to walk out the door, Shannon turned to me and said, "Oh, and I have been losing a lot of weight since I took your course too."

My face obviously registered that I failed to make the connection, because she followed up by saying, "I realized I had put on a lot of weight over the years so I would not be attractive to my husband and he wouldn't pester me for sex. Now, I am exercising regularly and I feel great." She paused for a moment and then got a big smile on her face. "He likes it too."

I found it remarkable that, as part of transformational process that took place in this woman's life while she took the course, she realized she no longer needed to hide herself from her husband. The healing that took place in her heart manifested itself in a new body.

Psychologists and nutritionists tell us that weight gain is often a symptom, rather than the problem, for many people. Experts will often point out that the weight gain was triggered by a traumatic event.[10] If you or your spouse has used weight to hide deeper issues, then recognizing this is the first step to freedom in this area of your lives. Get help from a pastor, therapist, and/or support group of friends as you work and pray through the root issue. In John 10:10 (NIV), Christ told us "The thief comes only to steal and kill and destroy; I have come that they may have life, and have it to the full." It is time for you to have freedom in this area of your life.

Letting Yourself Go

Women might find it surprising that in study after study,[11] men say they do not mind if their wives gain some weight after the wedding, but it disturbs them deeply when their wives "let themselves go." It is no surprise that men are visually wired. They have deep appreciation for how their wives look. When she ceases to make an effort about her appearance, he is often disheartened and frustrated. Usually, he is compassionate because he genuinely understands the circumstances that led his wife to this place (having and caring for children, the sheer number of responsibilities she carries, etc.). However, many times men can believe that their needs are at the bottom of their wives' priority lists. When a woman takes the time to take care of herself, her husband sees this as a gift she gives him.

Understand that what this "gift" looks like varies from man to man. Don't make the assumption that your husband's notion of what "attractive" looks like is built around models on the covers of magazines. For some men, it is important their wives get regular exercise. For others, it means putting on a bit of makeup or fixing her hair. My father, for example, loved it when my mother painted her toes. She went to her grave (literally) with bright red toenails because it was one of the last ways she told my dad she loved him.

Men, however, are not immune from the potential to "let themselves go." While a woman might not be wired for visual stimulation to the same degree, it is still important to women that their men put forth an effort. Many young, fit men get married, pack on the pounds, stop exercising, and think they look exceedingly sexy in sweats and a beer belly. Some women don't mind this transformation. Others do.

Personal Habits

Over the years, I have collected a list of personal habits extremely annoying to spouses I have spoken with. Items on this list have been shouted out during discussion times at speaking engagements, and whispered to me in quiet hallways by embarrassed spouses. They are habits that move beyond the annoying into the realm of "That's gross. How did I end up marrying to this person?"

- farting or burping
- going to the bathroom in front of each other
- biting your nails
- keeping your nails long with dirt underneath them
- swearing
- drinking directly from the milk container
- dropping clothes on the floor, rather than in the hamper
- going long stretches without brushing your teeth
- morning breath
- smoking and the lingering smell of smoke
- not shaving your legs.

Of course, this list is not exhaustive, but is a starting point for a conversation with your spouse about the habits that can be attraction killers.

Personal Hygiene

This is a category that inflames men and women alike. Thankfully, once it is acknowledged as an area of annoyance, it is relatively easy to fix.

Body Hair

One man I was speaking with was trying to find intimacy with his wife, but couldn't get past the sheer amount of hair. Very soon after they got married, she stopped shaving because it wasn't a high priority for her. (She had a "He should love me no matter what" attitude.) One night, he decided to try oral sex to please her, but had to stop when he couldn't tell where pubic hair stopped and leg hair started. It was such a turn-off for him, he gave up.

I always encourage couples to groom their body hair. There are many good reasons why both men and women might want to explore this option. (By the way, men, we call this "manscaping" for you.)

- In today's styles of skimpy bathing suits, shorts, workout clothes and even lingerie, trimming your pubic hair means you don't have to be worried about anything sticking out.
- If you are concerned about hygiene issues, the idea of less hair is most likely appealing.
- Most people find oral sex more enjoyable when they are well groomed.
- Intercourse takes on a host of new sensations when there is little or no barrier in-between.
- Less hair means more to see, and this can be very exciting – provided that the lights are on, of course.

If you decide to take the plunge, you have several options, three of which are the most popular:

- Trimming. Using scissors or a trimmer (hair or beard) is an option you can try at home. If this is your first time with a trimmer, start with a longer blade and then shorten it to the desired length. While it does not remove the hair completely, it does shorten the length and tidy up the area.
- Shaving. This is an easy option as most people keep a razor in the house. When shaving the pubic region, it is essential to have a sharp razor (brand new is best), and a good shaving cream or gel. If this is the first time to do any sort of upkeep in the pubic region, you will want to trim the area first so your razor isn't dull by the time you get to the sensitive areas. Go slowly, rinse the blade frequently, and try not to shave over the same area multiple times to avoid irritation to the skin.
- Waxing. The key to getting a good wax job is finding someone who really knows what they are doing. If possible, get a referral from a friend who has had a good experience. If not, make sure the salon is reputable, clean, and that your esthetician has experience giving pubic waxes.

Odors

The actor Matthew McConaughey caused quite a stir when he publicly admitted he never wears deodorant or cologne. Women were all a twitter about this revelation and, in many ways, deeply disappointed that the hottie they had secretly been swooning over, well, stinks.

Scientists have been researching the subject of smell and how it relates to attraction, and come upon some surprising discoveries. According to the research done in the "Sweaty T-Shirt Study," when women were given sweaty T-shirts to smell, they were more attracted to the men who had the most different immune system from their own.[12] In another study, men who were asked to smell the scent of a woman said they preferred her scent during her most fertile time of the month.[13] It appears we have been hard-wired to gravitate to partners who will be a good match for us.

There is no denying that scent can be an attraction enhancer on the home front. You might love to snuggle up to a piece of your lover's clothing while s/he is away on a business trip. Their smells are a comfort in their absence.

But smell can end up on the attraction killer list quite easily as well. While it might be true that we are originally attracted to a particular person because their sweat has properties to which we are unconsciously drawn, if we get too stinky in the bedroom, this can become a problem.

If you find that odors are a concern to you or your spouse, then take a shower, brush your teeth, and spray on a bit of cologne or perfume before you go to bed.

Attraction Enhancers

When I am coaching couples, I try to redirect their focus from what society says is attractive to what they find attractive in each other. Instead of scrambling to reach some unattainable cultural expectation, find out what your *lover* sees as beautiful, and what makes *you* feel attractive and sexy. Then set a goal to work on *those* things.

I love seeing what couples discover when they begin the process of bringing intentionality to their desire to be attractive to each other.

Know What an Attractive You Looks Like

Remember the Thoreau quote "I wanted to live deliberately"? This applies to the issue of attractiveness as well. It doesn't just happen. We often fall into the trap of believing that the really, really pretty people just feel attractive. But they don't. The beautiful people deal with their own insecurities as well. We have to be deliberate about finding our attractive selves.

Regina was one of my clients who shared her journey to finding her attractive self with me. She has terrible skin sensitivities and cannot wear makeup easily. Even hair products can be problematic. She always felt "less than" because she couldn't have glamorous hair and makeup. However, Regina discovered that she feels really attractive in skirts. So, she started to look for skirts that make her feel sexy. Sometimes they are long. Sometimes they are short. They have to be made of a fabric that feels good to her. She works with her husband, and so sometimes she goes to work with garters on under her skirts. This thrills him. Just knowing his wife is wearing garters is a complete turn-on to him.

Now, if you were expecting a woman who looked like she just stepped off the cover of *Vogue* magazine, you might not give her a second glance. But she feels attractive when she puts on her skirts, and her husband loves it. They have found what really works for them.

I have found that men often find their sexy self through exercise and being fit. Most men don't spend a lot of time doing their hair (of course, I can think of a few exceptions!), and they don't adorn their faces with makeup. Their physique, therefore, is the most common way for them to feel good about themselves.

Marketers have picked up on this desire. All you have to do is look at exercise programs such as P90X®, Insanity®, and Insanity: The Asylum™ to see these are no Jane Fonda workouts.[14] Rather than focusing on "muffin tops" and "saddle bags," the trainers in these programs home in on the number of pull-ups and push-ups you can do in one sitting. The spirit of competition is healthy and the testosterone is pumping. (If you listen carefully, you might be able to hear Tim "The Tool Man" Taylor from *Home Improvement* do his trademark grunting noise.) Needless to say, these fitness programs have become huge sellers.

As we develop healthy views of our attractive selves, our self-confidence grows, and this has a beauty all of its own. Many men have told me there is something remarkably sexy that takes place when their wives becomes confident in their own sensuality and sexuality. I do not mean she walks around with excessive amounts of cleavage hanging out. But when her husband is around her, she nonverbally communicates, "I am yours," and "We are on an incredibly romantic, sexy, and sultry journey together that no one else needs to know about."

This attractiveness does not just happen. It is a learned behavior. All the work you are doing in this book to break old habits and thought patterns gives you the practice you need to learn confidence.

However, attraction in marriage does not just involve us. It has to do with our spouses as well.

Know What an Attractive Spouse Looks Like

On one of our trips to Texas, my husband wanted to buy a new pair of cowboy boots. Now, he had been talking about it for years – since he wore his last pair out – and we decided we would get them on this trip. We walked into the boot store and it was immediately obvious that his thoughts on what constituted a good pair were vastly different than mine. All we had to do was look at the price tag and see what I had in mind was much more, well, *refined* than what he was thinking.

It wasn't long before I was able to find a pair that I fell in love with. However, they looked very different from what my husband had been thinking. He had been planning on getting a pair of "on the ranch" type of cowboy boots. I was thinking something a bit sexier. He sighed, but was willing to try on the boots I showed him because he has, over the years, learned to appreciate what I find attractive.

You see, when we first got married, I would get all dressed up for dates. In Texas, there is quite a tradition that a young lady follows when she goes on a date with a guy for the first time. She spends hours getting ready – trying on endless outfits, spending a long time in the shower, extending the process by calling friends and asking for their opinions, carefully applying makeup. And when the young man rings the doorbell, a member of her family answers because she is not ready. Ever. It doesn't matter if she has actually been ready for an hour. It is customary to make him wait.

During this time, the young man will usually be introduced to the young woman's father... and his gun. A conversation will then ensue which falls along the lines of "If you ever hurt my daughter, I will kill you. Most likely with this gun here. And I won't feel bad about it." Make no mistake – the rules of engagement are crystal clear when the couple leaves for their date.

Of course, as the relationship develops, things become a bit more casual. The father may actually invite the young man to watch a football game with him, and crack a few jokes. The young lady might actually be ready on time.

And so it went with our relationship. However, even after we got married, I still spent the time and effort getting dressed well for our dates. Eric just got comfortable. Ratty jeans and running shoes were common. This infuriated me. I did not find this attractive at all.

After years of disappointment and knock-down-drag-outs, it finally dawned on him that putting some effort into how he looked for me on our dates was important. The running shoes got tucked up on the shoe rack for things like, well, running. The jeans were clean and completely intact – no holes! He even ran a bit of gel through his hair. Because, while he might have thought that just being him was all it took to be attractive, I needed to see him dressed well. It was part of the whole package for me.

This learning curve is why he was so open to trying on the boots I found. He was putting an effort into listening to what I find attractive. And listen he did. In fact, he ended up getting the boots I liked, and he loves them. Perhaps it is all the compliments he has been getting (from men and women alike), or perhaps it is that I can't keep my hands off him when he wears them. Either way, it's working for him.

Attraction has to do with being in touch with what our spouse appreciates, and respecting them enough to put the effort into being attractive *to* them and *for* them.

Regardless of whether you are finding your own attractive self or recognizing what you appreciate most in your spouse, I recommend that everybody make exercise a priority.

Exercise

"America's Toughest Trainer" Jillian Michaels entered our lives in 2011. I had been swimming for years in British Columbia, but I was self-aware enough to realize that when winter in Ontario arrived, the thought of having to dig my car out of the snow before driving to the pool at 6am was going to be a big enough disincentive to make me roll over and go back to sleep. I needed something I could do in the warmth of my own home.

The decision came down to Jillian Michaels or a treadmill. Her DVD was cheaper, and she repeatedly tells me what an amazing job I am doing, so she won. So now, Eric and I begin our mornings by working out together. Not only are we encouraging each other in our pursuit for health and fitness, but evidently we are also making our sex life better.

Did you know swimmers in their sixties have the sex lives of people decades younger?[15] Did you know men and women who exercise two to three times a week rate their sex life as above average?[16] Or women have an easier time coming to orgasm[17] and men lower their chances of impotence[18] if they are exercising on a regular basis? In short, the more consistently you exercise, the better your sex life will be. Therefore, as you develop your list of attraction enhancers, you need to put exercise at the top.

In the midst of the weight loss debate raging in North America, it is easy to lose sight of the fact that exercise is essential to the proper mechanics of our bodies, even if you are not trying to lose weight. Even if you are a tiny person, you need to exercise. Our bodies were designed to move. They function better when they move. And yes, sex is more enjoyable too.

Study after study has concluded that exercise has a both a physical and psychological impact. Here are some of the sexual side effects of working out:

- Increased blood flow.[19] The science of arousal is all about blood flow. When you feel that tingling sensation in your genitals, that is blood engorging your tissues and heightening their sense of arousal. Since exercise increases circulation, arousal will be easier when you are having sex.
- Increased body satisfaction. A study in 2000 found when exercising regularly, you have higher self-confidence and self-image.[20] No matter what shape or size your body might be, if you are exercising consistently, you are going to feel better about yourself. This has a profound impact on how you respond when your spouse wants to take your clothes off.
- Increased strength, cardio-fitness and flexibility.[21] Not only will these benefits make your current sex life more comfortable, but if you would like to try a new position or extend the length of your lovemaking, all these factors come into play. The more fit you are, the more adventurous you can be.
- Lower stress.[22] Stress is one of the huge impediments to having a thriving sex life. Since the endorphins released during exercise drive down the stress hormone cortisol, you are more likely to say yes to sex. (Incidentally, the hormones released during orgasm drive down cortisol even further.)

A friend of mine recently commented, "I think that sitting is the new smoking. Move, people!" It is true that the ill side effects of smoking have permeated our cultural consciousness. This does not mean, sadly, everyone has kicked the habit. It is indisputable, however, how harmful smoking is to your health. We still have a way to go in recognizing and breaking our addiction to sedentary lifestyles. If your own personal wellness is not a big enough motivator for you, perhaps a fabulous sex life will be.

Working Together

It is highly possible that reading this chapter pushed buttons for one or both of you. The issue of attraction – what makes us attracted to each other and what we can ask of each other – is fraught with landmines threatening to explode at the slightest trigger.

However, if we truly want the freedom to express our deepest longings to our spouses, and also want the intimacy that brings, we must accept attraction as an essential part of our sex lives. Walking this out in a healthy way begins with permission to speak freely.

Permission to Speak Freely

As with all sensitive topics, *how* you approach the subject with your spouse is crucial. And since genuine change is a series of small but consistent steps, I recommend you each begin with one thing you would like your partner to change.

To be frank, there is nothing more vulnerable than sitting with your spouse, who has just asked you to change something about how you look, dress, appear, act or smell. If you happen to have shame issues around this particular topic, you could both be headed for some very tumultuous waters. This is why so many couples avoid this topic altogether.

If you feel one or both of you are simply not ready to venture into this area of your relationship, put this topic on the back burner until later. Practice your communication skills in other areas of your relationship so that, when you *are* prepared, you can address this issue.

However, when you come to the place that you would like to ask for change, there are a few ground rules for both of you.

The Request

Remember the story of the couple from the weekend marriage retreat? As they lay fuming in the darkness, the husband told God, "God, you have to admit that fight is 90 percent her fault." God responded, "Yes, but your 10 percent caused her 90 percent." You may have all the justification in the world to ask for change from your spouse, but if you do not ask well, it doesn't matter how valid your request might be. Here are a few tips:

- **Choose your timing well.** No request, no matter how reasonable, will be heard if you time it poorly. Add the fact you are about to make a request on this issue of attraction, and you have just increased the odds of blowing the request exponentially. So, if your spouse has just walked in the door from work, had a fight with the kids, or hasn't gotten much sleep the night before, these should all be situations when you delay your request for a better time. If the two of you are reading this book together, go on a date with the intention of tackling this subject. Make sure you have sufficient privacy so you can express what is on your hearts and minds without feeling exposed to outsiders.
- **Try side by side.** These sorts of requests are not for the faint of heart. It is tough to have this sort of conversation with your spouse. As such, I always recommend a side-by-side approach. Not having to maintain eye contact in the moment can help you process the information without it being so overwhelming. Taking a drive or going for a walk are great activities to engage in while you are having this conversation.
- **Get as specific as you can.** The more specific you can be, the better. How would you feel if your boss made a vague request, but it was going to be something on which your annual review was based next year? It would be extremely frustrating. You wouldn't know exactly what your targets were. Similarly, if you ask your spouse for change without specificity, you are not giving him/her the sufficient tools to succeed. I use the example of "letting yourself go," since it is a common complaint with couples and is extremely vague. Let's say a man looks at his wife and says, "Honey, you have let yourself go over the years and I want you to fix that." His wife may be thinking of numerous things she can do to change, but if it isn't what is important to her husband, she will fail. He has not given her sufficient targets for success. Instead, if he says, "Honey, when we first got married, I loved the fact you always put on a bit of makeup in the morning. I would love to see you do that again." Now his wife has a specific idea of what can reverse this "letting herself go" trend.

- **Phrase your request in a positive manner.** How you phrase your request is also crucially important. For example, approaching your husband and saying, "Don't you know your breath smells nasty?" is most likely not going to evoke a very positive response. However, if you approach him and say, "It makes me want to kiss you more when you come to bed with your teeth brushed. And you know how much I love to kiss you." This is also going to be much more effective. Here is a tip: If you can work in why you love it when your spouse does this for you, it goes a long way towards getting a positive response.

The Response

Let me give you a few pointers on how you can respond.

- **Give your spouse the benefit of the doubt.** If you are sitting across from your spouse having this conversation, it is most likely because your spouse loves you deeply and wants your relationship to have deeper intimacy. S/he genuinely is attracted to you, but wants to be attracted to you in all ways. Your spouse is giving you directions so you know exactly what you need to do to be the man or woman of his/her dreams. When you see your spouse's request as a tool to remove the uncertainty around the subject, you have the power to make changes.

- **Resist the temptation to get defensive or retreat within yourself.** Remember the different reaction styles to shame? There is every chance you might feel one of those responses when your spouse makes his/her request of you. Instead of having an immediate response, keep your mouth closed and allow your brain some time to process the request. If being physically active during this time is helpful to you, then jot down notes. Of all the topics I have mentioned in this chapter, weight is the one most likely to provoke defensiveness. It is an incredibly sensitive topic, and difficult for people to talk about and respond to well. So, when your spouse asks you to do something that is hard to hear, listen respectfully to the heart of what your spouse is asking. Keep your mind open and take note of what this issue looks like from your spouse's perspective. It takes tremendous maturity and courage, but will radically change your marriage.

- **Ask follow-up questions if you need clarification.** If you are not clear on what your spouse is asking, a good question to respond with is, "Could you describe a time when I did this for you?" Usually, people once had the attributes their spouse finds attractive, but it has been lost in the busyness of life over the years. If you can get a clear picture of a time when you possessed those qualities, you can find your way back. If your spouse has something attractive in mind that you never tried, make an agreement to discover it together. For example, if you would like for him to try a new style of clothing, go shopping together so he can see exactly what you like. (Husbands, if this is the case, view enduring the shopping process as well as making changes to your wardrobe your act of love to your wife.)

The Implementation

When I am coaching clients on opening up in this area, I always recommend they give each other permission to ask one thing of each other, and then spend the next six weeks working on it. Why six weeks? Because that will be enough time to form a new attractive pattern.

Furthermore, tackling one request at a time is less overwhelming. Can you imagine if you asked your spouse what s/he would like you to change, and s/he gave you a list twenty items long? That would be incredibly discouraging, and you would want to give up before you even started. When you each begin with one item, it is manageable and achievable. This will, in its own way, beget more success.

Once you have succeeded with the first item on each other's lists, have another conversation and choose new items. (Note: Don't stop doing the first ones!) Over the years, you will develop the pattern of having numerous candid conversations. When you give each other permission to speak freely, and it is done in a spirit of love and kindness, intimacy flourishes. Both of you have the confidence that your needs and desires will be taken seriously, and each of you will be working on the importance of being attractive to each other – in the way you both uniquely define "attractive."

As you practice these new habits, it is crucial you encourage each other along the way.

Are You Your Spouse's Saboteur or Cheerleader?

Rarely do we fully comprehend the power we have in our relationships. We can be the foundation of success for our spouse, or the path to their downfall. One woman wrote me, expressing her frustration with her husband over this issue.

> I have a question about sex in my marriage. We have sex regularly, but ever since I became overweight, I don't feel sexy. I was at a healthy weight before becoming pregnant with my fourth child. He is six months old, and I am still overweight. I am trying to lose weight, but feel like my husband is sabotaging me. He believes in eating unhealthy foods and tries to guilt me into eating them. I try to eat only healthy foods, but I hate the constant pressure because sometimes I feel guilty and eat the unhealthy stuff to make him happy. I would like to exercise more, but I don't have time. When I want to go to the gym, he says, 'Will you change the diaper and feed the baby first? Oh, I hate it when you leave. Come sit on my lap.' Then I don't end up going. He doesn't think he prevents me from going, but he does. How can I help him understand that I need him to help me by allowing me to leave to go to the gym, and not pressuring me to eat unhealthy foods, so that I can enjoy sex more because I will feel sexier, and so that I can be at a healthy weight?[23]

When I responded, I pointed out several ways she could reach her goal, and help her husband understand she greatly wanted his support as she worked to lose weight. However, this letter is an example of one person sabotaging the progress of his spouse.

When you ask for change, come alongside your spouse and be his/her greatest cheerleader. Did you ask for her to put on makeup? Then help her find the extra ten minutes in the day to make this a reality. (Yes, those ten minutes can be overwhelming to find at times!) If you asked him to change up his wardrobe, comment on how good he looks every time he wears one of his new outfits. If you asked her to shave her legs before she comes to bed, let her know how good it feels when she does. And, for goodness' sake, if you want your spouse to lose weight, pitch in and help with the kids, support healthy eating habits (this means you have to eat healthy foods too), and give encouragement along the way so s/he can succeed!

The Song of Songs illustrates a couple that is effusive in their praise for one another. This is a crucial ingredient for couples to incorporate into their marriages. Praise your spouse in his/her presence, to your children, and around friends and family.

Final Thoughts

Ecclesiastes 4:9-12 (NIV) is one of the most poetic depictions of marriage: "Two are better than one, because they have a good return for their labor: If either of them falls down, one can help the other up. But pity anyone who falls and has no one to help them up. Also, if two lie down together, they will keep warm. But how can one keep warm alone? Though one may be overpowered, two can defend themselves. A cord of three strands is not quickly broken."

The beauty of marriage is you are not in it alone. You have a partner to walk alongside you even as you stumble and make mistakes. As the two of you open up about what you find attractive in each other, and what changes you would like each other to make, do so with the understanding that this is a part of your journey together.

Bedwork: Attraction

PSA: _____

This week, answer at least two questions. If you have a strong emotional reaction to the questions, pick the one you love and the one you hate. If you do not have a strong reaction, pick an exercise your spouse will appreciate, or give them home field advantage. Don't forget to record your PSA.

1. **Negative Body Image.** Carve out some time by yourself with a notepad and pen. Reflect on these questions, jotting down notes as you do. What lies have I believed about body image? Who told me these lies? How were they conveyed? What do I love about my body? What is my favorite feature? What does my spouse love? How can I actively choose to change the negative self-talk that accompanies my poor body image so I begin to see myself in a better light?

2. **Negative Body Image.** Dr. Christiane Northrup suggests this exercise in her book, *The Secret Pleasures of Menopause*,[24] to help change the self-talk around body image over the next thirty days.

   So many times we look at ourselves in the mirror and say, "I am too fat," "My wrinkles make me look so old," or "I am so ashamed of my <body part>." The more we tell ourselves these things, the more we believe them. As we create the pattern of despising our bodies, it is difficult to believe our partners could appreciate our bodies, which ultimately cuts us off from receiving this gift from them.

   Each morning, stand in front of the mirror naked, look at yourself and say out loud, "I accept myself unconditionally right now." Start with your eyes and get used to the exercise over the first few days. As you get more comfortable, look at other areas of your body. Starting with your favorite parts is usually the easiest, and then move to areas you don't like as much. Practice saying, "I love you. You are fabulous."

   What are your favorite things about your body? Is it your smile? The warmth in your eyes? Your arms? Your waistline? Your biceps? Tell yourself what you love about those areas. Can you look at the areas that are not your favorites and see them in a different light? Perhaps you are not fond of your legs, but you can say to yourself, "These legs have carried me all over the country on great adventures. They have been strong when I have gone on explorations. I love what they have done for me."

   Ultimately (you might want to continue the exercise beyond thirty days), the goal is to look at your entire body naked with appreciation, love and respect. And when you enter the bedroom, take this newfound confidence with you.

3. **Attraction Killers.** When you were reading this section, did anything jump out at you? Did you think to yourself, "Oh, I do that!" Make a list of those things, and then write down what you can do to choose new behaviors over the next six weeks.

4. **Shame.** If this chapter pushed your shame buttons, answer these questions:
   - What does shame feel like to you? How do you know when your shame button has been triggered?
   - What triggers your shame button? (Think about things in your past that have caused a shame reaction within you for clues.)
   - How can you combat and reality-check it?
   - Who can you go to in moments of shame to safely share your story?
   - You might want to read Dr. Brene Brown's book *I Thought It Was Just Me (but It Isn't)*, on shame for further insight.

5. **The Attractive You.** What makes you feel attractive, beautiful, sexy or hot? Do you allow yourself the time, energy, or money to invest in this? How would your demeanor change if you did? Would your lover notice a difference? Would other people around you notice? Find one (even small) way you can feel more attractive this week, and do it.

6. **The Attractive You.** Buy an article of clothing that makes you feel incredible. How does it feel against your skin? What do you love about it? Is it the color, shape, fabric, or way you look in it? How does your lover respond when you wear it?

7. **Your Attractive Spouse.** What was the thing you found most attractive about your spouse when you first met her/him? When do you find him/her most attractive? Is there anything new you would like your spouse to try (clothing, hair style, shaving, etc.)? If your spouse is attractive to you just as s/he is, then write a note expressing your gratitude. If there are changes you would like to request, then consider doing exercise #9.

8. **Exercise.** Choose to move more this week. Pick one activity you can do each day, and do it. This might be walking for twenty minutes after dinner, taking the stairs at work, doing twenty jumping jacks or sit-ups, or going for a short run. The goal is to do something small but manageable, so you are consistent throughout the week. If you already engage in nominal activity, take it to the next level. Purchase an exercise program on DVD and begin to work out at home, extend your workout sessions at the gym, or increase the number of times you exercise each week.

9. **Permission to Speak Freely.** Go on a date with your spouse and do the communication exercise laid out in the chapter. Before you go, each of you should think what you would like to ask of each other. It can only be one thing, and it will be what s/he works on for the next six weeks. Be very clear about what you are asking so you can phrase your request compassionately and specifically to set your spouse up for success.

Part III: Making It Last

Making It Last

"If we did all the things we are capable of doing, we would literally astound ourselves."
Thomas Edison – Inventor

How did you do with your goal? Did you achieve it? Did you come close? Did you and your spouse find new avenues to intimacy during the book? Did your sex life change and grow? If you read through the entire book and faithfully did your Bedwork, I would bet your marriage is in a drastically different place today than it was twelve weeks ago.

The purpose of this chapter, therefore, is relapse prevention. I want to give you as many tools as possible to continue to build intimacy in the years to come, and get back on track if you find yourselves in a rut. Remember, ruts in your relationship are inevitable. Life happens. However, if you are an expert at recognizing you are in one, and know how to get yourself back on track, you will continue to see your sex life thrive over a lifetime together.

Graphing Exercise

Let's begin by graphing your personal satisfaction assessments. Flip back to all the Bedwork pages and record your PSAs on this graph. You can put a dot in the middle on the rectangle and then connect the dots, or just color in the appropriate rectangle for each chapter.

10												
9												
8												
7												
6												
5												
4												
3												
2												
1												
Chapters	Myth-Busting	Define Your Direction	Faith	Communication	Ritual	Mystery	Respect	Pleasure	Trust	Creativity	Passion	Attraction

What pattern emerged for you? What was better or different about weeks in which your number went up? Was it the subject matter? What was your highest number? When did you have your second highest number?

There is a growing field of psychology called positive psychology where professionals study what is going *right* in the lives of their clients instead of what is going *wrong*. The idea behind this field, to put it simply, is that when we identify and analyze the circumstances around success, we can duplicate them. Consider this graphing exercise to be your own window into positive psychology.

Through this graph, you will see a visual representation of significant breakthoroughs in your relationship. Let's say you hit a nine after reading and implementing the Ritual chapter. It seems that, for your relationship, learning the skills of clearing time and space for sex to happen was significant to you two. So, should you find yourselves in places of difficulty again, you can apply the solutions you discovered during the book.

When people relapse into old behaviors, it is not because the solutions they found are no longer effective. Most often, it is just that they forget to keep implementing the solutions. Perhaps they get busy, distracted, overconfident or just lazy. When I ask clients who are struggling for answers, "What worked last time you were in this position?" they can usually rattle off a list of solutions that worked. And yet, when I ask them whether they are implementing those solutions now, they say, "Oh! I haven't done that in a while!"

I am not immune from this tendency. When Riley was four, we moved to a new city and she began to have atrocious behavior. We understood *why* she was acting the way she was (she missed her friends, didn't feel settled in our new home that was still partially under construction, and had a very stressed-out mom), but her behavior was still unacceptable. Fairly quickly, Riley and I fell into an unhealthy pattern where she behaved poorly and I listed everything she did wrong. Needless to say, this caused her behavior to get even worse.

To break this pattern, we decided that Riley should have a "success journal." Riley and I went to the dollar store, picked out a journal, and she decorated the cover with stickers. Then, I kept the journal handy throughout the day, writing down all the things she did *well*. Each night, Eric would tuck Riley into bed and read all her successes aloud to her. Her behavior changed practically overnight.

All went smoothly until we ran out of pages. Since Riley had been doing so well, I put off going to the store for a second journal. It just never happened. Things remained status quo until Riley hit a rough patch with a friend at school. All of a sudden, her behavior began to tank again. Off to the store we went to buy another journal, and sure enough, she returned to her lovely Riley-self in no time flat. I could have spent a lot of time mulling over a new way to get her to turn her attitude around, but returning to a previously successful solution was all we needed.

The most important part of relapse prevention is staying aware. When we stop paying attention, we are vulnerable to falling into ruts and old patterns. As such, you might consider continuing to track your PSA. Each week, take note of how your sex life has been, and note any extenuating circumstances that might be affecting it (one spouse was out of town, the wife has her period, company was visiting from out of town, etc.). When your PSA begins to slide down the scale *and stays there*, look back and see what solutions were effective in the past and re-implement them.

Tools for Continuing Growth

When we think about change, many of us just want to be like Cinderella. We want to have a fairy godmother show up and say, "Bibbidi, bobbidi, boo!" In a moment, all our cares will disappear, and we will glide into a new glorious life.

Unfortunately, change does not work like that. Rather, it is a series of small but consistent steps. One small change, made consistently, will take you to a radically different place over time. Laura North of True North Coaching likes to say it is a matter of degrees. If you alter your course by one degree, in time you end up in a vastly different place than if you stayed on your original course. That's it – one degree.

My One Thing

In the movie, *City Slickers*, Mitch (Billy Crystal) is grappling with a mid-life crisis, and so his close friends gift him with a trip to a dude ranch. In the middle of a cattle drive, Curly (Jack Palance), the trail boss, has a conversation with him about the meaning of life.

> Curly: "You know what the secret of life is? [Long Pause] One thing. Just one thing. You stick to that and everything else don't mean [crap]."
> Mitch: "That's great. But what's the one thing?"
> Curly: "That's what you've got to figure out."

When I am speaking at conferences, I tell participants to listen for their "one thing." Your one thing is your moment of epiphany, your "ah-ha" moment. You had a moment of clarity, revelation or insight about your sex life. It is that something that sparked in your brain as you were doing the reading or practicing the Bedwork. Perhaps it was even a conversation you had with your spouse. Regardless how you came across it, it made an impact on you.

Perhaps you had several of these moments. Right now, take a moment and write notes on what they were. Don't forget them because you can sequentially work your way through your whole list. However, in order to grow in an area, you have to take one thing at a time. One degree.

Choose one of the items on your list and write it down on the My One Thing Worksheet later in this book. The next step is to clearly outline three ways you can put the knowledge of this one thing into practice to help deepen the sexual intimacy in your marriage.

Perhaps you realized you are a Cycle Two person – you do not realize you are in the mood until your body is fully aroused. This is a great revelation, but what are you going to do about it now? How is that insight going to change your life? What action are you going to take to bring about change in your relationship?

You might need to have baby steps as your three items. You don't want to create a list that seems completely overwhelming because that will undermine your hopes of success. If this is the case, you could write a list something like:

1. I will hug my spouse after I brush my teeth each night.
2. I will give my spouse a kiss as s/he leaves each morning.
3. I will verbalize my love for my spouse after dinner every night.

If you have already implemented those sorts of baby steps in your relationship, you might want to make your list a bit more challenging. For example, you might decide:

1. I will do a bit of research on what gets me sufficiently aroused so my brain understands I want to have sex.
2. I will try the Don't Say No Experiment.
3. I will share this revelation with my spouse so s/he can help me fully enter the experience of sexual intimacy.

Regardless how you construct your list, it is vital that you choose activities you can do so you can get to the fun part. In the third step in this exercise, you get to outline ways to celebrate your successes. Remember the research that our brains need rewards to motivate true change? Now you get to decide how you are going to reward yourself. Success begets success. Give yourself every opportunity to succeed by celebrating along the way.

Once you have clearly identified your one thing, the three action steps you will take to implement this new learning, and the three ways you plan to celebrate, work on your one thing for six weeks. As I mentioned in the Define Your Direction chapter, neuroscientists tell us it takes twenty-five to thirty days to solidify new patterns. Give yourself a bit more time to ensure you have solidly developed this new habit.

If you are a high achiever, pick a new thing every six weeks. (Don't stop doing the previous one!) Look back at that list you developed of all your epiphanies, and work through them one at a time. Over the course of a year, your relationship will be in a radically different place, one degree at a time.

(You can find the worksheet later in the book or visit www.erynfaye.com for a free electronic copy.)

The State of Our Union

On our anniversary each year, Eric and I do an assessment of our marriage. We call it "The State of Our Union" dinner. Typically, we go out for a fancy meal, order a glass of wine, and talk and talk. Sometimes we spend the night away in a hotel – other times we just sneak away for a few hours. Regardless what we choose, it is crucial to be *away* from the hustle and bustle of everyday life.

During our State of Our Union talks, we always look back over our past year of marriage, and discuss what we achieved together. What were our marital successes? What were our failures? Did we discover anything new that really worked for us as a couple? Did we like each other more this year than last? Did we like each other less? Did we still grow as a couple beyond our roles of mom and dad?

Then we look to the future and dream about what we want to see in the upcoming year. It is at this point that we each get to ask one thing of each other. Anything we want. And that is the thing we commit to working on in our marriage all year long. One year, I had to work on combating my selfishness. (This was early on in our marriage – I am completely cured of that now.) Another year, Eric had to work on helping around the house *without being asked.* (He had always been superb at doing what I asked, but I was tired of being the traffic cop in our relationship when it came to the house.) One year, I had to work on actually listening to and implementing the advice Eric had for my business. (Up until that point, I was incredibly adept at listening to the input from anyone else other than him – even if the advice was exactly the same.) Some years, we had very serious things to ask of each other. Other years, there were some small, yet significant irritants driving us nuts.

In essence, the State of Our Union is the My One Thing exercise on steroids. Instead of working on one issue of our own choosing for six weeks, we are committing to work on one issue of our spouse's choosing for a full year. It's pretty intense, but it has cultivated some of the most significant growth in our relationship. It enables us to identify the significant milestones in our relationship – milestones that make us uniquely *us.*

Here are some pointers to creating your own State of Our Union:

- Choose the same time each year. We choose anniversaries, but you might prefer to go out at a different time. Furthermore, you might prefer to do it twice a year or take a full weekend. The key is connecting at the same time(s) each year.
- Think about your request for several weeks before the event so you phrase it effectively, and have considered some solution-oriented strategies. For example, one year I asked Eric to stop checking his phone during dinner. The strategy we came up with was for him to take his phone off his belt when he came home, and set it on the counter. Don't get locked into your own strategies, though, because your spouse might have better ideas. You get to choose *what* to ask, but s/he gets to decide *how* to fulfill your request.
- Begin the evening by reflecting on the past year. Spend time talking about your successes and failures. Take this time to encourage each other about progress you have made together as well as acknowledge the struggles you experienced.
- Make your request and listen to your spouse's request. As you listen, pay attention to your spouse's heart on this matter and do not get defensive. This is an issue your spouse wants you to work on for a year – even if it seems silly or unimportant to you, it is a big deal.
- Chat about ways the two of you can work separately and together to fulfill the requests.
- Remember that your spouse is going to talk about how you did next year. This accountability can be very motivating.

The Essential Elements of Sex™ Wheel

In the years to come, you will want to do an assessment of how you measure up in the nine essential elements. Now that you have a solid understanding of what they are and how they operate, you can use this knowledge to track your progress.

The Essential Elements of Sex Wheel is a tool you can use (I recommend you use it once a year) to determine the areas you need to address to move to the next level of sexual intimacy. For example, you might not need to address your tolerance of mystery in the younger years of your marriage, but this area becomes crucial to analyze as you age.

This exercise has two parts. In the first, you do an assessment of your satisfaction with each element. When you do this, ask yourself, "How do I rank this element *right now*?" Not tomorrow, not last week, not the "average," but right now. Give each category a number from 1 to 10.

(1) means this element of your sex life is horrible or nonexistent.

(10) means this element of your sex life is phenomenal.

Color in the chart to the number that you ranked this area. All the way to the outer edge means you are a ten. You will quickly see the areas of imbalance in your sexual relationship so you can choose what area you would like to target for growth. Ask yourself:

- What is of value to you? What needs improvement in your relationship? What is really good in your relationship?
- When my spouse fills out the wheel, how is his/her perspective different than mine? What element is of higher priority to my spouse?
- How can we deepen the areas that are important to both of us?

(You can find the worksheet later in the book or visit www.erynfaye.com for a free electronic copy.)

Solutions Journal

A solutions journal is a very simple way to track what is working in your relationship. Go to the dollar store and pick up a notebook. As you continue to try new things to deepen your intimacy with your spouse, write them down. Then write down what works for the two of you. How did you feel? How did s/he respond? What were your breakthrough or "ah-ha" moments? What did s/he say or do that you enjoyed, loved, were turned on by? What evokes passion in you (even whispers of passion)? Focus on the things that are working for you so you can keep exploring them. Keeping track of your solutions will help you increase your effectiveness when working for change.

Accountability Group

Often we hide the less attractive parts of our relationship from our friends and family. (This might be to "protect" our spouse, out of embarrassment, or other such reasons.) However, we then cut off the potential for any support, encouragement and accountability we might receive.

Think about a friend (or friends) who believe in the importance of your relationship – including the sexual aspect of it – and can be a part of a same-gender accountability group with you. You do not need to go into the nitty-gritty details of your sex life, but through sharing where you are, they will be able to support you, as well as challenge you, if this important area of your relationship is beginning to slide back down to the bottom of your priority list.

More Bedwork

If you only did two questions each chapter and would like to further develop your skill set, go back through the book and do the rest. Need more questions? Visit my website at www.erynfaye.com for more Bedwork questions.

Final Thoughts

Eric and I recently had the privilege of celebrating the twentieth anniversary of some dear friends. As they reflected on two decades of marriage, they shared some advice that a mentor couple had once given them. "There is no coasting in marriage. If your relationship is not improving, it is deteriorating." Not only do I agree with that statement, it's the purpose of this book.

If you want your sex life to be better than average, beat out the dismal statistics we have in North America, and be everything God designed, you are going to have to be intentional about it. Consider it as ongoing maintenance. You don't wait until your car is out of oil before you go in for an oil change. Be proactive.

Going forward, develop a habit of checking in on your relationship. Ask yourselves:

- What season are we in right now?
- Is our communication better than it was a year ago? Five years ago?
- Are our rituals still working for us?
- Have we stumbled over a mystery box in our relationship?
- Is the respect that we have for each other deepening as we age?
- Are we still enjoying the pleasure that we give each other?
- Is our trust in each other deepening or eroding?
- Have we had practice sex recently and tried something new?
- Are we listening to the passions deep within us and allowing passion to thrive in our marriage?
- Have we remained vigilant about being attractive to and for each other?

As you consistently ask yourself these questions, you ensure that you do not coast. This does not mean that you won't have times of setback in your relationship. It just means that you will be more aware of these setbacks, and have the tools to get back on track.

You've already shown you are willing to put time and effort into your relationship. As long as you keep that focus and desire for more, you can have the sex life of your hopes and dreams. It's all part of God's design for you, and He has given you the tools to achieve it together. Never stop working together, and you'll never stop enjoying your relationship.

My One Thing Worksheet

Go back through the book and look through your notes. Choose one thing you believe will make the greatest impact on your marriage in the next six weeks. This might have been a personal revelation you had during the book, or an exercise useful to practice over time.

Then, choose three action steps you can take over the next six weeks to put your one thing into practical application. If you are a high achiever, choose a new item each six weeks so you are continually infusing your marriage with growth.

My one thing is:

_____

_____

Three practical steps I can take over the next six weeks:

1. _____

_____

2. _____

_____

3. _____

_____

Three ways I am going to celebrate my successes:

1. _____

_____

2. _____

_____

3. _____

_____

The Essential Elements of Sex™ Wheel Exercise

1. Look at The Essential Elements of Sex™ Wheel and rate your satisfaction levels with each area on a scale of 1 to 10 (1 = completely unsatisfied and 10 = totally satisfied).

    Communication: _____

    Ritual: _____

    Mystery: _____

    Respect: _____

    Pleasure: _____

    Trust: _____

    Creativity: _____

    Passion: _____

    Attraction: _____

2. Use those numbers to color in the graph on the next page. (All the way to the outer edge means you are a 10.)

3. How solid is your hub of communication?

4. Where are the areas of imbalance in your sexual relationship? What area do you want to target for growth over the next six weeks?

5. Fill in the My One Thing Worksheet to create an action plan to address this area.

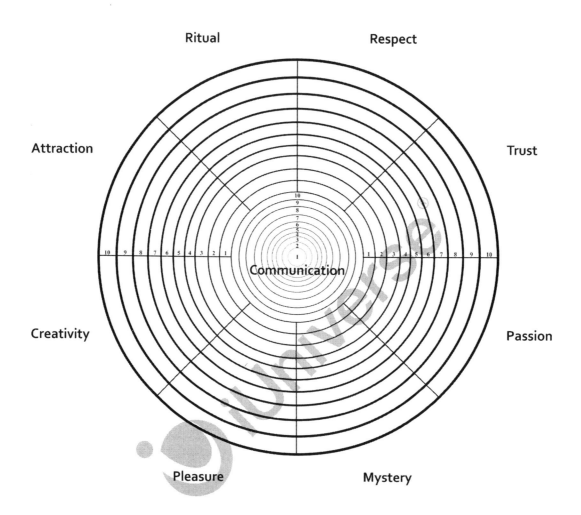

Bibliography

———◆———

Abrams, JJ. (2007). "JJ Abrams' Mystery Box." *TED*, March. http://www.ted.com/talks/j_j_abrams_mystery_box.html.

Alzate, H., & Londono, M.L. (1984). "Vaginal Erotic Sensitivity." *Journal of Sex and Marital Therapy*, Spring; 10(1): 49-56.

Amen, D. (1998). *Change Your Brain, Change Your Life: The Breakthrough Program for Conquering Anxiety, Depression, Obsessiveness, Anger, and Impulsiveness.* New York: Three Rivers Press.

Amen, D. (2007). *The Brain in Love: 12 Lessons to Enhance Your Love Life.* New York: Three Rivers Press.

Asthana, H.S., & Mandal, M.K. (1998). "Hemifacial Asymmetry in Emotion Expressions." *Behavior Modification*, 22: 177-183.

Auyeung, B., Baron-Cohen, S., et al. (2009). "Fetal Testosterone Predicts Sexually Differentiated Childhood Behavior in Girls and Boys." *Psychological Science*, 20: 144-148.

Bacon, C. G., Mittleman, M. A., & Kawachi, I. (2003). "Sexual Function in Men Older than 50 Years of Age: Results from the Health Professionals Follow-Up Study." *Annals of Internal Medicine*, 139: 161-168.

Baron-Cohen, S. (2003). "They Just Can't Help It." *The Guardian*, April 17. http://www.guardian.co.uk/education/2003/apr/17/research.highereducation/print.

Basson, R. (2005). "Women's Sexual Dysfunction: Expanded and Revised Edition." *CMAJ*, May 10, 172(10): 1327-1333. http://www.cmaj.ca/cgi/content/full/172/10/1327.

Bell, R. (2007). *Sex God: Exploring the Endless Connections between Sexuality and Spirituality.* Grand Rapids, MI: Zondervan.

Bolen, J. G. (1980). "The Male Orgasm: Pelvic Contractions Measured by Anal Probe." *Archives of Sexual Behavior*, 9(6): 503–521.

Boteach, S. (1999). *Kosher Sex: A Recipe for Passion and Intimacy.* New York: Doubleday.

Boteach, S. (2009). *The Kosher Sutra: 8 Sacred Secrets for Reigniting Desire and Restoring Passion for Life.* New York: HarperCollins.

Bowen, M. (1978). *Family Therapy in Clinical Practice.* Northvale, NJ: Jason Aronson, Inc.

Brizendine, L. (2006). *The Female Brain.* New York: Morgan Road Books.

Brizendine, L. (2010). *The Male Brain: A Breakthrough Understanding of How Men and Boys Think.* New York: Broadway Books.

Brown, B. (2008). *I Thought It Was Just Me (but It Isn't): Telling the Truth about Perfectionism, Inadequacy and Power.* New York: Penguin Group.

Brown, B. (2010). *The Gifts of Imperfection: Let Go of Who You Think You're Supposed to Be and Embrace Who You Are.* Center City, MN: Hazelden.

Cameron, J. (1992). *The Artist Way: A Spiritual Path to Higher Creativity.* New York: Penguin Putnam, Inc.

Canfield J., & Switzer, J. (2005). *The Success Principles: How to Get from Where You Are to Where You Want to Be.* New York: HarperCollins Publishers.

Carder, D., & Jaenicke, R.D. (1992). *Torn Asunder: Recovering from an Extramarital Affair.* Chicago: Moody Publishers.

Carder, D. (2008). *Close Calls: What Adulterers Want You to Know About Protecting Your Marriage.* Chicago: Northfield Publishing.

Castleman, M. (2009). "Desire in Women: Does It Lead to Sex? Or Result from It?" *Psychology Today,* July 15. http://www.psychologytoday.com/blog/all-about-sex/200907/desire-in-women-does-it-lead-sex-or-result-it.

Castleman, M. (2010). "Easier Orgasms for Women in the Missionary Position." *Psychology Today,* October 17. http://www.psychologytoday.com/blog/all-about-sex/201010/easier-orgasms-women-in-the-missionary-position.

Chapman, G. (1992). *The Five Love Languages: How to Express Heartfelt Commitment to Your Mate.* Chicago: Northfield Publishing.

Cloud, H., & Townsend, J. (1999). *Boundaries in Marriage.* Grand Rapids, MI: Zondervan.

Coady, D., & Fish, N. (2011). *Healing Painful Sex: A Woman's Guide to Confronting, Diagnosing, and Treating Sexual Pain.* Berkeley, CA: Seal Press.

Collins, J.C., & Porras, J.I. (1994). *Built to Last: Successful Habits of Visionary Companies.* New York: HarperCollins Publishers.

Corcoran, D. (2007). "On Desire: Interview with Helen Fisher." *New York Times,* April 10. http://video.nytimes.com/video/2007/04/09/science/1194817104832/on-desire.html?ref=sex.

Covey, S.R. (1989). *7 Habits of Highly Effective People.* New York: Free Press.

Davis Raskin, V. (2002). *Great Sex for Moms: 10 Steps to Nurturing Passion While Raising Kids.* New York: Fireside.

Day, T. "Psalm of Solomon – Song of Songs." *www.timday.org,* May 26. http://www.timday.org/writings/bible-study/old-testament-part-2/.

Dillow, L., & Pintus, L. (1999). *Intimate Issues: Conversations Woman to Woman.* Colorado Springs: Waterbrook Press.

Dixon, P., Rock, D., & Ochsner, K. (2010). "Turn the 360 Around." *Neuroleadership Journal,* 3: 78-86.

Doherty, W.J. (2001). *Take Back Your Marriage: Sticking Together in a World That Pulls Us Apart.* New York: The Guilford Press.

Ducklow, P. (2010). "70 Is My New 100." *www.theducklows.ca,* February 12. http://theducklows.ca/70-is-my-new-100/.

Dworkin-McDaniel, N. (2011). "Touching Makes You Healthier." *CNN,* January 5. http://www.cnn.com/2011/HEALTH/01/05/touching.makes.you.healthier.health/index.html.

Dye, M., & Fancher, P. (2007). *The Genesis Process: A Relapse Prevention Workbook for Addictive/Compulsive Behaviors,* 3rd ed. Auburn, CA: Genesis Addiction Process & Programs.

Eden, D. (1992). "Leadership and Expectations: Pygmalion Effects and Other Self-Fulfilling Prophecies in Organizations." *Leadership Quarterly,* 3(4): 271-305.

Eldridge, J. (2001). *Wild at Heart: Discovering the Secret of a Man's Soul.* Nashville: Thomas Nelson.

Esposito, K., Giugliano, F., et al. (2004). "Effect of Lifestyle Changes on Erectile Dysfunction in Obese Men." *JAMA,* 291: 2978-2984.

Farrel, B., & Farrel, P. (2001). *Men Are Like Waffles, Women Are Like Spaghetti: Understanding and Delighting in Your Differences.* Eugene, OR: Harvest House Publishers.

Feldhahn, S. (2004). *For Women Only: What You Need to Know about the Inner Lives of Men.* Sisters, OR: Multnomah Publishers.

Figueroa-Jones, M. (2012). "Plus Sized Bodies, What is Wrong with Them Anyway?" *Plus Model Magazine,* January 8. http://plus-model-mag.com/2012/01/plus-size-bodies-what-is-wrong-with-them-anyway/.

Finedgan, J.K., Bartleman, B., & Wong, P.Y. (1991). "A Window for the Study of Prenatal Sex Hormone Influences on Postnatal Development." *Journal of Genetic Psychology,* 150: 101-112.

Fisher, H., Aron, A., & Brown, L.L. (2005). "Romantic Love: An fMRI Study of Neural Mechanism for Mate Choice." *Journal of Comparative Neurology,* 493(1): 58-62.

Fisher, H. (2008). "Helen Fisher Studies the Brain in Love." *TED,* February. http://www.ted.com/talks/helen_fisher_studies_the_brain_in_love.html.

Fisher, H. (2009). *Why Him? Why Her? How to Find and Keep Lasting Love.* New York: Holt Paperbacks.

Fuchs, E. (1983). *Sexual Desire and Love.* New York: Seabury Press.

Gallup, G.G., Burch, R.L., & Platek, S.M. (2002). "Does Semen Have Antidepressant Properties?" *Archives for Sexual Behavior,* 31(3): 289-293.

Giedd, J.N., Castellanos, F.X., et al. (1997). "Sexual Dimorphism of the Developing Human Brain." *Progress in Neuro-Psychopharmacology and Biological Psychiatry,* 21(8): 1185-1201.

Gire, K. (1996). *Windows of the Soul: Experiencing God in New Ways.* Grand Rapids, MI: Zondervan.

Glass, S. (2003). *NOT Just Friends: Protect Your Relationship from Infidelity and Heal the Trauma of Betrayal.* New York: The Free Press.

Goldstein, J.M., Deidman, J.L., et al. (2001). "Normal Sexual Dimorphism of the Adult Human Brain Assessed by In Vivo Magnetic Resonance Imaging." *Cerebral Cortex,* 11: 490-497.

Gottman, J.M. (1994). *Why Marriages Succeed or Fail: And How You Can Make Yours Last.* New York: Simon & Schuster.

Gottman, J.M., Schwartz Gottman, J., & DeClaire, J. (2006). *10 Lessons to Transform Your Marriage.* New York: Random House, Inc.

Gottman, J.M. (2010). "Four Horsemen of the Apocalypse by John Gottman." *YouTube,* January 2. http://www.youtube.com/watch?v=CbJPaQY_1dc.

Goudarzi, S. (2006). "When a Woman Smells Best." *LiveScience,* January 18. http://www.livescience.com/553-woman-smells.html.

Gray, J. (1992). *Men Are from Mars, Women Are from Venus: A Practical Guide for Improving Communication and Getting What You Want in Your Relationships.* New York: HarperCollins.

Grilo, C.M., Masheb, R., et al. (2005). "Childhood Maltreatment in Extremely Obese Male and Female Bariatric Surgery Candidates." *Obesity Research Journal,* 13: 123–130.

Gross, G., & Krummrich, C. (2006). *Dirty Little Secret: Uncovering the Truth behind Porn.* Grand Rapids, MI: Zondervan.

Haltzman, S., & Foy DiGeronimo, T. (2006). *The Secrets of Happily Married Men: Eight Ways to Win Your Wife's Heart Forever.* San Francisco: Jossey-Bass.

Haltzman, S., & Foy DiGeronimo, T. (2008). *The Secrets of Happily Married Women: How to Get More Out of Your Relationship by Doing Less.* San Francisco: Jossey-Bass.

Hamann, S. (2005). "Sex Differences in the Responses of the Human Amygdala." *The Neuroscientist,* 11(4): 288-293.

Hartling, L.M., Rosen, W., et al. (2000). "Shame and Humiliation: From Isolation to Relational Transformation." *Work in Progress,* 88. Stone Center for Developmental Services and Studies. Wellesley, MA.

Hirsch, A.R. (1998). *Scentsational Sex: The Secret to Using Aroma for Arousal.* Boston: Element Books.

Hittelman, J.H., & Dickes, R. (1979). "Sex Differences in Neonatal Eye Contact Time." *Merril-Palmer Quarterly*, 25: 171-184.

Holloway, R.L., Anderson, P.J., et al. (1993). "Sexual Dimorphism of the Human Corpus Callosum from Three Independent Samples: Relative Size of the Corpus Callosum." *American Journal of Physical Anthropology*, 4: 481-498.

Hopkins, M., & Lockridge, R. (1997). *Intercourses: An Aphrodisiac Cookbook*. Memphis: Terrace Publishing.

Hughes, S.M., Harrison, M.A., & Gallup, G.G. (2007). "Sex Differences in Romantic Kissing among College Students: An Evolutionary Perspective." *Evolutionary Psychology*, 5(3): 612-631.

Hwang, S.J., Ji, E.K., et al. (2004). "Gender Differences in the Corpus Callosum of Neonates." *Neuroreport,* 6: 1029-1032.

Jobs, S. (2005). "Commencement Address to Stanford University." *Stanford University News,* June 14. http://news.stanford.edu/news/2005/june15/jobs-061505.html.

Katz, A. (2009). *Woman, Cancer, Sex*. Pittsburg, PA: Hygeia Media.

Kerner, I. (2004). *She Comes First: The Thinking Man's Guide to Pleasuring a Woman*. New York: HarperCollins Publishers, Inc.

Kerner, I. (2008). *Passionista: The Empowered Woman's Guide to Pleasuring a Man*. New York: HarperCollins Publishers, Inc.

Kerner, I. (2011). "How Porn Is Changing Our Sex Lives." *CNN,* January 20. http://thechart.blogs.cnn.com/2011/01/20/how-porn-is-changing-our-sex-lives/.

Kleinplatz, P.J., ed. (2001). *New Directions in Sex Therapy: Innovations and Alternatives*. Philadelphia: Brunner-Routledge.

Komisaruk, B., Beyer-Flores, C., & Whipple, B. (2006). *The Science of Orgasm*. Baltimore: The Johns Hopkins University Press.

Krucoff, C., & Krucoff, M. (2000). "Peak Performance." *American Fitness*, 19: 32-36.

Langer, G., Arnedt, C., & Sussma, D. (2004). "American Sex Survey." *ABC News (Primetime),* October 21. http://abcnews.go.com/Primetime/PollVault/story?id=156921&page=1#.T7WCYL-fI-8.

Laumann, E.O., Paik, A., & Rosen, R.C. (1999). "Sexual Dysfunction in the United States." *JAMA*, 281(6): 537-544.

Leeb, R.T., & Rejskind, F.G. (2004). "Here's Looking at You, Kid! A Longitudinal Study of Perceived Gender Differences in Mutual Gaze Behavior in Young Infants." *Sex Roles*, 50(1-2): 1-5.

Lehrer, J. (2009). "Don't!" *The New Yorker*, May 18. http://www.newyorker.com/reporting/2009/05/18/090518fa_fact_lehrer.

Leiblum, S., ed. (2007). *Principles and Practice of Sex Therapy*. New York: The Guilford Press.

Love, P., & Robinson, J. (1995). *Hot Monogamy: Essential Steps to More Passionate, Intimate Lovemaking*. New York: Penguin Group.

Love, P., & McFadden, K. (2006). "Hot Monogamy Workshop Training." *Smart Marriages,* June 24. http://www.smartmarriages.com/hot.html.

Love, P., & Stonsy, S. (2007). *How to Improve Your Marriage without Talking about It*. New York: Broadway Books.

Lutchmaya, S., Baron-Cohen, S., & Raggatt, P. (2002). "Foetal Testosterone and Eye Contact in 12-Month-Old Infants." *Infant Behavior and Development*, 25: 327-335.

Lutchmaya, S., Baron-Cohen, S., & Raggatt, P. (2002). "Foetal Testosterone and Vocabulary Size in 18- and 24-Month-Old Infants." *Infant Behavior and Development,* 24: 418-424.

Mason, M. (1985). *The Mystery of Marriage*. Portland: Multnomak.

Masters, W.H., & Johnson, V. (1966). *Human Sexual Response*. New York: Bantam Books.

McCarthy, B.W., & McCarthy, E.J. (2003). *Rekindling Desire: A Step by Step Program to Help Low-Sex and No-Sex Marriages.* New York: Brunner-Routledge.

McMahon, T., Kohler, N., & Stobo Sniderman, A. (2012). "How Canadian Are You? How Your Waist Size, Paycheque and Sex Life Measure Up." *Maclean's,* July 9.

McManus, E.R. (2008). *Wide Awake: The Future Is Waiting within You.* Nashville: Thomas Nelson.

Meston, C.M., & Buss, D.M. (2009). *Why Women Have Sex: Understanding Sexual Motivations – from Adventure to Revenge (and Everything in Between).* New York: Henry Holt and Company, LLC.

Mitchell, J. (2010). "NLSummit 2010 Insight: Making Sense of Others." *Neuroleadership Institute,* December 26. http://blog.neuroleadership.org/2010/12/nlsummit-2010-insight-jason-mitchell.html.

Morgentaler, A. (2009). "Men Who Fake Orgasms." *Psychology Today*, February 1. http://www.psychologytoday.com/blog/men-sex-and-testosterone/200902/men-who-fake-orgasms.

Murkoff, H., & Mazel, S. (2008). *What to Expect When You Are Expecting,* 4th ed. New York: Workman Publishing Company, Inc.

Northrup, C. (1994). *Women's Bodies, Women's Wisdom: Creating Physical and Emotional Health and Healing.* New York: Bantam Books.

Northrup, C. (2008). *The Secret Pleasures of Menopause.* New York: Hay House, Inc.

O'Hanlon, B., & Weiner Davis, M. (1989). *In Search of Solutions: A New Direction in Psychotherapy.* New York: W.W. Norton & Company.

Omartian, S. (1997). *The Power of a Praying Wife.* Eugene, OR: Harvest House Publishers.

Parker, S. (2007). *The Human Body: An Illustrated Guide to Its Structure, Function and Disorders.* New York: DK Publishing.

Pease, A., & Pease, B. (2001). *Why Men Don't Listen and Women Can't Read Maps: How We're Different and What to Do about It.* New York: Broadway.

Penhollow, T.M., & Young, M. (2004). "Sexual Desirability and Sexual Performance: Does Exercise and Fitness Really Matter?" *Electronic Journal of Human Sexuality*, October 5, 7.

Perel, E. (2006). *Mating in Captivity: Unlocking Erotic Intelligence.* New York: HarperCollins Publishers.

Rampell, C. (2010). "Women Now a Majority in American Workplaces." *The New York Times,* February 5. http://www.nytimes.com/2010/02/06/business/economy/06women.html.

Rankin, L. (2010). *What's Up Down There? Questions You'd Only Ask Your Gynecologist if She Were Your Best Friend.* New York: St. Martin's Press.

Rankin, L. (2011). "15 Crazy Things about Vaginas." *Psychology Today,* April 8. http://www.psychologytoday.com/blog/owning-pink/201104/15-crazy-things-about-vaginas.

Read, T.E. (2009). *Till Sex Do Us Part: Make Your Married Sex Irresistible.* Toronto: Key Porter Books Limited.

Roach, M. (2008). *Bonk: The Curious Coupling of Science and Sex.* New York: W.W. Norton & Company, Inc.

Robinson, T. (2008). *Small Footprint, Big Handprint: How to Live Simply and Love Extravagantly.* Boise, ID: Ampelon Publishing.

Rohr, R. (2002). "Grieving as Sacred Space." *Sojourners Magazine,* January-February. 31(1): 20-24.

Rohr, R. (2004). *Adam's Return: The Five Promises of Male Initiation.* New York: Crossroads Publishing.

Rosenthal, R., & Jacobson, L. (1992). *Pygmalion in the Classroom: Teacher Expectation and Pupils' Intellectual Development,* 2nd ed. New York: Irvington Publishers, Inc.

Sachs, A. (2008). "Help for Sex-Starved Wives." *Time,* April 7. http://www.time.com/time/health/article/0,8599,1728520,00.html.

Sample, I. (2011). "Female Orgasm Captured in Series of Brain Scans." *The Guardian,* November 14. http://www.guardian.co.uk/science/2011/nov/14/female-orgasm-recorded-brain-scans.

Schnarch, D. (1997). *Passionate Marriage: Keeping Love and Intimacy Alive in Committed Relationships.* New York: Henry Holt & Company.

Schneider, F., Habel, U., et al. (2000). "Gender Differences in Regional Cerebral Activity during Sadness." *Human Brain Mapping,* 9: 226-238.

Sheehy, G. (1998). *Menopause: The Silent Passage.* New York: Pocket Books.

Siegel, D. (2011). *Mindsight: The New Science of Personal Transformation.* New York: Bantam Books.

Skloot, R. (2007). "Why Is It So Damned Hard to Change?" *Oprah.com,* January. http://www.oprah.com/health/How-to-Change-Your-Bad-Habits/1.

Stafford, T. (1993). *Sexual Chaos.* Downers Grove, IL: InterVarsity.

Stanten, N., & Yeager, S. (2003). "Four Workouts to Improve Your Love Life." *Prevention,* 55: 76-78.

Story, L. (2007). "Anywhere the Eye Can See, It's Likely to See an Ad." *New York Times*, January 15. http://www.nytimes.com/2007/01/15/business/media/15everywhere.html.

Streib, L. (2007). "World's Fattest Countries." *Forbes.com,* February 8. http://www.forbes.com/2007/02/07/worlds-fattest-countries-forbeslife-cx_ls_0208worldfat_2.html.

Swanbrow, D. (2002). "American Study Finds Men Doing More Housework." *The University Record,* March 25. http://ur.umich.edu/0102/Mar25_02/16.htm.

Tennov, D. (1998). *Love and Limerence: The Experience of Being in Love. Chelsea, MI*: Scarborough House.

Toler, L. (2011). "How to Avoid Becoming a Victim of the Gray Divorce." *Huffington Post*, March 12. http://www.huffingtonpost.com/lynn-toler/how-to-avoid-becoming-a-v_b_834192.html?.

Tolkien, J.R.R. (1998). *The Hobbit.* London: HarperCollins Children's Books.

Ward, D. (2004). "We Had More Sex in the 50s Survey Says." *The Guardian,* August 6. http://www.guardian.co.uk/uk/2004/aug/06/gender.research.

Wedekind, C., Seebeck, T., et al. (1995). "MHC-Dependent Mate Preferences in Humans." *Proceedings of the Royal Society: Biological Sciences,* 260 (1359): 245–249.

Weiner Davis, M. (2001). *The Divorce Remedy: The Proven 7-Step Program for Saving Your Marriage.* New York: Simon & Schuster Paperbacks.

Weiner Davis, M. (2003). *The Sex-Starved Marriage: Boosting Your Marriage Libido.* New York: Simon & Schuster Paperbacks.

Weiner Davis, M. (2008). *The Sex-Starved Wife: What to Do When He Has Lost Desire.* New York: Simon & Schuster.

Weiner Davis, M. (2008). "The Sex-Starved Wife." *Redbook.* http://www.redbookmag.com/love-sex/advice/sex-starved-wife-5.

White, N. (2007). "Jennifer Love Hewitt: A Size 2 Is Not Fat!" *People,* December 2. http://www.people.com/people/article/0,,20163862,00.html.

Woller, L., & Woller, J. (2008). *The Skill.* Victoria, BC: The Vantage Group.

Index

C

change, true
  accountability 28, 29
  concept 19, 23
  defined target 24
  rewards 33, 216
clitoris
  facts about 128, 129, 130
  oral sex 135, 136
  sensate focus 133
  stimulation of 130, 173
contempt
  breaking patterns of 119, 186
  dangers of 62, 119
  in the culture 113, 124
corpus callosum 56, 61, 87
cortisol 49, 57, 59, 131, 203
criticism 119, 146, 186
Cycle One 8, 10, 20
Cycle Two 8, 9, 10, 20, 215

D

dangerous partner profile 159
defensiveness 119, 186, 205
depression
  andropause 147
  laughter 66
  menopause 146
  sexual side effects of 8, 12, 144
Designated Initiator 84, 85, 92
desire gap
  definition 5
  impact on marriage 6
  navigating it 8, 16, 46, 69, 85
differentiation 155, 166
divorce
  avoiding it 38, 98, 115
  in Christian marriages 3, 4
  risk factors 5, 6, 99, 102, 119
  statistics 4, 117, 160, 181
Don't Say No Experiment 85, 86, 92, 216
dopamine 6, 32, 33, 67, 128, 161

E

emotional fusion 154, 155, 166
empathy ix, 44, 45, 60, 69
erectile dysfunction 88, 127, 156

eroticism
  cultivating in marriage 94, 96
  delayed gratification 103, 107
  in Scripture 48, 52
  new perspectives 102
  pornography 48
  reignited by mystery 100, 101
  separateness 101, 102
estrogen 15, 139, 146

F

flirting 80, 91, 103
foreplay
  Bedwork 92, 148
  in Scripture 49
  necessity of 87
  oral sex 12, 134, 135
  respect 123
  ritual 27, 86, 87
  types of 81, 115, 130, 131
forgiveness
  healing broken trust xv, 161, 162, 163
  impact of 164
  process of 164, 167
Four Horsemen of the Apocalypse 119, 186

G

G-spot
  explanation of 136, 137
  male 138
  stimulation of 137, 138, 173, 177

H

habituation 98, 99, 107
Habituation 107
high achievers 13
High Desire Spouse
  Bedwork 21
  Designated Initiator 84, 85
  desire gap 5, 8
  Don't Say No Experiment 86
  role reversal 6, 7
  trust 157
  women 7, 8
hippocampus 57, 58
home field advantage xvii, 72
hormones
  andropause 15

Endnotes

Chapter 1: Myth-Busting

1. News Release. (2008). "New Marriage and Divorce Stats Released." *The Barna Group,* March 31. http://www.barna.org/barna-update/article/15-familykids/42-new-marriage-and-divorce-statistics-released?q=divorce.

2. McCarthy, B.W., & McCarthy, E.J. (2003). *Rekindling Desire: A Step by Step Program to Help Low-Sex and No-Sex Marriages.* New York: Brunner-Routledge, 4.

3. Haltzman, S., & Foy DiGeronimo, T. (2006). *The Secrets of Happily Married Men: Eight Ways to Win Your Wife's Heart Forever.* San Francisco: Jossey-Bass, 206.

4. Sachs, A. (2008). "Help for Sex-Starved Wives." *Time,* April 7. http://www.time.com/time/health/article/0,8599,1728520,00.html.

5. Schnarch, D. (1997). *Passionate Marriage: Keeping Love and Intimacy Alive in Committed Relationships.* New York: Henry Holt & Company, 141.

6. The psychologist Dorothy Tennov coined the term *limerence* to describe this phase in her book, Tennov, D. (1998). *Love and Limerence: The Experience of Being in Love.* Chelsea, MI: Scarborough House. Helen Fisher, a research professor at New Jersey's Rutgers University, calls this phase "romantic love."

7. Amen, D. (2007). *The Brain in Love: 12 Lessons to Enhance Your Love Life.* New York: Three Rivers Press, 63.

8. Weiner Davis, M. (2008). *The Sex-Starved Wife: What to Do When He Has Lost Desire.* New York: Simon & Schuster, 19. See also Weiner Davis, M. (2008). "The Sex-Starved Wife." *Redbook.* http://www.redbookmag.com/love-sex/advice/sex-starved-wife-5.

9. Masters, W.H., & Johnson, V. (1966). *Human Sexual Response.* New York: Bantam Books. Masters' and Johnson's sexual response cycle was expanded upon in the 1970s by Helen Singer Kaplan, a psychologist at Cornell University.

10. Although Dr. Basson has thus far only conducted her research on women, I have met many men who self-identified as a Cycle Two person as well.

11. Castleman, M. (2009). "Desire in Women: Does It Lead to Sex? Or Result from It?" *Psychology Today,* July 15. http://www.psychologytoday.com/blog/all-about-sex/200907/desire-in-women-does-it-lead-sex-or-result-it.

12. Basson, R. (2005). "Women's Sexual Dysfunction: Expanded and Revised Edition." *CMAJ,* May 10, 172(10): 1327-1333. http://www.cmaj.ca/cgi/content/full/172/10/1327.

13. (Name withheld for privacy), personal communication, May 1, 2010.

14. Amen, D. (2007). *The Brain in Love: 12 Lessons to Enhance Your Love Life.* New York: Three Rivers Press, 65.
15. Haltzman, S., & Foy DiGeronimo, T. (2008). *The Secrets of Happily Married Women: How to Get More Out of Your Relationship by Doing Less.* San Francisco: Jossey-Bass, 148.
16. According to The Global Erectile Dysfunction Poll (2011), the average Canadian couple has sex 1.26 times a week, and the average American couple has it 1.37 times a week. See http://www.skimgroup.com/skim-conducted-international-poll-for-lilly. See also McMahon, T., Kohler, N., & Stobo Sniderman, A. (2012). "How Canadian Are You? How Your Waist Size, Paycheque and Sex Life Measure Up." *Maclean's,* July 9.
17. Ward, D. (2004). "We Had More Sex in the 50s Survey Says." *The Guardian,* August 6. http://www.guardian.co.uk/uk/2004/aug/06/gender.research.
18. John 8:32 (NIV).

Chapter 2: Define Your Direction

1. Matthew 7:7 (NIV).
2. Collins, J.C., & Porras, J.I. (1994). *Built to Last: Successful Habits of Visionary Companies.* New York: HarperCollins Publishers. The term Big Hairy Audacious Goal ("BHAG") was coined by James C. Collins and Jerry I. Porras in their book.
3. News Release. (2007). "Study Backs Up Strategies for Achieving Goals." *Dominican University of California.* http://www.dominican.edu/dominicannews/study-backs-up-strategies-for-achieving-goals.
4. Palu won the $100,00 at-home challenge in season 9.
5. News Release. (2007). "Study Backs Up Strategies for Achieving Goals." *Dominican University of California.* http://www.dominican.edu/dominicannews/study-backs-up-strategies-for-achieving-goals.
6. Health Communications Inc.
7. (2005). New York: HarperCollins Publishers.
8. Skloot, R. (2007). "Why Is It So Damned Hard to Change?" *Oprah.com,* January. http://www.oprah.com/health/How-to-Change-Your-Bad-Habits/1.
9. Ducklow, P. (2010). "70 Is My New 100." *www.theducklows.ca,* February 12. http://theducklows.ca/70-is-my-new-100/.

Chapter 3: Faith

1. Gallup, G.G., Burch, R.L., & Platek, S.M. (2002). "Does Semen Have Antidepressant Properties?" *Archives for Sexual Behavior,* 31(3): 289-293.
2. Hughes, S.M., Harrison, M.A., & Gallup, G.G. (2007). "Sex Differences in Romantic Kissing among College Students: An Evolutionary Perspective." *Evolutionary Psychology,* 5(3): 612-631. For more information on the benefits of kissing, see Fisher, H. (2009). *Why Him? Why Her? How to Find and Keep Lasting Love.* New York: Holt Paperbacks, 217-219.
3. Fuchs, E. (1983). *Sexual Desire and Love.* New York: Seabury Press, 108.
4. Stafford, T. (1993). *Sexual Chaos.* Downers Grove, IL: InterVarsity, 37.
5. Mason, M. (1985). *The Mystery of Marriage.* Portland: Multnomak, 135.
6. Brown, B. (2008). *I Thought It Was Just Me (but It Isn't): Telling the Truth about Perfectionism, Inadequacy and Power.* New York: Penguin Group, 12. Dr. Brown differentiates between embarrassment, humiliation, guilt and shame, but the application of these definitions is the author's.

7. Hartling, L.M., Rosen, W., et al. (2000). "Shame and Humiliation: From Isolation to Relational Transformation." *Work in Progress,* 88. Stone Center for Developmental Services and Studies. Wellesley, MA.

8. Brown, B. (2011). "The Hustle for Worthiness." Presentation at the International Coach Federation Vancouver Chapter, September 30.

9. Editorial. (2006). "Before the Next Sex Scandal." *Christianity Today,* April, 50(4). http://www.christianitytoday.com/ct/2006/april/12.28.html?start=1.

10. Cloud, H., & Townsend, J. (1999). *Boundaries in Marriage.* Grand Rapids, MI: Zondervan, 17.

11. Day, T. "Psalm of Solomon – Song of Songs." *www.timday.org,* May 26. http://www.timday.org/writings/bible-study/old-testament-part-2/.

12. Dworkin-McDaniel, N. (2011). "Touching Makes You Healthier." *CNN,* January 5. http://www.cnn.com/2011/HEALTH/01/05/touching.makes.you.healthier.health/index.html.

13. Matthew 17:20 (NIV).

14. Brown, B. (2008). *I Thought It Was Just Me (but It Isn't): Telling the Truth about Perfectionism, Inadequacy and Power.* New York: Penguin Group.

Chapter 4: Element 1 - Communication

1. Gray, J. (1992). *Men Are from Mars, Women Are from Venus: A Practical Guide for Improving Communication and Getting What You Want in Your Relationships.* New York: HarperCollins.

2. Farrel, B., & Farrel, P. (2001). *Men Are Like Waffles, Women Are Like Spaghetti: Understanding and Delighting in Your Differences.* Eugene, OR: Harvest House Publishers.

3. Fisher, H. (2008). "Helen Fisher Studies the Brain in Love." *TED,* February. http://www.ted.com/talks/helen_fisher_studies_the_brain_in_love.html.

4. If you wish to expand on the science of the brain and how this science relates to relationships, here are some excellent books to read: *Mindsight* (Siegel, D. (2011). New York: Bantam Books.), *The Female Brain* (Brizendine, L. (2006). New York: Morgan Road Books.), *The Male Brain* (Brizendine, L. (2010). New York: Broadway Books.), *The Brain in Love* (Amen, D. (2007). New York: Three Rivers Press.), *Secrets of Happily Married Men* (Haltzman, S., & Foy DiGeronimo, T. (2006). San Francisco: Jossey-Bass.), and *Secrets of Happily Married Women* (Haltzman, S., & Foy DiGeronimo, T. (2008). San Francisco: Jossey-Bass.). There are many others – consider this a starter list.

5. Hamann, S. (2005). "Sex Differences in the Responses of the Human Amygdala." *The Neuroscientist,* 11(4): 288-293.

6. Amen, D. (2007). *The Brain in Love: 12 Lessons to Enhance Your Love Life.* New York: Three Rivers Press, 26.

7. Goldstein, J.M., Deidman, J.L., et al. (2001). "Normal Sexual Dimorphism of the Adult Human Brain Assessed by In Vivo Magnetic Resonance Imaging." *Cerebral Cortex,* 11: 490-497.

8. Finedgan, J.K., Bartleman, B., & Wong, P.Y. (1991). "A Window for the Study of Prenatal Sex Hormone Influences on Postnatal Development." *Journal of Genetic Psychology,* 150: 101-112.

9. Brizendine, L. (2010). *The Male Brain: A Breakthrough Understanding of How Men and Boys Think.* New York: Broadway Books, 14.

10. Hamann, S. (2005). "Sex Differences in the Responses of the Human Amygdala." *The Neuroscientist,* 11(4): 288-293.

11. Goldstein, J.M., Deidman, J.L., et al. (2001). "Normal Sexual Dimorphism of the Adult Human Brain Assessed by In Vivo Magnetic Resonance Imaging." *Cerebral Cortex,* 11: 490-497.

12. Sample, I. (2011). "Female Orgasm Captured in Series of Brain Scans." *The Guardian,* November 14. http://www.guardian.co.uk/science/2011/nov/14/female-orgasm-recorded-brain-scans.

13. Giedd, J.N., Castellanos, F.X., et al. (1997). "Sexual Dimorphism of the Developing Human Brain." *Progress in Neuro-Psychopharmacology and Biological Psychiatry,* 21(8): 1185-1201. See also Goldstein, J.M., Deidman, J.L., et al. (2001). "Normal Sexual Dimorphism of the Adult Human Brain Assessed by In Vivo Magnetic Resonance Imaging." *Cerebral Cortex,* 11: 490-497.

14. I personally love the book by Parker, S. (2007). *The Human Body: An Illustrated Guide to Its Structure, Function and Disorders.* New York: DK Publishing.

15. Love, P., & Stonsy, S. (2007). *How to Improve Your Marriage without Talking about It.* New York: Broadway Books, 12. Also see Hittelman, J.H., & Dickes, R. (1979). "Sex Differences in Neonatal Eye Contact Time." *Merril-Palmer Quarterly,* 25: 171-184.

16. Leeb, R.T., & Rejskind, F.G. (2004). "Here's Looking at You, Kid! A Longitudinal Study of Perceived Gender Differences in Mutual Gaze Behavior in Young Infants." *Sex Roles,* 50(1-2): 1-5.

17. Lutchmaya, S., Baron-Cohen, S., & Raggatt, P. (2002). "Foetal Testosterone and Eye Contact in 12-Month-Old Infants." *Infant Behavior and Development,* 25: 327-335.

18. Goldstein, J.M., Deidman, J.L., et al. (2001). "Normal Sexual Dimorphism of the Adult Human Brain Assessed by In Vivo Magnetic Resonance Imaging." *Cerebral Cortex,* 11: 490-497.

19. Love, P., & Stonsy, S. (2007). *How to Improve Your Marriage without Talking about It.* New York: Broadway Books, 14.

20. Baron-Cohen, S. (2003). "They Just Can't Help It." *The Guardian,* April 17. http://www.guardian.co.uk/education/2003/apr/17/research.highereducation/print.

21. Asthana, H.S., & Mandal, M.K. (1998). "Hemifacial Asymmetry in Emotion Expressions." *Behavior Modification,* 22: 177-183.

22. Schneider, F., Habel, U., et al. (2000). "Gender Differences in Regional Cerebral Activity during Sadness." *Human Brain Mapping,* 9: 226-238.

23. Haltzman, S., & Foy DiGeronimo, T. (2006). *The Secrets of Happily Married Men: Eight Ways to Win Your Wife's Heart Forever.* San Francisco: Jossey-Bass, 37.

24. Lutchmaya, S., Baron-Cohen, S., & Raggatt, P. (2002). "Foetal Testosterone and Vocabulary Size in 18- and 24-Month-Old Infants." *Infant Behavior and Development,* 24: 418-424.

25. Haltzman, S., & Foy DiGeronimo, T. (2006). *The Secrets of Happily Married Men: Eight Ways to Win Your Wife's Heart Forever.* San Francisco: Jossey-Bass, 172. Also see Pease, A., & Pease, B. (2001). *Why Men Don't Listen and Women Can't Read Maps: How We're Different and What to Do about It.* New York: Broadway, 80.

26. Amen, D. (2007). *The Brain in Love: 12 Lessons to Enhance Your Love Life.* New York: Three Rivers Press, 78. See also Holloway, R.L., Anderson, P.J., et al. (1993). "Sexual Dimorphism of the Human Corpus Callosum from Three Independent Samples: Relative Size of the Corpus Callosum." *American Journal of Physical Anthropology,* 4: 481-498. See also Hwang, S.J., Ji, E.K., et al. (2004). "Gender Differences in the Corpus Callosum of Neonates." *Neuroreport,* 6: 1029-1032.

27. Hebrews 11:1 (NLT) says, "Faith is the confidence that what we hope for will actually happen; it gives us assurance about things we cannot see."

28. The original experiment was conducted in 1965, and the two researchers wrote a book on their findings in 1968 (updated in 1992). See Rosenthal, R., & Jacobson, L. (1992). *Pygmalion in the Classroom: Teacher Expectation and Pupils' Intellectual Development,* 2nd ed. New York: Irvington Publishers, Inc.

29. Eden, D. (1992). "Leadership and Expectations: Pygmalion Effects and Other Self-Fulfilling Prophecies in Organizations." *Leadership Quarterly,* 3(4): 271-305.

30. Chapman, G. (1992). *The Five Love Languages: How to Express Heartfelt Commitment to Your Mate.* Chicago: Northfield Publishing. Visit Dr. Chapman's website, http://www.5lovelanguages.com/, to find out what your love languages are.

31. Mitchell, J. (2010). "NLSummit 2010 Insight: Making Sense of Others." *Neuroleadership Institute,* December 26. http://blog.neuroleadership.org/2010/12/nlsummit-2010-insight-jason-mitchell.html.

32. (Name withheld for privacy), personal communication, October 5, 2011.

33. Covey, S.R. (1989). *7 Habits of Highly Effective People.* New York: Free Press, 238.

Chapter 5: Element 2 – Ritual

1. Because the Christians in the country were uncomfortable with the literal meaning of this greeting, they would greet each other with "Jayamasi," which translates to "Christ has the victory."

2. Langer, G., Arnedt, C., & Sussma, D. (2004). "American Sex Survey." *ABC News (Primetime),* October 21. http://abcnews.go.com/Primetime/PollVault/story?id=156921&page=1#.T7WCYL-fI-8.

3. Need help getting your kids to bed on time? The National Sleep Foundation (www.sleepfoundation.org) has excellent resources.

4. Farrel, B., & Farrel, P. (2001). *Men Are Like Waffles, Women Are Like Spaghetti: Understanding and Delighting in Your Differences.* Eugene, OR: Harvest House Publishers.

5. Kerner, I. (2004). *She Comes First: The Thinking Man's Guide to Pleasuring a Woman.* New York: HarperCollins Publishers, Inc.

Chapter 6: Element 3 – Mystery

1. Abrams, JJ. (2007). "JJ Abrams' Mystery Box." *TED,* March. http://www.ted.com/talks/j_j_abrams_mystery_box.html.

2. Boteach, S. (2009). *The Kosher Sutra: 8 Sacred Secrets for Reigniting Desire and Restoring Passion for Life.* New York: HarperCollins, 149.

3. Rohr, R. (2002). "Grieving as Sacred Space." *Sojourners Magazine,* January-February. 31(1): 20-24.

4. Woller, L., & Woller, J. (2008). *The Skill.* Victoria, BC: The Vantage Group.

5. Toler, L. (2011). "How to Avoid Becoming a Victim of the Gray Divorce." *Huffington Post,* March 12. http://www.huffingtonpost.com/lynn-toler/how-to-avoid-becoming-a-v_b_834192.html?.

6. Perel, E. (2006). *Mating in Captivity: Unlocking Erotic Intelligence.* New York: HarperCollins Publishers, 37.

7. Abrams, JJ. (2007). "JJ Abrams' Mystery Box." *TED,* March. http://www.ted.com/talks/j_j_abrams_mystery_box.html.

8. Lehrer, J. (2009). "Don't!" *The New Yorker,* May 18. http://www.newyorker.com/reporting/2009/05/18/090518fa_fact_lehrer. See also (2011). "Marshmallow Test Points to Biological Basis for Delayed Gratification." *ScienceDaily,* August 31. http://www.sciencedaily.com/releases/2011/08/110831160220.htm.

9. Cyrus, M. (2009). "The Climb." *Hannah Montana: The Movie.*

Chapter 7: Element 4 – Respect

1. (Name withheld for privacy), personal communication, November 2009.

2. Brizendine, L. (2010). *The Male Brain: A Breakthrough Understanding of How Men and Boys Think.* New York: Broadway Books, 86-89.

3. Tyler, B. (1984). "Holding Out for A Hero." *Footloose.*

4. Rampell, C. (2010). "Women Now a Majority in American Workplaces." *The New York Times,* February 5. http://www.nytimes.com/2010/02/06/business/economy/06women.html.

5. Swanbrow, D. (2002). "American Study Finds Men Doing More Housework." *The University Record,* March 25. http://ur.umich.edu/0102/Mar25_02/16.htm.

6. For an interesting article on how mad women really are, see Brockenbrough, M. "Mad at Dad." *Parenting.com.* http://www.parenting.com/article/mad-at-dad.

7. Swanbrow, D. (2002). "American Study Finds Men Doing More Housework." *The University Record,* March 25. http://ur.umich.edu/0102/Mar25_02/16.htm.

8. Boteach, S. (2009). *The Kosher Sutra: 8 Sacred Secrets for Reigniting Desire and Restoring Passion for Life.* New York: HarperCollins, 108.

9. FAQs. "Who Initiates the Divorce More Often, The Wife or the Husband?" *Divorce Lawyer Source.* http://www.divorce-lawyer-source.com/faq/emotional/who-initiates-divorce-men-or-women.html.

10. Canfield J., & Switzer, J. (2005). *The Success Principles: How to Get from Where You Are to Where You Want to Be.* New York: HarperCollins Publishers, 229.

11. Amen, D. (1998). *Change Your Brain, Change Your Life: The Breakthrough Program for Conquering Anxiety, Depression, Obsessiveness, Anger, and Impulsiveness.* New York: Three Rivers Press. In this book, Dr. Daniel Amen lays out the various ways we indulge in ANTs and the ways we can break these unhealthy patterns.

12. Gottman, J. (2010). "Four Horsemen of the Apocalypse by John Gottman." *YouTube,* January 2. http://www.youtube.com/watch?v=CbJPaQY_1dc. See also Gottman, J. (1994). *Why Marriages Succeed or Fail: And How You Can Make Yours Last.* New York: Simon & Schuster, 68.

13. Genesis 1:27 (NIV) states, "So God created mankind in his own image, in the image of God he created them; male and female he created them."

14. Rohr, R. (2004). *Adam's Return: The Five Promises of Male Initiation.* New York: Crossroads Publishing.

15. Eldridge, J. (2001). *Wild at Heart: Discovering the Secret of a Man's Soul.* Nashville: Thomas Nelson.

16. Brizendine, L. (2010). *The Male Brain: A Breakthrough Understanding of How Men and Boys Think.* New York: Broadway Books.

17. Haltzman, S., & Foy DiGeronimo, T. (2008). *The Secrets of Happily Married Women: How to Get More Out of Your Relationship by Doing Less.* San Francisco: Jossey-Bass.

Chapter 8: Element 5 – Pleasure

1. Laumann, E.O., Paik, A., & Rosen, R.C. (1999). "Sexual Dysfunction in the United States." *JAMA,* 281(6): 537-544.

2. Experts say that about 10 to 15 percent of women have a condition called "primary anorgasmia," meaning they have never had an orgasm. This might be due to medications, health issues, psychological issues, etc. (Rankin, L. (2010). *What's Up Down There? Questions You'd Only Ask Your Gynecologist if She Were Your Best Friend.* New York: St. Martin's Press, 129). If both of you have tried consistently but unsuccessfully to bring the wife to orgasm, it might be time to get some professional help.

3. Alzate, H., & Londono, M.L. (1984). "Vaginal Erotic Sensitivity." *Journal of Sex and Marital Therapy,* Spring; 10(1): 49-56.

4. Durex Global Sex Survey, (2003). http://www.durexnetwork.org/en-GB/research/Pages/Home.aspx.

5. Rankin, L. (2011). "15 Crazy Things about Vaginas." *Psychology Today,* April 8. http://www.psychologytoday.com/blog/owning-pink/201104/15-crazy-things-about-vaginas.

6. Brizendine, L. (2010). *The Male Brain: A Breakthrough Understanding of How Men and Boys Think.* New York: Broadway Books.

7. Bolen, J. G. (1980). "The Male Orgasm: Pelvic Contractions Measured by Anal Probe." *Archives of Sexual Behavior,* 9(6): 503–521.

8. Rankin, L. (2011). "15 Crazy Things about Vaginas." *Psychology Today,* April 8. http://www.psychologytoday.com/blog/owning-pink/201104/15-crazy-things-about-vaginas.

9. McCarthy, B.W., & McCarthy, E.J. (2003). *Rekindling Desire: A Step by Step Program to Help Low-Sex and No-Sex Marriages.* New York: Brunner-Routledge, 78. The authors also say the average time for the entire lovemaking experience is 15 to 45 minutes.

10. Morgentaler, A. (2009). "Men Who Fake Orgasms." *Psychology Today*, February 1. http://www.psychologytoday.com/blog/men-sex-and-testosterone/200902/men-who-fake-orgasms.

11. Shmuley Boteach writes, "Long ago, well before Christianity enacted legislation forbidding its clerics from marrying or having sex, the ancient rabbis were giving explicit sexual advice to married men and women as to how they could enjoy pleasurable yet holy intimate relations. The rabbis made female orgasm an obligation incumbent on every Jewish husband. No man was allowed to use a woman merely for his own gratification." Boteach, S. (1999). *Kosher Sex: A Recipe for Passion and Intimacy.* New York: Doubleday, 10.

12. Dr. Ian Kerner coins this term in his book. Kerner, I. (2004). *She Comes First: A Thinking Man's Guide to Pleasuring a Woman.* New York: HarperCollins Publishers, Inc.

13. Dworkin-McDaniel, N. (2011). "Touching Makes You Healthier." *CNN*, January 5. http://www.cnn.com/2011/HEALTH/01/05/touching.makes.you.healthier.health/index.html.

14. Schnarch, D. (1997). *Passionate Marriage: Keeping Love and Intimacy Alive in Committed Relationships.* New York: Henry Holt & Company, 157.

15. Hughes, S.M., Harrison, M.A., & Gallup, G.G. (2007). "Sex Differences in Romantic Kissing among College Students: An Evolutionary Perspective." *Evolutionary Psychology*, 5(3): 612-631.

16. Fisher, H. (2009). *Why Him? Why Her? How to Find and Keep Lasting Love.* New York: Holt Paperbacks, 217-219.

17. Fisher, H., Aron, A., & Brown, L.L. (2005). "Romantic Love: An fMRI Study of Neural Mechanism for Mate Choice." *Journal of Comparative Neurology*, 493(1): 58-62.

18. Ian Kerner, Natalie Angier and others argue that because the clitoris extends deep within the body, stimulation in the G-spot region is merely massaging the internal part of the clitoris, and is thereby a clitoral orgasm.

19. Beverly Whipple, Barry Komisaruk and others maintain that the G-spot orgasm is different than the clitoral orgasm because stimulation of the G-spot region activates the *pelvic* nerve and induces orgasm, whereas the clitoral orgasm is triggered by the *pudental* nerve.

20. Komisaruk, B., Beyer-Flores, C., & Whipple, B. (2006). *The Science of Orgasm.* Baltimore: The Johns Hopkins University Press, 7.

21. Laumann, E.O., Paik, A., & Rosen, R.C. (1999). "Sexual Dysfunction in the United States." *JAMA*, 281(6): 537-544.

22. Sheehy, G. (1998). *Menopause: The Silent Passage.* New York: Pocket Books.

Chapter 9: Element 6 – Trust

1. Omartian, S. (1997). *The Power of a Praying Wife.* Eugene, OR: Harvest House Publishers.

2. (Name withheld for privacy), personal communication, February 13, 2012.

3. Mark 10:8 (NIV).

4. Bowen, M. (1978). *Family Therapy in Clinical Practice.* Northvale, NJ: Jason Aronson, Inc., as quoted by Rabstenjnek, C.V. "Family Systems and Murray Bowen Theory." http://www.houd.info/articles.htm.

5. Rosen, R.C. (2007). "Erectile Dysfunction: Integration of Medical and Psychological Approaches." Ed. Leiblum, S. *Principles and Practice of Sex Therapy.* New York: The Guilford Press, 288-293. See also Hall, K. (2007). "Sexual Dysfunction and Childhood Sexual Abuse: Gender Differences and Treatment Implications." Ed. Leiblum, S. *Principles and Practice of Sex Therapy.* New York: The Guilford Press, 355-359.

6. Carder, D. (2008). *Close Calls: What Adulterers Want You to Know About Protecting Your Marriage.* Chicago: Northfield Publishing, 19.
7. (2010). "Big Surge in Social Networking Evidence Says Survey of Nation's Top Divorce Lawyers." *American Academy of Matrimonial Lawyers*, February 10. http://www.aaml.org/about-the-academy/press/press-releases/e-discovery/big-surge-social-networking-evidence-says-survey-.
8. The website www.xxxchurch.com is devoted to keeping updated statistics on the growth and destructiveness of the porn industry. For up-to-date statistics, please visit http://www.xxxchurch.com/extras/stats.html.
9. (Name withheld for privacy), personal communication, March 17, 2009.
10. Kerner, I. (2011). "How Porn Is Changing Our Sex Lives." *CNN,* January 20. http://thechart.blogs.cnn.com/2011/01/20/how-porn-is-changing-our-sex-lives/.
11. Glass, S. (2003). *NOT Just Friends: Protect Your Relationship from Infidelity and Heal the Trauma of Betrayal.* New York: The Free Press.
12. Dye, M., & Fancher, P. (2007). *The Genesis Process: A Relapse Prevention Workbook for Addictive/Compulsive Behaviors,* 3rd ed. Auburn, CA: Genesis Addiction Process & Programs. Please see http://www.genesisprocess.org/.
13. Canfield J., & Switzer, J. (2005). *The Success Principles: How to Get from Where You Are to Where You Want to Be.* New York: HarperCollins Publishers, 214.
14. Schnarch, D. (1997). *Passionate Marriage: Keeping Love and Intimacy Alive in Committed Relationships.* New York: Henry Holt & Company.

Chapter 10: Element 7 – Creativity

1. Cameron, J. (1992). *The Artist Way: A Spiritual Path to Higher Creativity.* New York: Penguin Putnam, Inc.
2. Emperor Huang-Ti lived from 2697-2598 BC.
3. Castleman, M. (2010). "Easier Orgasms for Women in the Missionary Position." *Psychology Today,* October 17. http://www.psychologytoday.com/blog/all-about-sex/201010/easier-orgasms-women-in-the-missionary-position.
4. Pease, A., & Pease, B. (2001). *Why Men Don't Listen and Women Can't Read Maps: How We're Different and What to Do about It.* New York: Broadway, 220.
5. Christine Morton's lingerie has been featured in numerous magazines and new shows. Movie stars frequently are seen in it. You can purchase her lingerie online at http://www.christinelingerie.com/, at Holt Renfrew (Canada) or at Neiman Marcus (USA).
6. Hopkins, M., & Lockridge, R. (1997). *Intercourses: An Aphrodisiac Cookbook.* Memphis: Terrace Publishing. This book has a combination of recipes and beautiful photography.
7. Hirsch, A.R. (1998). *Scentsational Sex: The Secret to Using Aroma for Arousal.* Boston: Element Books.

Chapter 11: Element 8 – Passion

1. Love, P., & McFadden, K. (2006). "Hot Monogamy Workshop Training." *Smart Marriages,* June 24. http://www.smartmarriages.com/hot.html.
2. Bon Jovi, J. (1992). "Bed of Roses." *Keep the Faith.*
3. 2 Samuel 6:12-15 (NIV).
4. Tolkien, J.R.R. (1998). *The Hobbit.* London: HarperCollins Children's Books, 28.
5. Weir, P. (1989). Director, *Dead Poets Society.*
6. Minghella, A. (1996). Director, *The English Patient.*
7. Hardwicke, C. (2008). Director, *Twilight.*

8. McManus, E.R. (2008). *Wide Awake: The Future Is Waiting within You.* Nashville: Thomas Nelson, 19.

9. I Kings 19:11-13 (NIV).

10. Love, P., & Robinson, J. (1995). *Hot Monogamy: Essential Steps to More Passionate, Intimate Lovemaking.* New York: Penguin Group, 86.

11. Gottman, J.M. (1994). *Why Marriages Succeed or Fail: And How You Can Make Yours Last.* New York: Simon & Schuster, 41.

12. Gire, K. (1996). *Windows of the Soul: Experiencing God in New Ways.* Grand Rapids, MI: Zondervan, 71.

13. Psalm 139:14 (NIV).

14. Psalm 46:10 (NIV).

15. Robinson, T. (2008). *Small Footprint, Big Handprint: How to Live Simply and Love Extravagantly.* Boise, ID: Ampelon Publishing.

Chapter 12: Element 9 – Attraction

1. Brown, B. (2008). *I Thought It Was Just Me (but It Isn't): Telling the Truth about Perfectionism, Inadequacy and Power.* New York: Penguin Group, 93.

2. Story, L. (2007). "Anywhere the Eye Can See, It's Likely to See an Ad." *New York Times*, January 15. http://www.nytimes.com/2007/01/15/business/media/15everywhere.html.

3. Dove. (2006). "Dove Evolution Commercial." *YouTube.* October 15. http://www.youtube.com/watch?v=hibyAJOSW8U.

4. White, N. (2007). "Jennifer Love Hewitt: A Size 2 Is Not Fat!" *People,* December 2. http://www.people.com/people/article/0,,20163862,00.html.

5. Figueroa-Jones, M. (2012). "Plus Sized Bodies, What is Wrong with Them Anyway?" *Plus Model Magazine,* January 8. http://plus-model-mag.com/2012/01/plus-size-bodies-what-is-wrong-with-them-anyway/.

6. Psalm 139:14 (NIV) says, "I praise you because I am fearfully and wonderfully made; your works are wonderful, I know that full well."

7. Streib, L. (2007). "World's Fattest Countries." *Forbes.com*, February 8. http://www.forbes.com/2007/02/07/worlds-fattest-countries-forbeslife-cx_ls_0208worldfat_2.html.

8. (Name withheld for privacy), Facebook post, January 27, 2011.

9. I Corinthians 6:19-20 (NIV) says, "Do you not know that your bodies are temples of the Holy Spirit, who is in you, whom you have received from God? You are not your own; you were bought at a price. Therefore honor God with your bodies."

10. For example, in the United Kingdom, a disturbing 69 percent of people on a bariatric surgery waiting list have a history of childhood abuse. See Grilo, C.M., Masheb, R., et al. (2005). "Childhood Maltreatment in Extremely Obese Male and Female Bariatric Surgery Candidates." *Obesity Research Journal*, 13: 123–130.

11. Haltzman, S., & Foy DiGeronimo, T. (2008). *The Secrets of Happily Married Women: How to Get More Out of Your Relationship by Doing Less.* San Francisco: Jossey-Bass, 199. See also, Feldhahn, S. (2004). *For Women Only: What You Need to Know about the Inner Lives of Men.* Sisters, OR: Multnomah Publishers, 161.

12. Corcoran, D. (2007). "On Desire: Interview with Helen Fisher." *New York Times,* April 10. http://video.nytimes.com/video/2007/04/09/science/1194817104832/on-desire.html?ref=sex. Original study: Wedekind, C., Seebeck, T., et al. (1995). "MHC-Dependent Mate Preferences in Humans." *Proceedings of the Royal Society: Biological Sciences,* 260 (1359): 245–249.

13. Goudarzi, S. (2006). "When a Woman Smells Best." *LiveScience,* January 18. http://www.livescience.com/553-woman-smells-html.

14. This is not to say these programs do not have an attraction for women. In fact, I know a lot of women who prefer these programs to others on the market. However, because the programs have a very masculine bent to their marketing, they are tapping into an area that has long been reserved for muscle-filled gyms.

15. Krucoff, C., & Krucoff, M. (2000). "Peak Performance." *American Fitness*, 19: 32-36.

16. Penhollow, T.M., & Young, M. (2004). "Sexual Desirability and Sexual Performance: Does Exercise and Fitness Really Matter?" *Electronic Journal of Human Sexuality*, October 5, 7.

17. Stanten, N., & Yeager, S. (2003). "Four Workouts to Improve Your Love Life." *Prevention,* 55: 76-78. See also Penhollow, T.M., & Young, M. (2004). "Sexual Desirability and Sexual Performance: Does Exercise and Fitness Really Matter?" *Electronic Journal of Human Sexuality*, October 5, 7.

18. Bacon, C. G., Mittleman, M. A., & Kawachi, I. (2003). "Sexual Function in Men Older than 50 Years of Age: Results from the Health Professionals Follow-Up Study." *Annals of Internal Medicine,* 139: 161-168. See also Esposito, K., Giugliano, F., et al. (2004). "Effect of Lifestyle Changes on Erectile Dysfunction in Obese Men." *JAMA*, 291: 2978-2984.

19. Stanten, N., & Yeager, S. (2003). "Four Workouts to Improve Your Love Life." *Prevention,* 55: 76-78. See also Laumann, E.O., Paik, A., & Rosen, R.C. (1999). "Sexual Dysfunction in the United States." *JAMA*, 281(6): 537-544.

20. Krucoff, C., & Krucoff, M. (2000). "Peak Performance." *American Fitness*, 19: 32-36. Also see Penhollow, T.M., & Young, M. (2004). "Sexual Desirability and Sexual Performance: Does Exercise and Fitness Really Matter?" *Electronic Journal of Human Sexuality*, October 5, 7.

21. Krucoff, C., & Krucoff, M. (2000). "Peak Performance." *American Fitness*, 19: 32-36.

22. Ibid.

23. (Name withheld for privacy), personal communication, May 15, 2009.

24. Northrup, C. (2008). *The Secret Pleasures of Menopause.* New York: Hay House, Inc., 65.